BIDEN'S
CORRUPTION AND WAR:
THE TRUE STORY OF THE
1 BILLION DOLLAR PROSECUTOR

Viktor Shokin

With Forward by James Bradley

Commentary by Florita Toquero

BENI PRODUCTIONS
BREAKTHROUGH MEDIA

Laguna Hills, California

Published by Beni Productions LLC., 23046 Avenida de la Carlota Suite 600, Laguna Hills, CA 92653. Website: beniprod.com

ISBN 979-8-9932690-1-6

CONTENTS

FORWARD

BY JAMES BRADLEY, U.S. SENATE CANDIDATE
AND INVESTIGATIVE JOURNALIST

When I first encountered Viktor Shokin's relentless pursuit of truth described in his memoirs, I was struck by its raw courage and unflinching clarity. As a U.S. Senate candidate and investigative journalist, Shokin's work resonates deeply with my mission to hold those in power accountable. It is a problem when the actions of those in power undermine freedom and democracy—whether in Ukraine or in the United States. His book is a searing indictment of systemic corruption, a call to action, and a testament to the personal cost of standing up to the powerful.

Shokin's journey is laid out across the four parts of this book. Shokin exposes a web of corruption spun by Democratic operatives acting in the name of *securing democracy* and *energy independence*, with the Biden family at its center. Shokin's personal and public battles over his reputation as a prosecutor were stained *through* Democrats' exploitation of Ukraine as a hub for their financial schemes. His account of how figures like Joe Biden leveraged their influence for personal gain is chilling, yet familiar. They unfortunately shadow what I have discovered in many of my own investigations—a pattern of abuse disguised as diplomacy.

Shokin dives into the heart of the scandals that have weakened Ukraine by exposing how the Biden name became a currency for influence peddling. Shokin's meticulous documentation of Burisma's ties to U.S. aid and lobbying efforts echoes the stories I've pursued about foreign entities exploiting American resources. His work underscores a truth I've spoken about time and time again; corruption thrives in the shadows of unchecked power.

Shokin reveals how Joe Biden's influence extended beyond financial gain to reshaping Ukraine's political landscape for his benefit. His personal account, detailing the infamous quid pro quo that pressured Ukraine to oust Shokin himself, is a gut-punch. As someone who has faced political retaliation for exposing truth, I admire Shokin's resolve to document these events, even as he faced personal threats.

As he exposes the mechanisms of control, from the creation of Biden-aligned agencies like NABU to the manipulation of U.S. aid, we can see the other half of mismanaged U.S. diplomacy. It is a substandard and, for Ukraine, a predatorial diplomacy fueled by the misuse of American taxpayer funds abroad. I champion for ways to resolve these issues as a Senate candidate by giving those like Shokin a voice as a first step to a solution.

This book is a clarion call for Americans to confront the corruption eroding our institutions and those of our allies. Clearly, the last nine years spanning from 2016-2025 have taught Americans one thing. Regardless of one's desire to be a highly self-supporting, nationalist, isolationist country, our domestic policies are deeply tied to what our nation does abroad. Our country is and has been deeply tied to Ukraine for a long time, as Shokin reveals in his book. Ukraine is simply an example of the need for us to broaden our perspectives and become active participants in shaping what we do here and overseas. As you read *Biden's Corruption and War*, prepare to be outraged, inspired, and awakened to the urgent need for accountability and positive transformation. Viktor Shokin paid a steep price to tell this story—now it's up to us to act on it.

PREFACE

When U.S. Vice President Joe Biden called me a *son of a* bitch in January 2018 during his speech while on discussion panel at the prestigious Council on Foreign Relations, I decided to write a book about American corruption in Ukraine. I was not simply insulted but branded a liar and a corrupt official. My first memoir was published in 2020 and was re-released in June 2025 in Kiev. In my first book, I recounted my life story. However, that was not all that was in the book. The main theme was an attempt to understand how the Democrats turned my country into a giant *money laundering operation*. All this happened under the loud slogan of protecting and supporting the *fragile* Ukrainian democracy.

There was no more attentive observer in Ukraine than me, who closely followed the investigation into the Biden family's corruption schemes, which began in the U.S. in January 2023. This investigation was launched by the Committee on Oversight and Government Reform, the House Judiciary Committee, and the Ways and Means Committee of the U.S. House of Representatives. Their focus was on my *old and dear friend* Joe Biden and his relatives. U.S. Congressmen finally took an interest in what the President's son Hunter, Joe Biden's brother James, and many others were up to. The investigation was prompted by materials from Hunter Biden's lost personal laptop, which came to light amid the 2020 presidential campaign.

Literally, every morning I started with news from the U.S. And, no wonder why I was mesmerized by the media. I was at the forefront of the investigation into the Biden family's financial scandals in Ukraine. Seven years later, I watched as U.S. Congressmen took up the same cause. However, there was more than just a seven-year difference between their efforts and mine. I had to pay a high price for my courage in investigating crimes involving none other than the son of the U.S. President, Hunter Biden. In Ukraine, Joe Biden was called *the vice king*. During Barack Obama's administration, then Vice President Joe Biden oversaw Ukraine. Biden called the country's president Poroshenko, *his second wife*, because every night he had heart-to-heart talks with him with one goal in mind——to build a system of external control over Ukraine for his own personal gain. It must be admitted that Joe Biden succeeded admirably.

I first attempted to bring the truth about the Biden family's corruption schemes to the attention of the American public in early 2019. I was contacted by Donald Trump's lawyer, Rudolph Giuliani, who wanted to invite me to the U.S. to talk about the financial collusions of Joe Biden and his relatives. Unfortunately, that was not to be. The U.S. State Department refused to issue me a visa. Biden's supporters entrenched there understood that my testimony could be a political bombshell that would bury his chances of becoming the presidential candidate in the 2020 election. Incidentally, the U.S. ambassador to Ukraine at the time, Marie Yovanovitch, played a key role in denying me a U.S. visa. She understood better than anyone else what a threat my trip to the U.S. posed to the Democrats. She did everything she could to prevent me from visiting America.

The U.S. congressional investigation into the financial collusions of the Biden family prompted me to significantly revise my memoirs. I added new evidence using the allegations made by congressmen against the 46th president of the United States. I not only want to tell everything I know about Hunter Biden's corruption schemes but also want to open the eyes of Americans to the massive corruption entangled into my country led by Democrats. Sharing my long personal journey to an American audience is connected to another dream of mine. I want to clear my name of the mud that Joe Biden personally slung at me. He and his closest associates have spread these lies around the world. I want to file a lawsuit in the U.S. to protect my honor and dignity.

PART ONE:
THE LAY OF THE LAND

"I had to pay a high price for my courage in investigating crimes involving none other than the son of the U.S. President, Hunter Biden."

—Viktor Shokin, 2025

CHAPTER 1:

THE GOOD/BAD SHOKIN

I entered the justice system back in 1980. At that time, I believed that I could make the world a better place by fighting crime with the force of the law. After the fall of Viktor Yanukovych's regime, I had a historic opportunity to help rebuild the country, which had embarked on a successful and prosperous path of European modernization.

In 2015, I oversaw the prosecutor's office and began investigating the tragic events on the Maidan, as well as the corruption schemes that flourished under Yanukovych. The new Ukrainian government gave me a huge vote of confidence. My only fault is that I tried to justify their support by doing the job I had been doing all my life. The funny thing is that when I took office as Prosecutor General ten-years ago, I received high praise for my work from many influential politicians and officials, both in Ukraine and abroad.

In the summer of 2015, all my supporters acknowledged that under my leadership the Prosecutor General's Office (PGO) began to conduct effective

KNOWN RECORD:
2014 MAIDAN

Also known as the Revolution of Dignity, the 2014 Maidan civil protests in Ukraine led to the overthrow of Ukrainian President Viktor Yanukovych, which shifted politics. Considered corrupt, Yanukovych's presidency is often viewed as sympathetic to Russian ideals. Event reports suggest intimate involvement of Obama administration officials, like U.S. Ambassador, Geoffrey Pyatt, and Deputy Secretary of State, Victoria Nuland, who handed out cookies to protestors in events leading to Maidan.[1.2,1.3] George Soros linked NGOs are known to have supported protestors per Open Society and Renaissance Foundation websites.[1.4] The ousting of Yanukovych made way for Petro Poroshenko to take the presidency. Poroshenko was known to be more open to western ideals promoted by the EU, the Obama administration and the Open Society's Renaissance Foundation.[1.2,1.4]

KNOWN RECORD:
VIKTOR YANUKOVYCH

    Viktor Yanukovych was the Prime Minister of Ukraine then became the 4th President from 2010-2014.[1.5] Marked an authoritarian and corrupt president, civil protests over his administration fueled the Maiden events leading to his downfall. In February 2014, Yanukovych ordered shots fired among Maidan protestors killing several and wounding hundreds. In response, the Parliament voted to impeach him in February 20, 2014, opening the presidency to Poroshenko.[1.5]

    A Russian sympathizer, Yanukovych was backed by Russian President Vladamir Putin, during his presidential run in 2004, which he lost. After regaining influence and power in Parliament, he won the presidency in 2010. In 2013, Yanukovych pulled out of an agreement to join NATO sparking the Maidan events. During the Maidan uprising, Yanukovich's faction received funding from Putin.[1.5] investigations, established effective work, and embarked on reforms. At that time, Jan Tombiński, then Ambassador of the European Union to Ukraine, said in an interview, "We have not seen such reforms in Ukraine as those that have taken place in the last four months."[1.1]

Ambassadors and law enforcement officials from Germany, the United Kingdom, Sweden, Switzerland, Belgium, Latvia, Hungary, and other countries also spoke positively about my work. On February 19, 2015, during a working meeting with U.S. Ambassador to Ukraine Geoffrey Pyatt, he congratulated me on my appointment and praised the start of my work. I even received a positive response to a letter I wrote dated May 13, 2015, addressed to U.S. Secretary of State John Kerry concerning the improvement of the fight against corruption. In the reply I received from the U.S. State Department on behalf of Kerry, his deputy Victoria Nuland assured me that the United States "is impressed by Ukraine's ambitious program to reform the law enforcement system and fight corruption."[1.6] Yes, that's right, Victoria Nuland, the high-ranking U.S. official who handed out cookies on Maidan during the Revolution of Dignity wrote that. She emphasized "the importance of this historic moment in the fight against injustice through vigorous investigation and prosecution of Maidan cases, as well as the return

6

of stolen assets to the Ukrainian people."[1.6] Then suddenly everything changed overnight. While in Odessa during September 2015, Ambassador Pyatt, with whom I had a normal relationship, for no apparent reason brought up the *Burisma* case. He claimed that I was *not fighting corruption well* despite my office handling dozens, hundreds of corruption cases under active investigation! Pyatt stated:

> Even as we support the work of the new Anti-Corruption Commission and the recruitment of new prosecutors, we have urged Prosecutor General Shokin to empower Deputy Prosecutors Sakvarelidze and Kasko to implement reforms and bring to justice those who have violated the law, regardless of rank or status. We are prepared to partner with reformers within the PGO in the fight against corruption.
>
> —Geoffrey Pyatt, U.S. Ambassador,
>
> September 2015[1.7]

Burisma was just one case among countless others. Why did he remember this specific company? I will answer this question later in my book.

Known Record:
Petro Poroshenko

Form 2014-2019, Petro Poroshenko served in Parliament and was co-chair of the committee supporting the European Union (EU).[1.8] During that time he helped draw an agreement with the EU, which helped ignite the 2014 Maidan Events and secure the 5th presidency for him after Viktor Yanukovych's impeachment.[1.8,1.9] Shortly after taking office, Crimea was annexed into Russia as Putin sent forces to secure the land in a bloodless exchange.[1.8,1.10] More Ukrainian lands joined Russia after further skirmishes.[1.11]

In 2018, Poroshenko cemented NATO allegiance by proposing to change the constitution to allow Ukraine's entrance into NATO. Ratified by the Ukrainian Parliament in 2019, before Zelenskyy became president, it reversed the original 1989 post-cold war treaty to keep Ukraine a neutral state. Some believe the change influenced the February 2022 Russian invasion of Ukraine.[1.12,1.13]

Everything went downhill in my professional life when I started investigating the plots of the oil and gas company Burisma. From the very beginning, it became clear that we were dealing with a large-scale illegal scheme run by a company owned by Ukrainian oligarch *Mykola Zlochevsky*, former Minister of Ecology of Ukraine in the Yanukovych government. As we unraveled the web of corruption, we got closer and closer to its key players. All of them were members of the company's board of directors. Among them, stood out Hunter Biden, the son of then U.S. Vice President Joe Biden. This matter did not bother me at all. I did not even think about suspending the proceedings and going straight to the office of Ukrainian President Petro Poroshenko for advice on what to do given that we were getting close to the son of *Ukraine's best friend*, Joe Biden. I continued to conduct all the necessary investigative actions.

When I took office as Prosecutor General, I immediately began investigating the tragic events on the Maidan and the corruption scandals surrounding Yanukovych. Poroshenko fully supported me in this. However, the Burisma case involved high-level corruption, and it cost me dearly. Nevertheless first things first. Let's continue with my story.

KNOWN RECORD:
Mykola Zlochevsky

Ukrainian born Mykola Zlochevsky is the owner of the large oil and gas conglomerate Burisma Holdings Ltd. Zlochevsky, who built his oil and gas empire with his partner Mykola Luzin, also served in politics in Ukraine. During 2010-2012, Zlochevsky was the Minister of Ecology in Ukraine and in 2012-2014 he was the deputy secretary for Economic and Social Security of the National Security and Defense Council of Ukraine.[1.14]

Zlochevsky's name became infamously tied with Burisma when legal suits arose alleging possible embezzlement, laundering, and bribery activities occurring through company transactions benefiting Zlochevsky, company leadership, and public officials serving his interests.[1.15] Labeled among the Ukrainian oligarchs, Zlochevsky's Burisma became a household name during the 2020 U.S. election cycle when news broke of then former Vice President Biden's son. Hunter Biden, serving as a board member of the company.[1.16]

Known Records: Mykola Zlochevsky (continued)

Questions regarding Hunter Biden's role and possible illegal enrichment for the Bidens murmured around political circles, ultimately causing Hunter to leave the board shortly after Joe Biden shared his presidential run in April 2019.[1.17]

In 2019, The Derkach Tapes were featured in U.S. media revealing for the first time to many Americans Biden's request to remove then Ukrainian Prosecutor General, Viktor Shokin, from his post in exchange for receipt of loan guarantees funded by U.S. taxpayers.[1.17,1.18] Since then Burisma and the Bidens were topics broadcast in the U.S. media and politics as a constant tug-of-war of truth and ideologies.

Zlochevsky's Ukrainian business has international implications due to Burisma's nearly monopolistic hold of Ukrainian state-owned natural gas and oil resources. As a preferred vendor of the country, Burisma received financing through public funds, much of which was sourced as foreign aid from Europe and U.S. tax dollars, including USAID.[1.19]

The main activity of the investigation took place in 2015. During this period, searches were carried out, including at Zlochevsky's residence. Evidence was actively gathered, interrogations were performed, and expert examinations were conducted. We established the use of a whole network of shell companies and complex schemes to transfer funds abroad, including through banks in Latvia, Lithuania, and Russia.

The investigation came to an unequivocal conclusion. Mykola Zlochevsky was engaged in *large-scale illegal activities*. My firm position on this case was based on a simple conclusion. Foreign members of Burisma's board of directors were used as a *shield* for the company's financial schemes. Among these figures, Hunter Biden, his partner Devon Archer, and former Polish President Aleksander Kwasniewski played key roles.

The investigation was reaching its climax. Interrogations of all those involved, including foreign members of the board of directors, were imminent. Subpoenas were being prepared for Hunter Biden, Alexander Kwasniewski, and Devon Archer. That's when the real storm began. Somehow, this information reached U.S. Vice President Joe Biden. He and his partner in late-night conversations, Ukrainian President Petro Poroshenko, were seriously alarmed.

The situation began to develop rapidly. Immediately after February 3, 2016, when Burisma's office was searched and its assets were seized as part of an investigation into financial fraud, President Petro Poroshenko personally intervened in the situation. Poroshenko summoned me to his office and said, "You have to leave, you understand why." He directly referred to the Burisma case.

As a result of Joe Biden's direct interference in Ukraine's internal affairs and under enormous pressure from the president, I was forced to sign a letter of resignation.[1.20] Afterward, the closure of all criminal cases related to Burisma followed. My resignation was illegal, and the closure of the cases was a crime.

I want to emphasize that I submitted my resignation on February 19, 2016. However, I was not dismissed until April 3, 2016. In my opinion, the reason for the delay was telling. The Verkhovna Rada did not have the necessary votes to dismiss me within the two-week period required by law.[1.21] I regard this delay as evidence of the real support I enjoyed both within Ukraine and from a number of international partners.

Ten years later, I cannot fail to note that after *Shokingate*, I retained the support of many influential figures both in Ukraine and abroad. In the US,

KNOWN RECORD:
Devon Archer

Devon Archer is the former business partner of Hunter Biden and former member of the Burisma Board of Directors. He was born August 17, 1965.[1.22] In 2009, Devon formed a law firm called Rosemont Seneca with his two Yale classmates, Chris Heinz and Hunter Biden. Chris Heinz is the Heinz ketchup heir and stepson to former U.S. Secretary of State John Kerry. Hunter Biden is the son of former U.S. President and Vice President Joe Biden. Devon came to fame when he and Hunter joined the board of Burisma Holdings in 2014.[1.22] In 2022, Archer was indicted and imprisoned for fraudulently issuing and selling more than $60 million of tribal bonds.[1.23]

politicians from the Republican Party spoke out on my behalf. These include Congressman James Comer of the House Oversight Committee and Congressman Jim Jordan of the Judiciary Committee. U.S. President Donald Trump also expressed his bewilderment at my resignation in a declassified transcript of a conversation with Zelensky in 2019.[1.25] Former U.S. Attorney Scott Brady investigated unconfirmed allegations by an FBI whistleblower about alleged bribes paid to the Bidens by Ukraine in 2020 and testified about this to lawmakers in the House of Representatives. He found some of the material *credible enough* to pass it on to the prosecutor leading the criminal investigation into Hunter Biden.[1.26]

During the impeachment debate against Biden, Democratic Representative Jamie Raskin shook Congress with his speech, "You have tens of thousands of documents, dozens of hours of questioning, but no evidence of Joe Biden's guilt!"[127] Doesn't the existence of such evidence prove that the American power machine is seriously ill? Would you find such a wealth of incriminating material on George Bush, Richard Nixon, or even Barack Obama? Hardly. Biden has surpassed all American presidents, leaving behind him a fantastic number of *toxic episodes* in various corners of the globe, like Ukraine, Kazakhstan, Russia, China, and Romania.

All the charges brought against me are trumped up and politically motivated. However, the truth is like water, and it is already making its way to the U.S. Congress. Perhaps even to the courtroom. As Woland said in Mikhail Bulgakov's timeless novel *The Master and Margarita*, "Manuscripts don't burn."[1.28] Ukraine is waiting for the moment when the authors of this corrupt *work of art* will face justice. Although the investigation into Burisma was interrupted and the cases were effectively closed, I am convinced that the evidence gathered was preserved.

Therefore, I will take the liberty of slightly paraphrasing Bulgakov—*archives do not burn*. I am confident that if the opportunity arises to resume this investigation, it can and must be brought to a lawful and just conclusion. Be that as it may, my personal investigation continues.

CHAPTER 2:
HOW DEMOCRATS MASTERED CORRUPTION IN UKRAINE

"My story is about a system where war became a commodity, American aid became a currency for kickbacks, embassies became branches of lobbying firms, and democratic ideals were sacrificed for personal gain."

—Viktor Shokin, 2025

It was late at night in Kiev on February 21, 2014. The air was thick with black smoke from Maidan. The gates of the luxurious residence of Ukrainian President Viktor Yanukovych, Mezhyhirya, were swung open well after midnight. A motorcade of Mercedes S-Class cars, with their headlights off, drove Viktor Yanukovych away into the unknown. In the abandoned office of the president, a report from the National Bank is laid on the floor. The last page drily stated that more than *$3 billion* in gold and foreign currency reserves have evaporated. This large sum was only a fragment of the country's assets that *disappeared* while this administration was in power.

> For example, in 2011–2013, Yanukovych's government issued $3.25 billion in dollar-denominated government bonds. The bonds were bought up by a small circle of individuals to legalize the corrupt income of Yanukovych and his entourage.

At that moment, amid a geopolitical storm, no one paid attention to the fact that the state treasury was empty. According to a modest estimate by the IMF, Ukraine needed no less than *$35 billion* to avoid plunging into a severe financial crisis. Yanukovych's hasty departure was only the beginning of the *great robbery*. In the air above Maidan, saturated not only with gunpowder but also with hope, another smell appeared. The scent of easy prey lingered also and marked a division, which just begun.

Meanwhile, across the ocean and in the west wing of the White House, then U.S. Vice President Joe Biden met with Victoria Nuland, likely with a map of Ukraine on screen. "This is our chance to reset Eastern Europe," Biden or Nuland might write in their memoirs someday. Together with their patrons from the U.S. Democratic Party, a *new Ukrainian elite* took over, seizing Bankova Street where the home of the Ukrainian government sits. A window of opportunity opened for the creation of an unprecedented system of corruption and rent-seeking. The noble slogans of the *Revolution of Dignity* became nothing more than a beautiful cover for it.

After 2014, then Vice President Joe Biden, who oversaw Ukraine since 2009, effectively became the *vice-king* of the former Soviet republic by exploiting the current a power vacuum in Kiev. His power is not enshrined in any agreements, but it is clearly audible in recorded telephone conversations with President Petro Poroshenko. An excerpt from the famous *Biden Tapes* replays Biden's words, "`Petro, you won't get a billion if you keep the prosecutor general.`" The tone brooks no argument. This is the voice of a man who knows the value of his power and knows how to capitalize on it, both figuratively and literally.[2.1]

Cynical and cold calculations dominated the U.S. White House, the offices on Capitol Hill, and the corridors of the State Department. Ukraine, with its vast resources, crumbling institutions, and desperate need for Western support was rapidly turning from a geopolitical prize into a feeding trough for the U.S. Democratic Party. All the slogans about *defending democracy and fighting corruption* became nothing more than pretty phrases designed to create a smokescreen for the launch of a complex mechanism for extracting *corruption rents*.

This scenario is not a conspiracy theory. It is a harsh reality, confirmed by thousands of pages of financial reports, emails, witness testimony, and U.S. congressional investigations. In particular, the investigations led by the tireless

Congressman James Comer and Congressman Jim Jordan are among the most telling to-date. As a result of their work, they have managed to expose much of the giant corruption machine created by the Democrats in Ukraine. At the center of all this intrigue is Joe Biden and his family.[2.2] Hunter Biden became a key cog in this corruption scheme, which I was determined to expose when I became Ukraine's Attorney General.

It became clear to me very early on that the *Revolution of Dignity* had very quickly taken a wrong turn. As early as 2016 foreign auditors were questioning where the billions in international aid were going.[2.3] In 2014-2016 alone, the EU allocated billions of euros to Ukraine to support the budget. Then at the end of the Obama era, the European Court of Auditors admitted that *it could not say exactly where the money had been spent*. I understand their political correctness, but I can say with certainty that the money disappeared into the good old Ukrainian corruption system, which has been taken under the wing of the U.S. Democratic Party. This is the essence of the changes that took place in 2014. The schemes that flourished under Yanukovych were safely inherited by the new government and their curators, led by Joe Biden.

In 2017, the Ukrainian Accounting Chamber published a report entitled *On the Results of the Analysis of the Effectiveness of the Use of International Technical Assistance by State Administration Bodies.* According to the report, since 2015 a total of *440* international technical assistance projects worth *$5.3 billion* have been implemented in Ukraine. In the document, the auditors concluded that the effectiveness of international assistance is extremely low. They noted that the Ukrainian Ministry of Economy did not perform the functions of coordinator and controller of foreign funds expenditure.[2.4]

How was such negligence in the use of American taxpayers' money possible? On August 5, 2015, Arseniy Yatsenyuk's government issued *Resolution No. 553: On Amendments to the Procedure for Attracting, Using, and Monitoring International Technical Assistance.*[2.4] With a light touch from Prime Minister Yatsenyuk and Verkhovna Rada Chairman Volodymyr Groysman, special exemptions were immediately introduced for monitoring projects funded by USAID.

Here are the most glaring legal innovations. For example, procurement plans for USAID projects are approved by the donor (i.e., USAID) and the contractor, *without any coordination with Ukrainian government agencies.* Simply put, this means that there is virtually no control over the spending of funds. The response to violations *depends on the goodwill of USAID itself.* Or, in extreme cases, the response to violations relies on the contractor suddenly admitting that the money was not spent for its intended purpose. In turn, law

KNOWN RECORD:
Arseniy Yatsenyuk

Appointed Ukrainian Prime Minister in 2014, Arseniy Yatsenyuk oversaw domestic affairs after President Yanukovych's removal and replacement by President Poroshenko.[2.5] Nearly two-years afterwards, President Poroshenko asked Yatsenyuk to resign in February 2016. However the Verkhovna Rada did not approve the request. Yatsenyuk remained as Prime Minister for another two months before he resigned and was swapped with Volodymyr Groysman.[2.5]

Volodymyr Groysman

In the wake of the 2014 Maidan, Volodymyr Groysman was Chair of the Ukrainian Parliament, before replacing Yatsenyuk as prime minister. At age 38, he was the youngest prime minister until he left in August 2019.[2.6,2.7] As prime minister, his relationship with Poroshenko was rocky due to his support of de-regulation efforts, which Poroshenko did not favor.[2.7] enforcement oversight was virtually absent from the resolution. The document assigned monitoring functions *solely to the Ukrainian Ministry of Economic Development*. This situation excludes from the audit and control procedure specialized agencies such as the Ukrainian Ministry of Internal Affairs, the PGO, and the State Bureau of Investigations (GBR) The recently *created* Specialized Anti-Corruption Prosecutor's Office (SAPO) and National Anti-Corruption Bureau of Ukraine (NABU), *which were established at Biden's initiative,* were also excluded from these same monitoring functions.

Here is a real-life example of how this worked in practice. I have before me a procurement plan for a program called *Effective and Responsible Policy in Ukraine* implemented with USAID funds on behalf of the Verkhovna Rada Committee on Foreign Affairs. The program budget is $6,150,000. This amount seems to have been plucked out of thin air. There is no breakdown of expenses. Many of the expenses seem absurd. Millions of dollars were allocated for PR and transaction costs. Of course, there are no reports on this program. It is also unclear what effect the program had and where this tidy sum has gone. Most importantly, everything is within the law, thanks to that very same Resolution No. 553.[2.4]

Incidentally, this program was signed by Irina Lutsenko, a member of the Verkhovna Rada and the Foreign Affairs Committee in Ukraine. She made amendments and approved the plan for the procurement of goods, work, and

23

services under this program. Irina is the wife of former Prosecutor General Yuriy Lutsenko, about whom you will read more later in this book. Essentially, it would not be an exaggeration to say that *Resolution No. 553 legalized corruption in the use of U.S. foreign aid.* Steal all you want! You won't be held legally responsible. As a servant of the law, such innovations seemed outrageous to me. All interested parties, like corrupt foundations and officials, were officially given the green light to steal American money that could have served Ukraine's interests.

Why did the state remove itself from control over foreign financial aid? Because Yatsenyuk and Groysman, who came to power on the wave of the Maidan, proved to be faithful executors of all instructions *from above*, which were instructions from the Obama administration.

Against this negative backdrop, a series of highly revealing episodes unfolded. Hunter Biden unexpectedly appeared in Ukraine, skillfully embedded in the heart of the corrupt oil and gas sector, and in partnership with a corrupt official from the Yanukovych era, former Ukrainian Minister of Ecology Zlochevsky. I had to personally untangle the web of corruption schemes of the former minister. Then it became clear how and why Hunter Biden appeared in his entourage.

Today, the archives of the U.S. Senate and House of Representatives contain countless witness statements about all the fuss Joe Biden made over his son's Ukrainian business. Thanks to Hunter's forgetfulness, his laptop, which was sent for repair with a bunch of compromising material and *confidential* correspondence, became public property. The laptop, which was gutted by the American media, confirmed the testimony of witnesses and facts that had been accumulating since 2014. Thanks to all this new information, the puzzle of *Biden's Ukraine*, the pieces of which I had been trying to put together since I retired, instantly fell into place. What I saw revealed a vivid and damning picture. That's when I fully realized why Joe Biden ran me over like a steamroller.

Here is an excellent admission from one of the witnesses. It shows the extent of Biden's involvement in his son's affairs, not only in Ukraine, but also in other high-profile episodes, including stories related to deals with the Chinese. Hunter Biden's partner, Devon Archer, testified to Congress in July 2023. He candidly recounted how Joe Biden joined Hunter's business dinners with his partners. Joe Biden was either present in person or joined the conversations via speakerphone. There were more than twenty such instances.[28]

The story did not end with Hunter. As U.S. Congressman James Comer's investigation revealed, there was a whole network of companies and accounts through which money was distributed among members of the Biden clan, their friends, and their partners. A whole system of monetizing the political influence of the father emerged.[2.7]

A lot of water has flowed under the bridge since I started digging into the Biden family's corruption schemes in Ukraine. It took more than 10-years to obtain new evidence of the financial scams perpetrated by this *noble* family. James Comer published a book on January 2025 called, *All the President's Money: Investigating the Secret Foreign Schemes That Made the Biden Family Rich*. In it, Comer states in black and white that his investigation revealed nearly *$30 million* transferred to the Biden's family account.[2.9]Comer's findings are based on SAR (Suspicious Activity Report) bank reports, which paint a truly phenomenal picture worthy of a crime novel.[2.10] I would like to note that a significant portion of these sums *flashed* before my eyes in the investigation materials during my years working in the prosecutor's office. For those interested in seeing the entire timeline of the Biden family's corruption episodes, I recommend James Comer's well- illustrated infographic of the investigation called, *The Bidens' Influence Peddling Timeline*.[2.2]

KNOWN RECORD:
The Hunter Biden Laptop

In April 2019, Hunter Biden turned in his laptop to a local repair shop in Delaware due to water damage but never returned to pick it up. After receiving no contact from Hunter, the repairman submitted the laptop to the FBI in December 2019.[2.11, 2.12] The laptop contained alleged illegal contents, which included evidence of Biden family business deals in China and Ukraine, and illicit photos. The contents were then verified by the FBI as authentic and belonging to Hunter.[2.13]

In October 2020, news of Hunter's laptop and its scandalous contents broke in a *New York Post* article on the eve of the 2020 U.S presidential elections with Trump vs. Biden.[2.14] Yet, the laptop was dismissed as Russian collusion by Biden's campaign team, media outlets, and social media. Branded as a hit piece from the Trump campaign, media labeled the news *unverifiable* by intelligence agencies.[2.13-2.15]

Known Record: Hunter Biden Laptop (continued)

Further investigations into the laptop by U.S. legislators revealed a large coverup coordinated among major media outlets, social media and U.S. intelligence agencies. During Congressional meetings, correspondence shared supported allegations to defeat Trump in the 2020 elections.[2.13-2.17]

The Hunter Biden laptop marked rising negative impacts of censorship on U.S. politics that grew distrust in U.S media and government. Such concerns in time lead to the sale of Twitter to Elon Musk.[2.12,2.13] Government distrust, especially round Joe Biden and his family was reflected in a poll after Biden took office. The poll showed 54% of voters for Biden as president would have voted another way if the Hunter laptop story was deemed true.[2.18]

Although the contents of the laptop could serve as strong evidence of illegal self-enrichment by the Bidens, no accountability for the mishandling of evidence or the coverup occurred.[2.12] However, Senator Grassley requested the release of all FBI correspondence about the laptop in April 2025.[2.19]

Burisma was not the only company involved in extracting *rent*. American taxpayer money was being stolen through USAID. This once noble instrument of global aid, created under President Kennedy, turned into a *money shower* for corrupt officials from various countries. They received American money but spent it completely for purposes other than those intended.

I saw millions of U.S. dollars go to various funds and charitable organizations with poor reputations. Funds were allocated to USAID *democracy development* and *anti-corruption* projects for organizations that were registered just the day before, with minimal experience and dubious connections. The reports on these grants were either fictitious or non-existent, thanks to *Resolution No. 553!* A significant portion of the money simply disappeared. All these problems are reflected in the reports of the Accounting Chamber of Ukraine, which were prepared when there were still people there who were capable of calling a spade a spade, rather than passing off failures as *successes in democratization.*[2.20]

Under Ambassadors Pyatt and Yovanovitch, Obama/Biden appointees, the U.S. Embassy in Kiev turned from a diplomatic mission into a branch of Washington lobbying firms. They promoted the interests of Hunter, his partners, and other figures associated with the U.S. Democratic Party. The embassy actively interfered in the internal personnel decisions of the Ukrainian government.

Embassy members lobbied for the appointment of *its own* people to key positions in the prosecutor's office, to anti-corruption agencies (NABU, SAPO), and even to positions in state-owned enterprises(such as Naftogaz). These appointees were often accountable to the embassy rather than to the Ukrainian people. This embassy's influence even went as far as the transfer of sensitive information classified as confidential. I will discuss this in more detail in Chapter 20.

American *advisors* were embedded in Ukrainian law enforcement and anti-corruption structures. They effectively controlled the course of reforms in the law enforcement system and key investigations, especially those that could affect the interests of Burisma and its owner, or companies receiving grants from USAID. Any investigation that ran counter to the interests of the Democratic Party was blocked on the pretext of *not being in line with the spirit of the reforms.*

Bank records examined by U.S Congressman Comer show how money from Burisma and other Ukrainian sources, such as *oligarchs seeking protection*, flowed through a maze of offshore companies. These offshore

KNOWN RECORD:
James Comer

Elected to Congress in 2016 for the 1st Congressional District in the state of Kentucky, James Comer, continues to serve as Chairman of the House Committee on Oversight and Government Reform.[2.21]

On September 28, 2023, Congressman Comer began impeachment inquiries into President Joe Biden, focusing on evidence showing how the president benefited from his son's business activities.[2.22] With core support from the Republican party, the hearings exposed records, reports and testimony evidencing illegalities, including publicly released payments to the Bidens from Russia, Kazakhstan, and Ukraine.[2.23]

Yet, opposing Democratic party members backing Biden, mocked the effort, claiming that evidence presented lacked credibility to move a trial forward.[2.21,2.24] In March 2024, Comer's attempts to impeach President Biden fell short. Instead of pursuing the matter further, he mentioned passing on his gathered evidence for criminal referrals.[2.25] companies included the infamous Rosemont Seneca Bohai, linked to Hunter Biden and Devon Archer. These same monies also flowed across accounts in various jurisdictions, like China, Romania, Mexico, and the US. I believe that some of this money was then used to support Joe Biden's political ambitions and finance his allies.[2.19] *It was a classic influence peddling scheme.*

Ukraine became not just an ally on the geopolitical chessboard for the ruling elite of the U.S. Democratic Party, but *an object of systematic extraction of corrupt rents*. Under the slogans of supporting democracy and fighting corruption, a machine was created and fine-tuned where:

- *The political influence of Joe Biden as U.S. Vice President and as President through his administration* was sold to Ukrainian oligarchs, like in the case of Burisma, and corrupt officials.

- *U.S. taxpayer money allocated to USAID* was used inefficiently and often stolen through dubious grant schemes and inflated contracts, feeding loyal contractors and lobbyists.

- *Diplomatic leverage* (e.g., activities exercised through the embassy or the threat of freezing aid) was used to pressure the Ukrainian government in the interests of American *beneficiaries* and to protect schemes.

All this shows not just isolated missteps, but a system deeply rooted in the Democratic Party's approach to Ukraine from 2014-2021. This system turned a country fighting for survival and a European future into a source of enrichment for the select few. The price of this *influence* for Ukraine is deepening corruption, undermining trust in real reforms, and ultimately weakening its sovereignty on the eve of a major war. For America, it is a serious blow to its moral authority and trust in its institutions.

The model of support for Ukraine built under Obama has turned into a systemic crisis. USAID programs and the personnel policy of the U.S. Embassy have not eradicated corruption but, on the contrary, have legalized many new schemes that were previously unheard of. Under the guise of *reforms*, spheres of influence were redistributed in favor of loyal oligarchs and contractors linked to the U.S. Democratic Party, such as Viktor Pinchuk, Petro Poroshenko, and a whole galaxy of small oligarchs from his orbit.

The country's de facto sovereignty was eliminated. Key decisions, ranging from the appointment of the prosecutor general and heads of anti-corruption agencies to the management of state-owned enterprises, were made under the dictation of the U.S. embassy in the interests of American beneficiaries. Joe Biden's ultimatum to me was no exception. Rather, his ultimatum confirmed the rule, finally cementing Ukraine's status as a state critically dependent on external influence.

The corrupt system established in the early years after Maidan played a major role in severely undermining Ukraine's defense capabilities in the run-up to Russia's attack. Billions in military and financial aid were stolen or used inefficiently, as confirmed by numerous reports from the U.S. Government Accountability Office (GAO).[2.26] The lack of equipment and the supply of poor-quality equipment to the Armed Forces of Ukraine on the eve of 2022 were a direct consequence of the emergence of the *Biden system*. I am convinced that many of these problems were laid down during the active intervention in key areas of the state by *reformers* from the team of the former U.S Vice President.

In the following chapters, I would like to tell you more about the episodes of corruption and political intrigue that unfolded before my eyes when I was Prosecutor General, which I know firsthand.

PART TWO:

THE BIDEN BRAND INC. SCAM IN UKRAINE

"In Ukraine, Joe Biden was called the vice king...Biden called the country's president Poroshenko, his second wife, because every night he had heart-to-heart talks with him with one goal in mind...to build a system of external control over Ukraine for his own personal gain."

—Viktor Shokin, 2025

CHAPTER 3:

IT'S GREAT TO BE HUNTER BIDEN

"The value that Hunter Biden brought to Burisma was, in theory, corporate governance, but obviously, *given the brand*, he was a big part of the value. I think that was a key component of the value…"

—Devon Archer Testimony to U.S.

Congress, July 2023[3.1]

Hunter Biden's history at Burisma is not just a shameful episode. It is the key to the Democratic Party's *corruption machine*. One only needs to look at Hunter's *career biography* to come to an obvious conclusion. This womanizer and big spender was simply lucky to be born the son of an influential father.

People started talking about Joe Biden's nepotism over 20-years ago. Even Wikipedia gives a detailed description of the family. After graduating from Yale in 1996, Hunter got a job as a consultant at MBNA America Bank.[3.2] In less than two years, he became the company's senior vice president. Even then, I knew people in the U.S. were saying, "Sure, a lot of kids with influential parents get good jobs. But the Biden situation is a bit concerning."

Hunter was indeed lucky with his father, as noted by former Polish President and Hunter's partner at Burisma, Aleksander Kwasniewski. In an interview with the Associated Press, he once confided, "If you don't have a name, you're nobody. Being Biden isn't bad. It's a good name," Kwasniewski said candidly. Well, at least he's honest.[3.2]

On April 22, 2014, Vice President Biden visited Kiev and held a meeting with representatives of the Ukrainian authorities. Just three weeks later, on May 12, 2014, it was announced that his son Hunter joined the board of directors at Burisma. The Revolution of Dignity had just overthrown the pro-Russian Yanukovych. Ukraine was on the brink of collapse, with a military conflict unfolding in the southeast between Kiev and pro-Russian separatists. As Devon Archer testified before Congress, it was around March 2014, while the ashes of the Maidan were still warm, when Hunter was in Moscow. Hunter was there to discuss new business projects in light of the prospects which opened up for the Bidens after friendly forces came to power in Ukraine.[3.3] It is noteworthy that the meeting took place on March 14, 2014, the day Russia invaded Crimea. Interestingly, Archer claimed in his testimony that Hunter's future employer Mykola Zlochevsky was also present at that meeting in Moscow.[3.3] It was Zlochevsky, a figure in criminal cases, who would lead to Archer's arrest.

After these cynical meetings in Moscow on such a tragic date for my country, I was doubly shocked by the appointment of Hunter Biden to the board of directors of Burisma. He was a man with zero experience in energy and a scandalous reputation. According to declassified documents from the U.S. National Archives and correspondence from Hunter's laptop, the media asked Joe Biden whether it was ethical for his son to be employed by a company linked to a corrupt former official in Viktor Yanukovych's administration. Moreover, at that time, Zlochevsky was under investigation in London for money laundering. State Department officials tried to convey the toxicity of this situation to the vice president. Among them, was high-ranking department official George P. Kent.[3.4]

It is also interesting to recall the statements of former White House stenographer Mike McCormick, who flew with the vice president on Air Force Two and overheard his conversations on the eve of Joe Biden's visit to Ukraine in April 2014. The vice president discussed how to promote Burisma's business. *Just a few days before that conversation*, Hunter became a member of the company's board of directors.[3.5] Official correspondence from Joe Biden published by the U.S. National Archives showed that he maintained contact with Hunter's partners (i.e., he was actively involved in his son's affairs, contrary to his denials). Records also show that starting in 2014 Joe Biden was aware that Mykola Zlochevsky had serious legal problems.[3.6]

"Family Golf." Pictured: Devon Archer (far left) with Joe and Hunter Biden

Additionally, it is now known that Biden's press secretary Kendra Barkoff monitored publications about corruption schemes, particularly those related to Burisma's money laundering. Meanwhile, Hunter wrote a letter to Vadim Pozharskyi at Burisma, asked about the allegations against Zlochevsky, and was interested in "who could put an end to these attacks."[3.7] Yet, against the backdrop of seven corruption cases involving Zlochevsky, his company Burisma signed a memorandum of cooperation with USAID. I will return to this little-known episode a little later.

Here is an interesting detail from Hunter's leaked correspondence. In a letter dated May 13, 2014, Hunter's partner Eric Schwerin writes that he received a call from Demetra Lambros, an advisor to Joe Biden. Demetra asked Eric to remove a photo of Devon Archer with Joe Biden from the Burisma website.[3.7] I wonder how the advisor justified her delicate request? It turns out that Joe Biden himself could have asked her to do so. So Biden is concerned about his photo on the Burisma website? Why, if the vice president did not consider anything that linked this Ukrainian company to his name to be a problem? Or did Biden realize that the company was toxic and that such a photo could compromise him? This episode confirms once again that officials in the Biden administration were in contact with his son's partners and, presumably, kept contact on the instructions of the vice president.

In addition, a June 11, 2023, article in *The New York Post* reported that Hunter partially used White House documents which were possibly classified.[3.8] The full version of these materials was posted on Twitter by Miranda Devine.[3.9] In addition, the letter she quoted mentions a certain person named Alex who was supposed to help *reestablish contact with the boxer.* Could this be a reference for Kiev Mayor Vitali Klitschko? He is, of course, a boxer. All of this suggests that Hunter freely took advantage of his father's connections in the White House, including his ability to establish contacts with Ukrainian politicians. Today, it is known that Joe Biden understood perfectly well who he was dealing with in Ukraine but deliberately avoided uncomfortable questions on the subject.

Be that as it may, Hunter Biden and his buddy Devon Archer, Americans with *zero experience in energy* and scandalous reputations, suddenly joined the board of directors of Burisma, a large Ukrainian oil and gas company with a tarnished reputation. What's more, their salaries *were many times higher* than the standard salaries of Ukrainian top managers at the time. Hunter Biden's official salary at Burisma was $50,000 per month.[3.10] At the same time, Hunter's main place of work remained the law firm Schiller & Flexner LLP, located in New York. Simultaneously, Hunter also held the position of chairman of the U.S. Coalition for Global Leadership, chair of the Center for Security Policy, and chair of the National Democratic Institute. All this occurred while Burisma owner Mykola Zlochevsky faced criminal charges in the UK for money laundering and had his accounts, worth $23 million, frozen.

Bank records obtained by Congressman Comer show that this *dream team* received $3.3 million from Burisma through Hunter and Archer's company, *Rosemont Seneca Bohai*, between April 2014 and the end of 2015.[3.11] Together with payments through other firms linked to Biden, *the total amount reaches more than $6.5 million.* This figure was cited by Joseph Ziegler, a special agent with the U.S. Internal Revenue Service's Criminal Investigation Division, in his testimony to Congress on July 19, 2023.[3.12] It must be assumed that Special Agent Ziegler had full visibility of *all* payments made to the Bidens from abroad.

Clearly, the vice president's son was not paid for consulting, as Hunter Biden's defenders claimed, but for access to his father. What is this, if not *influence peddling?* Emails published by Comer, among others, show direct requests from Burisma's management to Hunter for *help* in resolving the company's problems with the Ukrainian authorities. This was precisely the reason for bringing in Hunter, who had never had anything to do with the energy sector before. It was not Hunter's talent that was important to Burisma, but his surname. With a surname like that, you can move mountains and get away with it.

Not convinced? Ask someone without a famous last name. Meet lawyer, John Buretta. In June 2025, the *Daily Mail* published an article with

KNOWN RECORD:
The Oversight Project

The Oversight Project is a student led online blog produced in coordination with a seminar offered at the American University Washington College of Law in Seattle, Washington.[3.13] Published blogs reflect examinations in of the *"oversight and accountability communities,"* which include "Inspector Generals, Office of Government Ethics, Office of Special Counsel, Government Accountability Office, and the Office of Management and Budget," among others. On Occasion, blogs from community professionals are posted.[3.13]

On September 19, 2017, the Oversight Project analyzed inconsistencies among FARA reports submitted by Burisma-related lobbyists. The firm, Cravath, Swaine & Moore, under which John Burreta worked while representing Burisma, was forced to retroactively submit a FARA. In contrast, Hunter Biden was not required to file a FARA. This double-standard suggested possible covert activity related to Hunter and foreign lobbying efforts.[3.14] the intriguing allegation, "Hunter Biden helped develop a plan to 'shut down' Viktor Shokin's investigation into Burisma." [3.15] The article literally explains why *it's good to be a Biden*. New documents from the U.S. Department of Justice highlighted in the article indicated that lawyer John Buretta, who lobbied on behalf of Ukrainian energy company Burisma, was forced to register as a foreign agent under the FARA law. The conservative research organization named, The Oversight Project, obtained these documents and claimed that Burisma Board Director Hunter Biden *avoided filing a FARA solely because of his surname.*

Data from the Oversight Project confirms that in 2022-2023, the Justice Department established that Buretta represented Burisma in 2016. During that time, Buretta held meetings with high-ranking U.S. officials, including representatives of the U.S. State Department and the U.S. Justice Department. In these meetings, Buretta attempted to influence their position on Burisma owner Mykola Zlochevsky. This type of activity falls under the FARA law requiring the registration of foreign agents. [3.15]

Incidentally, the findings uncovered by The Oversight Project shows that while Hunter still held a seat on Burisma's Board, he tried to meet with then U.S. Deputy Secretary of State Anthony Blinken in May 2015. Later in July

2016, Hunter also sent an email to Blinken's wife, Evan Ryan, while trying to connect Blinken with Blue Star Strategies, a lobbyist hired by Burisma. Hunter also lobbied for the company's interests by organizing meetings between its representatives and U.S. officials, as evidenced by letters from his laptop. The Oversight Project insists that Hunter Biden's actions for Burisma were *identical* to those of a lawyer, like Buretta.[3.12]

Despite the obvious parallels between Biden and Buretta's activities, Hunter did not register under FARA. The Oversight Project accused the U.S. Justice Department, including Special Counsel David Weiss, of deliberate inaction due to a desire to avoid scandal for the president's family. They also cite testimony from IRS whistleblowers who claimed that an investigation into possible FARA violations by Hunter Biden was blocked. During court proceedings in other cases active in 2023 which involved tax claims and allegations of illegal possession of weapons, the Justice Department acknowledged the possibility of prosecuting Hunter Biden for violating the FARA law. However, no official charges under this law were ever filed. Yet, Buretta and the Blue Star Strategies lobbying firm, which were both hired by Burisma with Hunter's involvement, were forced to register retroactively.[3.12] The Oversight Project alleges that these FARA filing inconsistencies are evidence of a double standard and of corruption. I fully agree with their conclusions. I will try to explain why.

CHAPTER 4:

GOOD GUY KOLYA AND HIS FRIEND, THE FORMER PRESIDENT OF POLAND

"So, Kolya is a good guy."

— Petro Poroshenko from recorded

conversations with Oleksandr Onyshchenko[4.1,4.2]

I will start with an intriguing question. Why did Vice President Biden need *my head*—that is the *head* of the Ukrainian Prosecutor General? To answer that question, we need to answer these questions. What is Burisma, and why did it have such influence on high politics? And, how did this mysterious Mykola Zlochevsky (a.k.a. Kolya) bring the son of the vice president and other famous names into his company?

Mykola Zlochevsky was entrenched in politics and business since the 1990s, but his *moment of glory* came during Viktor Yanukovych's presidency, when he became Minister of Ecology of Ukraine. His rise to the top of Ukrainian business was not trivial. Zlochevsky founded Burisma together with his partner Mykola Lysyn in 2002. However, at that time, the company did not

KNOWN RECORD:
Burisma

Burisma is one of Ukraine's largest private companies for extraction of hydrocarbons, primarily natural gas. At its peak, it controlled over 30% of Ukraine's mineral resources for private use. It held 35 licenses for extraction in all gas-bearing regions of the country. In the mid-2010s, it provided more than 30% of all-natural gas produced in Ukraine – over 1 billion cubic meters yearly. All gas produced was sold on the chronically deficient domestic market.[4.3]

Burisma Holdings Ltd. unites twelve domestic companies engaged in deep exploration, production, and sale of natural gas. The largest of these is Esco-Pivnich (also known as Esco-North), with a monthly production level of around 37 million cubic meters. Other companies in the holding include Pari, First Ukrainian Oil and Gas Company, Aldea, and Technokomservice.[4.3]

Burisma (continued)

The Burisma holding company is owned by Brociti Investments Limited, which is registered in Cyprus. The actual owner is Mykola Zlochevsky.[4.3] The holding company also owns the large production company Kub-Gas, which Zlochevsky bought after the 2015 death of its former owner, Jan Kulczyk, considered Poland's richest man.[4.3]

Burisma became a household name in the U.S. during the election involving Trump vs. Biden. Media covered Hunter's role at Burisma before Joe Biden officially announced he was running, presenting questionable ties suggesting corruption.[4.4] The name Burisma was circulated in the news again, during the infamous 2019 phone call with Trump and Zelenskyy. After U.S. Congressman Adam Schiff proclaimed the conversation as quid pro quo, Burisma became tied to the first impeachment of President Trump in 2020, repeatedly surfacing in the investigations.[4.4,4.5] The Burisma issue was resurrected in the 2023-2024 impeachment inquiry against President Biden led by the U.S House of Representatives, and again when Trump faced-off Biden in the 2024 elections.[4.4] have the right to develop fields independently. It drilled wells and extracted gas under contracts with state-owned enterprises.

The business began to grow rapidly in late 2003, when Zlochevsky lobbied the National Security and Defense Council of Ukraine (NSDC) to create *a State Committee on Natural Resources*, which he effectively headed.[4.6] The newly appointed chairman launched tenders for the sale of special permits for the right to use subsoil resources. It is not difficult to guess whose companies participated in these tenders with 100% success. Esco-Pivnich received its first license for the development of oil and gas fields in July 2004, the second three weeks later, and the third in October of the same year. Pari, also part of the Burisma group, received five more permits for gas production.

When Oleksandr Onyshchenko came to power in the Ukrainian Parliament in 2005, Zlochevsky was removed from his position as head of the State Committee for Natural Resources. The rapid development of his gas business came to a halt for a while. Meanwhile, the owner of Burisma bet on the Party of Regions and was elected to parliament in 2006. When Yanukovych came to power, Zlochevsky headed the State Committee for Material Reserves of Ukraine, and finally, in 2010 he regained his position

KNOWN RECORD:
Oleksandr Onyshchenko

Oleksandr Onyshchenko was in Parliament under President Yanukovych, then an advisor to President Poroshenko.[4.6] Considered the original whistleblower who exposed taped conversations between Joe Biden and Poroshenko, he was subpoenaed to testify in the first Trump impeachment hearing to present these facts. Yet, he was arrested by German law enforcement for money laundering prior to leaving for the U.S.[4.6,4.7] He was imprisoned for half a year. In 2020, he survived a failed assassination attempt.[4.7] He is exiled in Spain, after Ukraine failed to extradite him for alleged corruption and money laundering.[4.7]

Party of Regions

This political party in the Ukrainian Parliament was most influential in the Yanukovych era and supported his presidential run in 2004 and 2010.[4.8] With the party's support, Zlochevsky secured a seat in Parliament and regained his title as Minister of Ecology in 2010.[4.9] as *Minister of Ecology of Ukraine*. He was interested in this ministry not because the gas trader was passionate about ecology and the environment, but because the duties of the head of the Ministry of Ecology included control over mineral resources, including the issuance of licenses for their development.

In 2011, Zlochevsky's partner, Mykola Lysin, was killed in a car accident in Kiev while driving his Lamborghini. After Lysin's death, all property rights passed to Zlochevsky. The years 2010-2012 were a golden age for Burisma. Its subsidiaries received more than two dozen licenses for the development of oil and gas fields during that time.

It is very convenient when you are the Minister of Ecology of Ukraine, overseeing the issuance of licenses for the exploitation of mineral resources, while owning an oil and gas company that needs these licenses. Subsequently, the licenses allowed Esco-Pivnich to grow tenfold. From a modest gas producer with an annual gas production of 30 million cubic meters in 2010, Burisma became a major player by 2014 with an annual production of 400 million cubic meters. In the 2024 rankings published by *Den'ga UA*, Zlochevsky retains a strong financial position. He ranks 17th among Ukrainian oligarchs with a fortune of $515 million.[4.10]

Of course by Ukrainian standards, Zlochevsky cannot be called a top oligarch. However, he did quite well for himself during Ukrainian President

Yanukovych's time in power. Thus, another functionary-businessman from the Yanukovych era burst onto the Ukrainian business scene. In this way, the *bad guy* who was a pillar of the corrupt regime, very quickly turned into a *great guy*, Hunter's partner, and a friend of the Biden family. In 2023, The *New York Post* published joint photos of Hunter Biden's daughter Naomi and Mykola Zlochevsky's daughter Karina together with their fathers.[4.11] In fact, his friendship with the Bidens *whitewashed* the corrupt Zlochevsky.

The 2014 Maidan Revolution swept through Yanukovych's entourage. Its *architects* passed a lustration law. As a result, activists threw former officials and businessmen from the Yanukovych era into trash cans and opened criminal cases against a number of officials. However, this fate *miraculously* bypassed Mykola Zlochevsky. Of course, the *miracle* was that after the coup he fled the country, realizing who the Maidan bells were tolling for.

However, not everything went smoothly for the former minister. In March 2014, the UK Anti-Fraud Office took an interest in him. A separate closed investigation was also conducted by the British Serious Crimes Office. Zlochevsky was accused of money laundering. The amount mentioned in the investigation materials was impressive, totaling $50 million in funds.[4.12]

British investigators established that between December 19, 2013, and January 22, 2014, $35 million was transferred to the corporate accounts of

Burisma Holdings Ltd. and Brociti Investments Ltd. (Cyprus). A portion of that amount, a cool $15 million, was transferred to Zlochevsky's accounts at LGT Bank in Switzerland. On April 16 and May 28, 2014, the Central Criminal Court of London imposed restrictions on Zlochevsky's use of $23.5 million held in four accounts belonging to Burisma and Brociti at BNP Paribas. As a result of this case, according to the decision of the Central Criminal Court of London (Old Bailey), *$23.5 million was frozen.*[4.13]

Naturally, proceedings against the former Minister Zlochevsky began in the Ukrainian justice system. On March 27, 2014, investigators from the PGO of Ukraine opened the first criminal case against Zlochevsky for embezzlement of state funds during his tenure as minister. The facts, as they say, were right there on the surface. Mykola was charged with embezzling 49.38 million hryvnia. He was notified of the charges on December 30, 2014.[4.14]

Between April and December 2014, four more criminal cases were opened involving the former *minister of deep drilling* (my ironic nickname for Zlochevsky), his wife, his daughter, and the companies aligned under the Burisma holding company. A complex and confusing scheme was uncovered for transferring funds from the accounts of some Burisma subsidiaries to the accounts of others, from where the money was transferred, to offshore accounts, and to ending up in the pockets of the former minister and members of his family.[4.14]

If I am not mistaken, seven cases were opened against Zlochevsky before I was appointed head of the PGO. Most of them were combined into a single case under number *42014000000000805*.[4.14] All the details and evidence in this case were compiled into several volumes. Information gathered contained specific episodes of fraudulent schemes involving money, in which the Yanukovych family and the young oligarch Sergei Kurchenko were also involved. Ukrainian investigators actively dug into Zlochevsky, uncovering more and more evidence of crimes.

A serious threat loomed over Zlochevsky's oil and gas empire. But Mykola quickly realized that to save his empire from collapse, he needed to lean on political heavyweights. Therefore, in the spring of 2014, Burisma's board of directors was replenished with a whole galaxy of famous people, in addition to Biden's son Hunter. Despite the numerous criminal cases against Zlochevsky, Hunter and his *celebrity* board members were unmoved and were indifferent.

Among the celebrity crew on the Burisma board was former Polish President Aleksander Kwasniewski. How did the former leader of Poland end up on the Burisma board? That's a good question and a very important detail in our story to realize how Zlochevsky won influence among European Union officials. To understand how this happened, we need to go back in time to Ukrainian President Yanukovych's rule in 2012.

In 2012, a special commission was established in Ukraine in accordance with an agreement between the Ukrainian government and the leadership of the European Parliament. This commission included former EU Parliament President Pat Cox and former Polish President Aleksander Kwasniewski. The group's mission was to find a compromise that would lead to the freedom of the convicted and imprisoned former Ukrainian Prime Minister Yulia Tymoshenko.[4.15] The commission worked until Viktor Yanukovych's opponent, Tymoshenko, was released from prison following the Maidan victory. It was believed that the fate of the agreement between Ukraine and the EU depended on the success of the *Cox-Kwasniewski mission*. Therefore, the work of the commission was closely monitored by the Ukrainian authorities.

The commission and its work on the *Cox-Kwasniewski mission* was supervised by then Ukrainian Prime Minister Mykola Azarov on behalf of Ukraine and then European Parliament President Martin Schulz on behalf of the European Parliament. Prime Minister Azarov along with other Ukrainian officials viewed the commission members as honored guests and quickly realized that the guests had to be given a reception befitting their status. To understand the reason behind all the fuss over the commission members, you must understand the heart of Ukrainian hospitality! Guests cannot be left alone. Guests must be entertained, pampered with boat trips on the Dnieper, taken fishing and hunting, treated to borscht with pampushki and salo, and stuffed with gorilka. The richer the cultural entertainment and the more abundant the feasts are, the better. I have no information about how Pat Cox spent his time in Ukraine. However, I have heard a lot about Kwasniewski and know that he really enjoyed all these traditional gatherings and feasts, especially because Kwasniewski speaks Russian perfectly.

What does EU support and Burisma have to do with the Ukrainian style pampering of Cox and Kwasniewski? As they say in Ukraine, the whole point is that the role of the hospitable Ukrainian host was assigned to the then deputy head of the National Security and Defense Council of Ukraine (NSDC) who was none other than owner of the oil and gas company Burisma, Mykola Zlochevsky! It was the good guy Kolya who paid for all the entertainment for the commission members out of his own pocket and rubbed elbows with them. It was no trouble at all for him.

KNOWN RECORD:
Aleksander Kwasniewski

Polish born Aleksander Kwasniewski was a minister during the Soviet Union's Cold War reign in the 1980s. After the fall of the Berlin Wall and end of the Cold War in 1989, Kwasniewski led the post-communist progressive political party named the Social Democracy of the Republic of Poland. He was President of Poland from 1995 until 2005.[4.16,4.17]

Kwasniewski's presidency showcased his pro-western ideals in his rapid modernization projects, his effort to redraft the Polish constitution, and his success in Poland joining NATO. In 2003, he approved the treaty joining Poland to the European Union.[4.16,4.18] Considered a long-time supporter of Ukraine with a pro-western influence, he helped broker the mediation efforts in the 2004 Orange Revolution in Ukraine, which resulted in Yanukovych losing his first attempt at the Ukrainian presidency. In 2020, a public poll in Poland identified him as one of the greatest Presidents of Poland.[4.16,4.18]

KNOWN RECORD:
Yulia Tymoshenko

Yulia Tymoshenko was the first female Prime Minister of Ukraine, serving from 2005-2010. She strongly supports Ukraine joining the European Union and opposes any Russian-Eurasian efforts.[4.19] Tymoshenko co-led the Orange Revolution, a political uprising in Ukraine occurring November 2004-January 2005 that was one of Soros's supported color revolutions.[4.20,4.21] The Orange Revolution cost Yanukovych the election in his first run for president to Viktor Yushchenko and secured Tymoshenko's seat as Prime Minister in 2005 under his administration.[4.20] In 2010, she lost the Ukrainian presidential race to her opponent Viktor Yanukovych. Shortly after, she was imprisoned from 2011-2014 allegedly due to political persecution by the Yanukovych administration. With the assistance of EU President Cox and Kwasniewski, Tymoshenko regained her freedom after the events in Maidan.[415]

It is difficult to recall exactly when Kwasniewski became friends with Zlochevsky. Regardless, months of feasting did not go to waste, and their friendly relations grew into business ones. That is how in February 2014 before the victory of the Maidan a token missionary of the European Union Parliament, Aleksander Kwasniewski, joined the Burisma Board of Directors.

Once Kwasniewski was onboard Burisma, a door leading to the Bidens shortly after was opened. There are a few stories circling about which describe how the Biden family became acquainted with Zlochevsky and Burisma. According to one account, it was Kwasniewski who helped Zlochevsky get in touch with the Bidens. The Polish president had extensive international contacts. Kwasniewski, who spoke both Russian and English, could have acted as a mediator between Biden and Zlochevsky. Incidentally, Zlochevsky does not speak any foreign languages.

However, another account of how the relationship between the Bidens and Burisma originated is based upon the testimony of Hunter's partner Devon Archer.[4.22] This version of the story contradicts the claims made by members of the Biden family and those parroted by the liberal press because it claims that Hunter Biden's acquaintance with Mykola Zlochevsky was not accidental. According to Devon Archer, Burisma was on the list of Rosemont Real Estate Acquisition Fund One (RREAF).[4.22]   This list was compiled by Tri Global (cap-intro company), which acted as a broker. However, correspondence from the laptop refutes Archer's statement. In other words, he lied in his testimony to Congress.

> A cap-intro company is also known as a capital introduction. It is a brokerage company that introduces hedge fund clients to hedge fund investor bonds that were bought up by a small circle of individuals to legalize the corrupt income of Yanukovych and his entourage.

A third account describes Hunter and Joe Biden's acquaintance with Burisma as being facilitated by a certain individual named Alexander Kotlarsky, a Russian-speaking Jew from Brooklyn, presumably with roots in Odessa. Interestingly, Mykola Zlochevsky's brother, Vladislav Zlochevsky, was deputy head of the Odessa Regional Police and also had business interests in the region. It is a minor detail that helps bring some validity to this story. Added support for this version of the Biden-Burisma hookup exists in correspondence between Devon Archer, Eric Schwerin, and their lawyer Kenneth Levinson, who advised Rosemont Seneca on tax matters. Levinson recalled that Kotlarsky helped Hunter secure the board seat at Burisma in exchange for a commission.[4.23] Kotlyarsky, allegedly a consultant to Tri Global, is a dark horse whose exact role is unknown as to whether he was a supplier of contacts or a middleman. In any case, he was involved in establishing contacts between the Bidens and businessmen from Russia and Ukraine. He also appears in Hunter's correspondence as a participant in Archer's visit to Moscow to meet with Russian billionaire Elena Baturina, and in another meeting involving Mikhail Shishkanov who is the nephew of Russian oligarch Mikhail Gutseriev.[4.23]

However, it is not so important how Zlochevsky got in touch with the Bidens. One thing is certain. For Zlochevsky, the meeting was worth it!

Interestingly, Hunter's emails also revealed that Rosemont, Archer, and Biden had been doing business in Moscow since 2010 and even received payments from Russia, which bothered me. The discovery fueled a burning question inside me. If Hunter Biden was receiving payments from Russia since 2010, then why did U.S. law enforcement agencies not initiate a *Bidengate* investigation? The Mueller Commission was not interested in the dubious deals that Hunter and his partners were trying to make in Russia and Kazakhstan, building partnerships with corrupt local businessmen and officials. Perhaps the infamous *Russiagate* appeared to purposely cover up *Bidengate*?

Let's return to Zlochevsky. It took almost three years to settle issues with the British justice system. Judging by all appearances, personnel changes on Burisma's board of directors have paid dividends. In January 2017,

Zlochevsky returned to Ukraine because all lawsuits and criminal cases against Burisma were dropped. Back in January 2015, a British court had to unfreeze Zlochevsky's $23 million because *the Ukrainian prosecutor's office refused to provide the necessary documents for the investigation.*[4.13] We will talk more about these episodes later, dear readers.

Thus on January 21, 2015, the Ukrainian court complied with the British court's decision that Zlochevsky was not involved in financial fraud and withdrew him from the international wanted list. Foreign partners really tried to clean up the image of the company's boss, and they succeeded. Kwasniewski insisted on the amnesty for Zlochevsky and proposed that his business would help Ukraine become energy independent. Kwasniewski even linked the success of the case to the ideals of the Ukrainian revolution, for which blood was shed on the Maidan.

Shortly after Hunter Biden's candidacy was approved, Kwasniewski had a brief telephone conversation with Hunter in which he told Hunter that one of Burisma's tasks was to rid Ukraine of its energy dependence on Russia. The company produced 25-30% of the gas on the Ukrainian market. According to former President Poroshenko, those volumes could increase gas production to reduce dependence on Russia.[4.24] To Kwasniewski, this reasoning justified the dismissal of all charges against Zlochevsky. In my humble opinion, *the road to hell is paved with good intentions*. Although a valuable asset, Burisma could not claim to be a company *cleansing* Ukraine of Russian gas. This issue clearly required a completely different approach, and a legal one.

In fact, it was the collective efforts of foreign members of Burisma's board of directors that pulled Zlochevsky out of the clutches of British justice. The role of *Mykola's celebrity friends* was doubly confirmed by Petro Poroshenko in the so-called Onyshchenko tapes, in which his views on this matter were recorded in conversations with former Parliament member, Oleksandr Onyshchenko.[4.1,4.2] The recordings were made during January 2016 in Poroshenko's office. One of the conversations was devoted to Mykola Zlochevsky. A part of the audio records indicates the Ukrainian leader stated, "So Kolya is a good guy. I'll think about what can be done. It's just that the Americans have been stirring things up around him lately."

Onyshchenko replied, "In theory, they shouldn't have taken any action against him because Biden's son is on the board of his company. And Kwasniewski too. So when I spoke with Kolya, there should be no moves from the Western side."[4.1,4.2]

However, Poroshenko was clearly being disingenuous with his complimentary assessment of Kolya. He did not like Zlochevsky very much because he had ingratiated himself with the Biden family and was able to use Hunter to conduct his personal affairs bypassing the Ukrainian president. Malicious tongues claim that Poroshenko did not stand aside either. The president demanded that Zlochevsky supply gas to the glass factory that Poroshenko owned, and possibly free of charge since such a service as preserving business and freedom is very expensive.

Chapter 5:

How George Kent Investigated a Bribe Paid to the Prosecutor General

To better understand how rotten the law enforcement system is in Ukraine, I will recount an incident involving my predecessor Prosecutor General Vitaly Yarema. He was accused of receiving a large bribe. I know a lot about this episode. It perfectly complements the picture of the *unblemished* reputation of Mykola Zlochevsky, who was *whitewashed* by the entire U.S. Democratic Party. However, not allAmerican officials in Ukraine were initially involved in this dirty game.

I will start with the fact that Yarema's subordinate, Deputy Prosecutor General Vitaly Kasko, was responsible for the PGO's relations with foreign partners. He oversaw what I call the *Georgian landing party* that arrived at the Ukrainian PGO. The Georgian landing party is a group of reformers from the country of Georgia. It was led by former Georgian President Mikheil Saakashvili, who became Poroshenko's advisor in 2015 and then governor of the Odessa region in Ukraine.[5.1] I will discuss the *Georgian invasion* of the Ukrainian authorities in more detail later in Chapter 19.

So, the *Georgian landing party* is a team of *reformers* sent to Ukraine to carry out *reforms*. Among them was a character named David Sakvarelidze. In 2015, he was *assigned* by Joe Biden's team as deputy prosecutor general to oversee the reform of the PGO.[5.2] Of course, there was no question of any real reforms. Nevertheless, carrying out Biden's requests and orders was his main *strength*. Sakvarelidze oversaw all activities related to the sphere of competence of Vitaly Kasko, who was responsible for international affairs.

I am sure that Kasko deliberately delayed providing documents to the British side in the case of Zlochevsky's laundering of millions frozen in England. He did this with full knowledge of the facts. Without a response from the Ukrainian PGO on the Zlochevsky investigation, the British colleagues' investigation would reach a dead end. Kasko was clearly working in Biden's interests. He first delayed the response to the British for several months and then got away with a form letter. In addition, during the hearings in London in December 2014, lawyers for Mykola Zlochevsky's presented a statement from the PGO about the *uncertain legal status and absence of any notifications of suspicion*. The case against Zlochevsky collapsed.[5.3]

In my opinion, *Zlochevsky's money was unfrozen* thanks to Kasko's efforts. Having received no information from Ukrainian investigators, the London court was forced to lift the arrest on Zlochevsky's accounts. Kasko

KNOWN RECORD:
Marie Yovanovitch

Canadian born American Marie Yovanovitch was the former U.S. ambassador to Ukraine under President Trump's first term. Her career includes years of service as part of the U.S. Foreign Service many of them spent in U.S. State Department posts. She was Deputy Assistant Secretary for the Bureau of European and Eurasian Affairs from 2012–2013 and began her Ukrainian ambassadorship in 2016.[5.4]

Despite claims that a disinformation campaign resulted in Trump removing her, local officials in Ukraine allege that she blocked efforts to combat corruption.[5.5] Among them include her denial of U.S. visas for Ukrainians involved in Rudolph Giuliani's investigations. News that she gave a *Do Not Prosecute List* to Ukrainian Prosecutor General Yuriy Lutsenko, was later clarified by Lutsenko as a disagreement between the two.[5.6–5.8] Zelensky during his infamous 2019 phone call with Trump, also expressed his disapproval of the ambassador.[5.9]

KNOWN RECORD:
George P. Kent

George P. Kent is an American diplomat and member of the U.S. Foreign Office, which included his work serving as ambassador to Estonia. During 2015-2018, Kent was the deputy political counselor in Kiev, Ukraine, and was deputy chief of mission in Kiev. This assignment included his role as the Senior Anti-Corruption Coordinator in the State Department's European Bureau from 2014-15. His efforts lead to the development and advocacy of anti-corruption messages across Europe and Eurasia. He was the U.S. Deputy Assistant Secretary of State for European and Eurasian Affairs in 2018-2021.[5.10,5.11]

On October 15, 2019, he testified in the U.S. Senate during the impeachment trial of Donald Trump. He shared his concern about a conflict of interest arising from the fact that Hunter Biden, as the son of the vice president, had joined the board of Burisma. He recorded these concerns in official governmental email correspondence.[5.12] seems to have successfully accomplished what Joe Biden lobbied. After I was forced to resign, the criminal case against Zlochevsky for money laundering in England was closed in Ukraine as well. It is clear who benefited from this. It would be worth asking former Ambassador Marie Yovanovitch about her role in resolving Zlochevsky's problems.

However, it is worth remembering that the wheels of Ukrainian justice always turn with a squeak. Therefore, they need to be *oiled* so that they turn faster. American patronage alone is not enough. The history of the last ten years has shown that this influence is worthless without money— whether it be formal channels for obtaining money, such as the IMF or USAID, or informal ones, such as bribes to the prosecutor general for help in closing criminal cases.

I found it very interesting to study the U.S. Congress materials, which shed light from *the other side* on events that many in narrow professional circles in Kiev have heard about. This information confirms that not only I, Viktor Shokin, sensed something was wrong with Zlochevsky and Burisma's schemes. It also bolstered the criticisms of George Kent, a high-ranking U.S. State Department official, who sounded the alarm.

During U.S. congressional hearings in 2019, Kent recounts the apparent activities of Deputy Inspector General Vitaly Kasko on pages 81-82 of his transcribed testimony:

> In December 2014, someone in the Ukrainian Prosecutor General's Office—to be clear, this was before Lutsenko, before Shokin, a different corrupt, ineffective prosecutor who inexplicably had shut down the criminal case that had been the basis for a British court to freeze $23 million in assets held by Mykola Zlochevsky.
>
> That was an issue of our interest because we had made a commitment to the Ukrainian Government in 2014 to try to recover an estimated tens of billions of dollars of stolen assets out of the country. The first case that U.S., U.K., and Ukrainian investigators worked on was a case against Zlochevsky, and that's because the British Serious Crimes Office had already opened

up a case, an investigation against Zlochevsky.

—George Kent, Testimony to U.S.

Congress 2019[5.13]

Kent then revealed some very interesting information. He stated that the U.S. State Department allocated *half a million dollars* to the FBI to investigate Zlochevsky's schemes. The specific figure mentioned by George Kent is extremely important, which was mentioned on pages 80-81 of his testimony, "We spent roughly half a million dollars of State Department money in support of the FBI and this investigation and to build capacity to track down stolen assets."[5.13]

A little further on, Kent repeats his statement about the hundreds of thousands of dollars spent and says that the U.S. government took this investigation very seriously, but someone *covered up* the case with a bribe. On page 82 of his testimony, Kent states, "But I want to make very clear the seriousness with which the U.S. Government takes this because we spent months and hundreds of thousands of dollars trying to help your country get your stolen assets back, and somebody in your office took a bribe and shut a case, and we're angry."[5.13]

According to Kent, his concerns about Zlochevsky's devices and bribery were ignored by Joe Biden's administration. At that time, the Biden family was going through a personal tragedy due to the illness of Joe's eldest son, Beau Biden. On this basis, Kent was advised not to bother Joe with this issue.

The exchange between Kent and Republican Counsel Stephen Castor at the hearing describing this request is recorded on page 227 of the testimony as follows:[5.13]

Castor: And what did the person on the other end of the line tell you?

Kent: The message that I recall hearing back was that the Vice President's son Beau was dying of cancer and that there was no further bandwidth to deal with family-related issues at that time.

Castor: Was that pretty much the end of it?

Kent: That was the end of that conversation.

Here's the most interesting part. Kent is aware that in 2014 Ukrainian Prosecutor General Vitaly Yarema may have received a $7 million bribe to close the case against former Minister of Ecology Mykola Zlochevsky and his oil and gas company Burisma. This is also mentioned in a report by the U.S. Senate Committee on Homeland Security and Governmental Affairs and the Committee on Finance. The report states that Biden's son Hunter served on Burisma's board of directors when Zlochevsky could have paid $7 million to *close the case against himself.*[5.14]

In February 2015, George Kent met with Deputy Prosecutor General Yarema Anatoliy Danylenko. At the meeting, Kent asked Danylenko a question about the bribe. In the senate report, he recalls, "`[Kent asked] How much was the bribe, and who took it? Danylenko laughed and replied, 'That's exactly what President Poroshenko asked us. last month.' I asked, 'What did you tell the president?' And he replied, '$7 million.' And that was last May [2014], before our team came to the [PGO] office.`"[5.14]

On page 29 of the senate report, Kent shares that the above bribe occurred in December 2014, *seven months after Hunter joined Burisma's board.* After learning about the bribery, he and the Resident Legal Advisor reported this allegation to the FBI. He reported that "`Hunter Biden was` serving on Burisma's board (supposedly consulting on corporate governance and transparency) when Zlochevsky allegedly paid a $7 million bribe to officials serving under Ukraine's prosecutor general, Vitaly Yarema, to shut the case against Zlochevsky."[5.14]

Kent's senate testimony also mentions the collapse of the investigation into Zlochevsky in Britain. On page 28 of the report, it stated, "George Kent, a career diplomat who served in a number of roles at the State Department over his career, including several tours in Ukraine, did not hold Prosecutor General Yarema or his team in high regard. In fact, he testified, '[Yarema's] team failed to bring a single prosecution over a seven-month period, and which allegedly took a bribe from Zlochevsky to close the case against him and collapse our effort to recover the $23 million frozen in the United Kingdom.'"[5.14]

George Kent reported the bribe to the U.S., but there was no response from the Justice Department or the FBI, led by James Comey. Page 29 of the report has Kent's ordeal recorded. "Kent told the Committees that after the meeting with Danylenko, the DOJ official at the U.S. Embassy in Kiev reported the allegation — that Zlochevsky paid the PGO a $7 million bribe — to the FBI…At this time, the Committees are seeking an explanation from the FBI about what, if any, actions they took after receiving this information from the U.S. Embassy in Kiev."[5.14] There are also excerpts from the official email correspondence between Kent and Yarema.[5.15]

The term Avakov's police refers to the law enforcement actions prominent under the leadership of Arsen Avakov, Minister of Internal Affairs of Ukraine during 2014-2021. Law enforcement under his supervision was criticized for its failures to reform. In 2020, Avakov was under fire due to repeated reports over the years of corruption, unjust, and cruel punishment, including torture imparted by law enforcement officials on those suspected of crime.[5.16]

For my part, I could add one interesting detail to Kent's account. Once while I was still serving as his deputy, Yarema asked me to take Zlochevsky's case from the prosecutor's office to the police. I told him that this was illegal because the case was being investigated by the prosecutor's office and would be returned to us. That is exactly what happened. The case was returned to our desk. So it's a good question. What motives did Yarema have for trying to get rid of this case? Perhaps Yarema was trying to take the investigation to another level by *killing* it in the prosecutor's office. It would have been easier to destroy a case that ended up in the hands of Avakov's police. However, I am not claiming that Yarema tried to close the case by passing it on to the police.

It is possible that Yarema and his deputy Danylenko were not involved in this bribery at all. The bribe could have been given during the tenure of Yarema's predecessor, Oleg Makhnitsky. It was Makhnitsky who was appointed prosecutor general immediately after the Maidan, under the quota of a right-wing political party of the Ukrainian Parliament called Svoboda. The reason why no one has brought the case against Zlochevsky to a conclusion may be related to the success of overthrowing Yanukovych. As compensation for their active participation in street protests occurring during Maidan, the position of prosecutor general was given to radicals from the Svoboda party and resulted in Oleg Makhnitsky's appointment. That is why the political *umbrella* of the Ukrainian authorities, represented by foreign supporters like then U.S. President Obama and then U.S. Deputy Secretary of State Nuland, thwarted the investigation into these episodes.

In support of the above version as a possible scenario of who received the bribe, I can note that Danylenko would not have been so bold as to tell George Kent about the payment if he was uncertain that the money was paid to the previous prosecutor general. Remember that Danylenko served as a deputy under Prosecutor General Yarema. If Yarema had taken the bribe, Danylenko would not have given Kent such dangerous information about his boss, which could have harmed him as well.

In summary, the following picture emerges based upon these excerpts of Kent's testimonies I have shared with you. The Deputy Assistant Secretary of State for European and Eurasian Affairs George Kent consistently warned USAID, the embassy, and the Biden administration about the corrupt reputation of Burisma and Zlochevsky. Meanwhile, the FBI is conducting an investigation and spending $500,000 of U.S. taxpayer money on it. The fact that one of the world's most powerful special services is involved in the case suggests that there are serious grounds for investigating Zlochevsky's suspicious manipulations at the highest level. However, Kent's warnings went unheeded. The FBI, under the leadership of James Comey, began to obstruct the Republicans' investigation into the ties between Zlochevsky and the Biden family. To help this conundrum sink in, I would like to revisit the statement by U.S. Ambassador Geoffrey Pyatt, in which he lamented the inaction of the Ukrainian PGO:

> For example, in the case of former Ecology Minister Mykola Zlochevsky, the UK authorities had seized $23 million in illicit assets that belonged to the Ukrainian

people. Officials at the PGO's office were asked by the UK to send documents supporting the seizure.

Instead, they sent letters to Zlochevsky's attorneys attesting that there was no case against him. As a result, the money was freed by the UK court and shortly thereafter the money was moved to Cyprus.

The misconduct by the PGO [Prosecutor General's Office] officials who wrote those letters should be investigated, and those responsible for subverting the case by authorizing those letters should – at a minimum – be summarily terminated.

—Geoffrey Pyatt, U.S. Ambassador to Ukraine, Commentary 2022[5.17]

Pyatt nodded in my direction when talking about Zlochevsky's *lawlessness*, but it is obvious that the investigation had been paralyzed long before I became head of the PGO. In the end, both the ambassador and his superiors in Washington simply turned a blind eye to the breakdown in communication between the Prosecutor General of Ukraine and the British investigation.

Be that as it may, I believe that the episodes involving Zlochevsky's bribes were not properly investigated. Neither the U.S. Congress nor Kent fully understood some of the details of this story. Zlochevsky paid bribes so many times to have criminal cases against him closed that it created confusion about the facts. Therefore, I would recommend that the U.S. Congress committees revisit these episodes, specifically by raising the issue of the FBI's misappropriation of funds. Of course, it is necessary to talk to Mr. Kent again about what kind of bribe the FBI itself was interested in and why the whole thing was swept under the rug. I think this story would also be of great interest to the current FBI Director Kash Patel.

Incidentally, Zlochevsky's first move was to approach the newly appointed member of the board of directors, Hunter Biden, and ask him to use his father's influence to have all criminal cases closed. The kind-hearted Hunter immediately responded to this request. He sent a letter to Burisma board advisor Vadim Pozharskyi, inquiring about the allegations against Zlochevsky.[5.18]

As reported by the British *Daily Mail* on May 12, 2014, the day before Hunter's appointment to Burisma's board of directors was publicly announced, Zlochevsky's lawyer Pozharskyi sent Hunter an email informing him that Mykola Zlochevsky was under criminal investigation in Ukraine. "We urgently need your advice on how you could use your influence to send a message/signal, etc., to stop what we believe to be politically motivated actions," Pozharskyi wrote. The lawyer continued, "If we do not cooperate, i.e., do not provide cash, [Zlochevsky's] gas business will be shut down." He added, "After unsuccessful attempts to obtain funds from us, they moved on to concrete actions." [5.18] The point here is to unfreeze the money frozen in Zlochevsky's British accounts. To do that, the criminal cases had to be closed.

Incidentally, the Biden family's *corruption collection* includes another very similar episode. With his father's support, Hunter tried to get Romanian businessman Gabriel Popoviciu out of prison. In 2015-2016, Hunter, using his father's position, offered *legal assistance* to Romanian businessman Gabriel Popoviciu. He was facing prison for fraud involving state-owned land.

To avoid punishment, Popoviciu hired Hunter, as well as former FBI director Louis Freeh. In turn, Hunter, brought in a trusted confidant of his family, former U.S. ambassador to Romania and then U.S. ambassador to the EU Mark Gitenstein. Popoviciu promised Hunter *millions of dollars* to resolve the issue. Using his diplomatic connections, Gitenstein arranged a meeting between Vice President Joe Biden and then Romanian President Klaus Johannis in Washington in September 2015. This scheme was described in detail in a lengthy article in the *New York Post* in 2022.[5.19]

Now, let's return to Ukraine.

CHAPTER 6:

BURISMA, THE BIDEN FAMILY BUSINESS

On the frosty morning of January 16, 2017, a plane carrying U.S. Vice President Joe Biden landed at Boryspil Airport in Kiev. The important American guest went to meet with Prime Minister Volodymyr Groysman and Ukrainian President Petro Poroshenko. On January 17th, Biden left Ukraine as quickly as he had arrived.

Many Ukrainian experts found Biden's lightning visit to Ukraine strange. For example, Alena Getmanchuk, director of the Kiev-based Institute of World Policy, said in an interview with *DW* that Biden's visit was more of a symbolic gesture of his remaining five days of support for Ukraine before Donald Trump's inauguration as U.S. president. She added that she did not fully understand the *added value* of this visit.[6.1] Indeed, nothing new was said. Instead, he repeated the same old statements about continuing cooperation with the IMF, bringing order to the banking sector, and carrying out reforms in the energy sector *to eliminate Ukraine's dependence on Russian gas.*[6.1]

However, there was one curious passage in Biden's speech. The U.S. vice president called on Ukrainians to understand that the fight against corruption is a matter of national survival, as he mentions, "Russia has used corruption against Ukraine for the past ten-years as a tool of coercion to keep the state vulnerable and dependent."[6.2] Biden also noted that state anti-corruption agencies need to be strengthened and that they themselves must "root out those who want to return Ukraine to the abyss of nepotism and kleptocracy."[6.2] Joe Biden was being disingenuous. This was more of a Freudian slip. The U.S. vice president was more concerned with another issue—how to close all criminal cases involving the company where his son worked.

Following the talks, Biden made routine statements about the need to stand up to Russia, fight corruption, and carry out economic reforms.[6.3] Many media outlets described the vice president's trip as completely meaningless. Why fly across the ocean to repeat the well-known key points of the U.S. foreign policy agenda on Ukraine? What makes it even more pointless is the fact that in just four days, on January 20, 2017, Biden will step down and Donald Trump's team will take over the White House. Apparently, there were very compelling reasons why the second most powerful man in the U.S. decided to fly across the ocean to visit a distant country.

It is interesting to note that Joe Biden made six visits to Kiev during his tenure as vice president, five of which took place between 2014 and 2017. Curiously, many U.S. states did not receive as many visits from Joe Biden, even when he was the U.S. president.[6.4] Certainly, no American vice president has visited Ukraine more often than Biden. His colleague and predecessor, Dick Cheney, visited Ukraine once as vice president in September 2008 after the conflict between Russia and Georgia.[6.5] Al Gore came to Kiev to meet Leonid Kuchma, and visited Chernobyl on an inspection tour.[6.6, 6.7]

However, all these dry protocol meetings cannot compare to Biden's colorful visits. He set another record when he became the first high-ranking American official in the history of Ukraine's independence to speak from the rostrum of the Verkhovna Rada. Biden commented on *his* almost maniacal attraction to Kiev during Petro Poroshenko's inauguration with a humorous remark. "You must be getting tired of seeing me as often as you do."[6.8]

However, the love and reverence for Ukraine cannot be explained solely by the Obama Administration and Joe Biden's personal concern for the fate of their ally on Russia's border. At the very moment when Joe Biden was climbing the steps of the government plane to visit Kiev for the last time before his resignation, news spread rapidly in the Ukrainian and then global media about the closure of all proceedings and court cases against the Ukrainian oil and gas holding company Burisma Group and its key beneficiary, Mykola Zlochevsky.[6.8]

Of course, this news caught my attention. Images flashed before my eyes of piles of criminal case files, transcripts of interrogations, financial documents, names of money laundering companies in Latvia, transactions in Hunter's name, and so on. The work on these damning materials was never brought to a logical conclusion. "To hell with it, take the Bidens out of the criminal cases. It's the US's business after all." I thought as I looked through the news. Yet, I frustratingly pondered, "But what about Zlochevsky's money laundering, which has been confirmed by Ukrainian investigators, verified by the London courts, and finally noticed by George Kent and the all-powerful FBI as a potential episode of corruption?"

I have only one explanation for Joe Biden's farewell visit to Ukraine. He needed to make sure once again that all the cases in which Hunter Biden could have been involved in one way or another were not just closed but destroyed. Poroshenko understood this perfectly well. Conveniently, all the high-profile criminal cases were closed just in time for Biden's farewell visit in January 2017.

Hunter Biden's position in a Ukrainian company might not have caused such a public outcry had it not been for the fact that the appointment became known a few weeks after his father's visit to Kiev on April 22, 2014. Suspicions of nepotism immediately arose. At the time, the German press often wrote about the dubious involvement of former German Chancellor Gerhard Schröder in the business of Russia's Gazprom.[6.9] A new term even appeared to refer to a type of German lobbying in Russia called *Schröderism*. However, for some reason, the European and U.S. media ignore the lobbying by the owner of Burisma, and the role of European influence played by Kwasniewski occurring in plain sight. And, regarding the relations between Burisma and the U.S.—Joe Biden himself gave his son the green light to become a member of the board of directors of the Ukrainian company. Joe publicly attempted to justify his decision by saying that his son had never discussed his business dealings with him. As noted earlier in Chapter 2, materials from recent years have proven that Hunter Biden did discuss these topics with this father, that Hunter took Pozharskyi to meet his father at Cafe Milano in 2015, and that everyone in the White House was whispering about the Bidens' Ukrainian affairs.[6.10]

Lawyers who are familiar with the realities of energy companies in the post-Soviet space cite two main reasons for attracting people with well-known names in the West. First, it is a matter of reputation. Imagine that a gas production company needs to obtain a loan from a foreign bank. Not a Cypriot bank, but one of the world's top ten banks. To do this, it needs to go through the Know Your Customer regulatory procedure as a means of validating the bank's business and standing. So it's very nice when the first few clicks online reveal that the company's board of directors includes *Western authorities*.

"The fact that Biden's son worked for such a company is bad. And not so much because sitting on the board of directors supposedly gives the company influence in the West," British journalist Edward Lucas noted in a 2019 commentary for BBC News Ukraine that I encountered. "Who has heard of Hunter Biden in the UK, the EU, or even the US? But this is a signal within Ukraine; don't touch this company because we bought a 'big Western name' for it," the expert said.

Hunter could have sat quietly at Burisma for years, turning his new job into a cushy position with a monthly salary of $50,000 and drawing only grumbling from opponents of nepotism. However, that was too small for him. The Burisma story brought to light far more unsavory facts and far more significant sums of money. Payment documents for payments to Biden were first mentioned in the sensational U.S. Senate report released in September 2020. The report is still available on the Senate website under the title *Hunter Biden, Burisma, and Corruption: The Impact on U.S. Government Policy and Related Concerns.*[6.11] The document is based on both publicly available information and confidential documents that shed light on the financial transactions of Biden and his associated companies. Its contents expose the full extent of the relationship between Burisma and the Biden family. Prepared by two Republican senators, Ron Johnson and Chuck Grassley, the report has been unjustly forgotten today. When the report first appeared amid the U.S. presidential campaign, Biden's campaign team called it another attempt to *harm a political opponent and interfere in the electoral process*. What did the American senators publish that was so explosive?

The authors of the report managed to obtain information on all payment transactions between Burisma Zlochevsky and Hunter Biden, which are listed on page 65 of the report.[6.11] One payment of interest occurred on April 15, 2014, before Hunter Biden joined the board of directors of Burisma Holdings. Zlochevsky's company made two transfers totaling $112,758.15 to Rosemont Seneca Bohai

Hunter Biden, Burisma, and Corruption: The Impact on U.S. Government Policy and Related Concerns

U.S. Senate Committee on Homeland Security and Governmental Affairs

U.S. Senate Committee on Finance Majority Staff Report

Screenshot of the famous U.S. Senate report[6.11]

LLC, a company owned by Hunter and his colleague Devon Archer, who would also later serve on the Burisma board with Hunter. On May 7, 2014,

Burisma also made a payment of $250,000 to the Washington law firm Boies, Schiller, and Flexner LLP (Boies Schiller), where Hunter Biden was still working at the time. Just a week later May 12, 2014, Hunter's appointment to Burisma's board of directors was officially announced. Then on September 16, 2014, another payment of $33,039.77 was made to the Boies Schiller law firm.[6.11,6.12]

These transactions were just a *trial run* because further transfers will be made regularly and to the intended target—precisely into the pockets of Joe Biden's son Hunter. Specifically, between May 15, 2014, and February 12, 2016, Burisma made 48 payments to Rosemont Seneca Bohai LLC. Curiously, 39 of the 48 transfers that amounted to $83,333.33 each were classified as *consulting services*.[6.12] You don't need to be an expert in corporate finance to ask yourself this question. Why did Hunter Biden receive money for *consulting services* in addition to his compensation for his work on the board of directors? These funds were not paid directly to Hunter, but to companies associated with him. The answer is obvious. Such large payments, even at a reputable company like Burisma, could not have been justified.

Where did Biden's substantial fees go after being transferred to Rosemont Seneca? The answer to this question is just as obvious. Between June 5, 2014, and October 5, 2015, Rosemont Seneca Bohai LLC made 38 payments totaling $701,979 to three personal accounts belonging to Hunter Biden. In total, according to Ukrainian investigative materials, between April 2014 and October 2015, Burisma transferred $4,817,000 to Rosemont Seneca Bohai LLC.[6.12]

Subsequently, the scheme for transferring money from Zlochevsky to Biden changed. The blame lies with one unpleasant story. In May 2016, Devon Archer was arrested on suspicion of securities fraud. The U.S. Securities and Exchange Commission accused Archer and six of his partners of defrauding investors by selling fictitious bonds issued in 2014 and 2015 worth more than $43 million.[6.13] Nice guys, though, Hunter's partners and friends. As a result, starting on January 25, 2016, Burisma began transferring fees to the law firm Owasco PC, owned by Hunter.

Between January and November 16, 2016, Hunter Biden received a total of $752,054.99. Admittedly, all these transfers look like a substantial addition to Hunter's main salary, which was officially $50,000 per month and should have amounted to $900,000 for the period from May 2014 to October 2015. Even if we discount the funds that were paid to Archer's salary that went through Rosemont Seneca's accounts because he was its co-owner, it still does not add up to $4 million. Who received the remaining amounts and for what achievements?

KNOWN RECORD:
Ron Johnson and Chuck Grassley

In 2019, Wisconsin Senator Johnson and Iowa Senator Grassley joined forces to investigate Hunter Biden's role in Burisma and potential conflicts of interest.[6.14-5.16] Their work sparked a series of subpoenas for individuals to testify in congress.[6.17]

In Sept. 2020, part of the findings were announced then summarized in a final report.[6.17] Deemed by Democrats as a politicized effort to negatively influence Biden's 2020 presidential campaign, Johnson and Grassley closed the investigations due to lack of cooperation from other agencies.[6.11] The media reports were split on the investigation findings.[6.18, 6.19]

It is still unclear why Burisma rewarded Hunter so generously. An amateur in the energy sector, he could not possibly have improved the performance of an oil and gas company with his advice, given that he knew nothing about its business. You will not find any photos of Hunter in dirty rubber boots inspecting sites for drilling rigs in the Ukrainian steppes. Hunter never even visited Kiev during his *work* at the Ukrainian company. Zlochevsky organized *off-site meetings* with the board of directors, as was also revealed in Hunter's leaked correspondence. One meeting was held in Norway, another in Monte Carlo.[6.20]

You might say that we live in the age of the internet and *remote work*. However, nothing is known about how Hunter could have been useful outside Ukraine. Maybe he helped get a loan from a reputable Western bank? Or attracted Western investment in Ukraine's oil and gas sector? All these *meetings* in Monte Carlo speak of the *incredibly laborious work* that Hunter did *with the sweat of his brow* for Burisma, without ever showing up at his workplace.

A lack of knowledge in the energy sector is only half the problem. Hunter Biden didn't know much about how to cover up suspicious transactions either. Thanks to his lack of skills, the payments became public knowledge. Incidentally, in my experience of corruption investigations, Kolya Zlochevsky did not help his partner Hunter hide dubious transactions, although Zlochevsky knows perfectly well how to do so. As an investigator with extensive experience, I can responsibly state that it was in Zlochevsky's interest for Hunter to make his payments *openly* to companies affiliated with him and to his personal accounts. This gave Zlochevsky two advantageous options. First, if third parties found out about the payments, Hunter would be *up to his ears* in Zlochevsky's shady dealings. To save Hunter, Zlochevsky would also have to be saved (which is what Biden Sr. did). Second, if no one ever found out about the payments, Zlochevsky could blackmail the Bidens with his *knowledge* of their financial transactions in the event of any disagreements. Zlochevsky thus obtained unique *insurance* for his own safety. This is another reason why energy companies in the post-Soviet space would attract people with well-known names in the West.

However, let's think about it a little further. Imagine that Zlochevsky knew more about the Bidens than we thought. Imagine that Zlochevsky, wanting to *raise his stock even higher*, shared with Zelensky information about the Bidens' corruption that no one else knew about. In this way, it would be possible to blackmail not just the vice president, but the entire U.S. presidency from 2021-2024 and gain additional benefits from this. Given the scale of U.S. funding for Ukraine after Russia's invasion, we are talking about colossal sums. Of course, I support the provision of all this aid and am infinitely grateful for it. However, as a lawyer, I would like to point out that there should be no abuse here.

I digressed a little again. So, let me return to the heroes of this chapter. I have before me a very convincing piece of evidence confirming the fact of cash transfers to our heroes. During the investigation into Zlochevsky's plots, some Latvian financial intelligence reports came to light. They contain information about transfers of funds from Burisma to two offshore shell companies, to Hunter Biden and to his partner Devon Archer.

According to some sources, the total amount of funds that left Burisma's Ukrainian accounts is $16.5 million. This figure may include not only the Bidens' money, but also Zlochevsky's laundered capital. The amount exceeds what is known about Hunter's Ukrainian fees. Be that as it may, the most interesting thing here is that Latvian financial intelligence not only discovered payments to the *honest American businessman* Hunter but also saw signs of corruption in the movement of this money. It is surprising that Latvian financial intelligence, which is generally loyal to the Americans, came to these conclusions. Apparently, these transactions were extremely blatant, as I describe in the discussion below.

KNOWN RECORD:
Eric Sherwin

Eric Sherwin was a business partner with Hunter at Rosemont Seneca after he joined in 2009.[6.21] Sherwin and Hunter Biden were close. Sherwin claimed that he served as a financial advisor to the Biden family at the time. Their families had ties until their falling out in 2017.[6.21] Emails from Hunter's laptop showed that Joe Biden emailed Sherwin several times when Joe visited Ukraine.[6.22] In his congressional testimony, Sherwin claimed he was unaware of any financial conduct between Joe and his son Hunter when Sherwin corresponded with Joe Biden just prior to Hunter joining Burisma.[6.22]

Yes, this story did not develop further. Yet, all these documents, comprising Morgan Stanley statements and Latvian financial intelligence files, have not been refuted by anyone to date. Neither the State Department, nor the White House under President Joe Biden, nor members of his family have filed a lawsuit against the Latvian operatives of this special service who pointed out the criminal component in transactions related to the Biden companies.

I would like to note that for the Biden family, their involvement in transactions with Latvian money laundering companies could result in severe criminal penalties. This includes the fact that none of them paid taxes on this income. In the US, tax evasion is a very serious crime. In December 2020, it became known that the U.S. Department of Justice and the Delaware State Attorney General's Office were conducting an official investigation into Hunter's transactions during his time at Burisma.[6.23]

In early 2019, the U.S. Internal Revenue Service (IRS) filed claims for tax evasion against Hunter Biden and his wife. The amount in question is a considerable $400,000.[6.24] Moreover, Hunter was well aware that he had to fulfill his civic duty and pay taxes on his Ukrainian fees.

This information came to light from Hunter's email correspondence, which was obtained by Robert Costello, a lawyer working for Rudolph Giuliani.[6.22] Costello, in turn, received this information along with other files from the famous laptop, which the forgetful Hunter failed to collect from the repair shop in time, making its entire contents public knowledge.

In one of the letters, the president of Rosemont Seneca Partners, Eric Schwerin, informs Hunter, "In 2014, you joined the board of directors of Burisma, and we still need to amend your 2014 income data to reflect unreported income."[6.22] The income, as reported in the letter, amounted to a hefty $1.2 million, including $400,000 received from Burisma. Interestingly, the letter is dated January 16, 2017, the date of Joe Biden's last visit to Kiev.[6.22] Obviously, against the backdrop of his imminent resignation, Joe gave orders to his close lawyers to start cleaning up any rough edges that could turn into serious problems in the future. However, Hunter's sloppiness ruined everything.

On April 13, 2016, tax specialist Ken Levinson wrote a letter to Eric Schwerin. The letter detailed some of the financial arrangements between Rosemont Seneca Bohai LLC, Burisma, Owasco, and private individuals, which included Hunter Biden, Schwerin himself, Devon Archer, and a certain Alex (probably former President of Poland, Aleksander Kwasniewski mentioned in Chapter 3). The correspondence refers to Alex returning the money paid to him from the Rosemont

Seneca Bohai LLC account RSB as a commission. Incidentally, this was allegedly a commission for Hunter's employment at Burisma. In short, the commission had to be returned to the RSB accounts to pay taxes on it.[6.29] However, Schwerin replies that the money has already gone to Alex, and he cannot reverse the transaction. In the end, the correspondents agreed that the debt to Alex was Hunter's personal debt, and that he himself had to deal with tax issues related to these payments.[6.29] Judging by subsequent events, Hunter never resolved the tax issues. The IRS took serious action against him.

As is well known, on June 11, 2024, Hunter was found guilty on three counts related to the illegal acquisition of weapons and pleaded guilty to several tax crimes, including *tax evasion in the amount of $1.4 million.*[6.30] A few months later, his father attempted to forgive him for all these crimes through a pardon, as well as any other crimes he may have committed between January 1, 2014, and December 1, 2024.[6.25] In turn, at the time of Hunter's financial manipulations, the White House ignored all these facts and took Joe Biden and his adult son under their wing. They said it was just business and not to politicize the issue for your own dirty interests.

KNOWN RECORD:
Presidential Pardon of Hunter Biden

On December 2, 2024, outgoing President Joe Biden issued a full and unconditional pardon for his son Hunter. He was convicted on federal gun and drug charges, and also plead guilty on tax evasion in 2024.[6.23,6.24] The edict included clemency for Hunter Biden on these and any future crimes discovered from 2014-2024. In his official statement, Joe Biden claimed he kept his word and did not interfere with any legal actions against Hunter, but believed Hunter was treated unfairly in the courts, which drove Joe's pardon.[6.25]

In his first term, Trump openly pardoned his son-in-law's father, setting a precedent to pardon family members. Additionally, President Gerald Ford pardoned disgraced President Richard Nixon for any future crimes found during Nixon's time servicing as President.[6.26]

Recently, issues surrounding Joe Biden's pardons have surfaced. The discovery of Biden's advanced cognitive decline and autopen use for specific presidential approvals, like pardons, made

KNOWN RECORD: Presidential Pardon of Hunter Biden
(continued)

the validity of these actions questionable.[6.27] On *Real America's Voice*
John Solomon recently uncovered records showing Biden delegated
activities, like issuing pardons, to his aides.[6.28] Opponents to the Biden
presidency, claim the president must perform certain actions personally,
which includes pardons. In an interview, Congressman James Comer
pledged to investigate the legality of Biden's pardons.[6.27,6.28]

CHAPTER 7:

THE BILLION-DOLLAR PROSECUTOR FOLLOWS THE DEMOCRATS' MONEY

"Follow the money."

—Deep Throat from film *All the President's Men*, 1976[7.1]

When the character reporter Bob Woodward, in the movie *All the President's Men*, receives the above message from his anonymous source Deep Throat, it was clear that his source understood the mechanics of a pay-to-play system in politics.[7.1] Money leads to influence, and influence is bought with money. So, between April 2014 and October 2015, $4.8 million was transferred from Burisma's accounts to Rosemont Seneca's accounts.

To understand what happened to these funds, we must follow the transferred money in these transactions. Among these payments, I would like to highlight the most odious ones that required thorough investigation in this chapter. Accounts of suspicious activities involving the Bidens and Burisma are peppered across media and various reports. In 2020, the following information appeared in the American publication *Just The News*, "...in 2016, the authorities of the former Soviet republic of Latvia identified a number of 'suspicious' financial transactions involving Hunter Biden and his colleagues from a Ukrainian gas company [Burisma] and asked Kiev for help in investigating them. A warning dated February 18, 2016, regarding Ukraine was received from the Latvian prosecutor's office responsible for investigating money laundering, and it specifically raised the question of whether the youngest son of Vice President Joe Biden and three other Burisma Holdings officials were potential beneficiaries of suspicious funds." [7.2] The Latvian agency, called The Financial Intelligence Unit of Latvia (FIU), included the following statement in a written notice to its Ukrainian counterparts, "The Office for the Prevention of Money Laundering is currently investigating suspicious activities by Burisma Holdings Limited." [7.3]

The U.S. Financial Crimes Enforcement Network (FinCEN) also drew attention to suspicious transactions, as noted in the 2022 U.S Congressional report. "There have been recent alarming reports that numerous international business transactions involving Hunter and James Biden, the brother of President, have been flagged in the Financial Crimes Enforcement Network (FinCEN) through suspicious activity reports (SARs).At the same time, the Biden administration is restricting Congress' access to SARs. This departure from long-standing policy raises serious questions about the motives behind the changes, including whether they are intended to protect Hunter Biden."[7.4] This statement written in the report was from senior House member James Comer and addressed to Department of the Treasury Secretary Janet Yellen.[7.4] Comer also mentions that "More than 150 international business transactions involving Hunter or James Biden have been flagged by U.S. banks in SAR reports filed with the U.S. Department of the Treasury. The sheer number of flagged transactions in this case is highly unusual and may indicate serious criminal activity or a threat to national security. We are particularly concerned that these transactions may be related to business with firms or organizations, including those with direct ties to foreign governments hostile to the interests of the United States."[7.4]

Additionally, all payments to the Bidens, down to the last dollar, are reflected in a Morgan Stanley report. The report disclosed the correspondent accounts of Rosemont Seneca Bohai.[7.5] What is important in this document is the transactions to Rosemont Seneca's accounts through the Latvian branch of PrivatBank (*AS PrivatBank*). It was this bank and two Latvian companies, which I will mention below, that Zlochevsky used to launder money.

Another document from my archive is the testimony of a person who provided Zlochevsky with services for *legalizing* money through Latvian banks and companies, in which the witness states, "Since 2010, together with other people, I have been providing services to some Ukrainian and Russian businessmen to legalize their illegal income and evade taxes...One of my clients from 2009 to 2010 was a holding company whose beneficiary was Mykola Zlochevsky."[7.6] Other excerpts from the testimony describe the contact person and the handling of cash, "Mykola Zlochevsky's contact person was his representative, Oleg Nelin...In Ukraine, Mykola Zlochevsky had a lot of *unaccounted cash* – *black cash* – unaccounted cash in Ukrainian currency (hryvnia) hidden from taxes. We are talking about up to $10 million per month..."[7.6] The witness then talks about the companies that were involved in money laundering, including Zlochevsky's money intended for Hunter:

> We also organized fictitious foreign economic contracts, which were never actually executed, between the aforementioned companies and offshore companies controlled by us, WIRELOGIC TECHNOLOGY A.S. and DIGITEX ORGANIZATION LLP, which had dollar accounts with AS PrivatBank in Latvia...Between November 2014 and October 2015, I noticed strange recurring payments that I made with Mykola Zlochevsky's money on Oleg Nelin's instructions. I sent them from the account of BURISMA HOLDINGS LTD in AS PrivatBank in Latvia to the account of the U.S. company ROSEMONT SENECA BOHAI LLC...I did not have any contract confirming these payments. Oleg Nelin sent me a sample

111

payment order by email, which I had to fill out using the Client-Bank system and transfer from the account of BURISMA HOLDINGS LTD in Latvia's AS PrivatBank to the account of the American company ROSEMONT SENECA BOHAI LLC...I have already explained that these were not targeted payments from Ukraine and that at a certain stage, the money of many clients associated with Ukrainian and Russian businesses was mixed in the accounts of WIRELOGIC TECHNOLOGY A.S. and DIGITEX ORGANIZATION LLP. After that, I transferred them to the account of BURISMA HOLDINGS LTD at AS PrivatBank in Latvia.[7.6]

Note, these are not all the documents at my disposal. Here is another one. This document was provided to me by former colleagues, titled *Summary material No. 0145/2016/DSK of the State Financial Monitoring Service of Ukraine*. The document contains a complete description of the financial transactions of Zlochevsky's shell companies, including transactions to transfer laundered funds to the accounts of the Biden family and their partners.[7.7]

I am holding in my hands the indictment issued by the PGO of Ukraine against Mykola Zlochevsky. It contains facts about the transfer of funds between December 16, 2014, and August 19, 2015, to the accounts of Aleksander Kwasniewski, former president of Poland and member of the board of directors of Burisma, in the amount of €1 million for consulting services. This indictment also cites facts confirmed by the Latvian Financial Monitoring Service showing that between November 18, 2014, and November 16, 2015, $3,404,000 was transferred to Rosemont Seneca's account at Morgan Stanley Bank for *consulting services*.

The originals of the documents mentioned are part of criminal case *No. 42014000000001590*. What's worse is once this investigation began, someone started pulling the right strings, and the work in this direction was stopped. Once upon a time when the organization had not yet lost its spirit of justice, the Ukrainian prosecutor's office would have drawn the obvious conclusion from these and other facts that Mykola Zlochevsky was guilty of embezzlement and financial fraud on a particularly large scale through the creation of a criminal organization.

Chapter 8:
Burisma Alone is Not Enough, So What is Naftogaz?

Brushing off the initial revelations in the American press and by Republican senators as if they were annoying flies, both father and son Biden did not even consider winding up their financial schemes in Ukraine. During the Cold War, the mere mention of the U.S. vice president's patronage of any foreign company in which his son worked would have instantly caused a scandal and could have cost him his political career. Nonetheless, Biden got away with a simple comment that neither he nor his son had ever discussed Burisma's affairs and that the American public had nothing to worry about. It worked then. However, a U.S. congressional investigation found that Joe Biden lied to the American public. He was fully aware of his son's activities, and he *traded his influence* with him.

Moreover, the Biden family's partnership with Zlochevsky was probably just the tip of the corruption iceberg. Joe Biden was aiming for something bigger—*the entire oil and gas sector in Ukraine*, and not only that. Biden's priorities included promoting the business of the oil and gas corporation Burisma. Work in this direction began back when Molotov cocktails were flying at Ukrainian police officers on the Maidan, and sniper bullets were flying at protesting citizens.

On March 18, 2014, Joe Biden, who was visiting Poland, discussed with Prime Minister Donald Tusk the possibility of reverse gas supplies to Ukraine.[8.1] The new Ukrainian authorities, who had not yet gotten used to the corridors of power, were immediately puzzled by the U.S. vice president's plans for *energy reform*. Biden demanded that the new Ukrainian Prime Minister Arseniy Yatsenyuk immediately begin replacing direct gas supplies from Russia with reverse supplies from Eastern Europe.

Why was Biden in such a hurry? There was not much time left before the U.S. 2016 presidential election. Even then, a Democratic victory did not seem so certain. This is the only explanation for the rush to implement Ukrainian *reforms* and for Biden's three visits in April, June, and November 2014.

It was during these *blitz visits* that loyal democrats were placed in key positions in the Ukrainian government, without whom external control would have been impossible. Thus, on March 26, 2014, at a government meeting chaired by Arseniy Yatsenyuk, a young former employee of the company, Andriy Kobolev, was approved as chair of the Naftogaz board. As The Wall

KNOWN RECORD:
Reverse Gas Supplies

It should be explained what reverse flows are. Gas reverse flow (*from the Latin reversus, meaning "backward"*) is a mechanism for supplying gas whereby energy resources are delivered to one country via an intermediary *rather than directly from another*. Historically Ukrainians rely on gas from Russia, due to limited supply of gas in Western Europe. A reverse flow is when Russian gas flows through pipelines to Ukraine and is pumped into Ukrainian underground storage facilities. Part of the gas is reserved for purchase by a European gas trader. The trader then pumps part of the purchased gas to European territory for further sale to consumers in Europe and sells part of the gas to Ukraine. Meanwhile, gas intended for Ukraine sits in Ukrainian underground storage facilities. Per documents, Ukraine supposedly "imports" gas from the EU and buys it from a European trader—it is exactly the same gas from Russia. Yet, reverse gas has a markup from the trader, plus a corruption markup from Naftogaz and shell companies.

Street Journal correctly noted, the Ukrainian gas giant was headed by a *newcomer*.[8.2] However, it was precisely such an impressionable and controllable manager who was the ideal candidate for gas schemes under the patronage of Biden and the U.S. State Department.

Since spring 2014, Prime Minister Arseniy Yatsenyuk had eagerly implemented Biden's instructions to diversify gas import sources. In October 2014, through the Slovak operator Eustream, Naftogaz began purchasing gas from the Norwegian company Statoil, the German companies EON and RWE, the French company GDF Sue, and the American trader TrailStone.[8.3] The final green light for European reverse gas was given in April 2015 after the parliament passed the Natural Gas Market Law.[8.4] Incidentally, Burisma sharply increased its portfolio of licenses for the development of new gas fields in Ukraine around the same time with Ukrainian Prime Minister Yatsenyuk's assistance.

The Ukrainian press began to actively discuss how Ukraine was getting rid of its dependence on Russia in the gas sector. However, in practice, the *gas reform* did not lead to a reduction in dependence on Russia. Europe does not produce enough gas to share with Ukraine.

The Supervisory Board of Naftogaz played a key role in the *reverse gas* story. Such bodies in Ukrainian state-owned companies were strengthened in 2016, when the Ukrainian parliament passed a law expanding the powers of supervisory boards in state-owned enterprises. The legislative innovations were accompanied by statements about bringing the management of state-owned companies into line with the standards of the Organization for Economic Cooperation and Development (OECD).[8.5] However, as it turned out, this was not the goal of Biden's team.

In a recording of a conversation between Joe Biden and Petro Poroshenko on February 11, 2016, published on May 19, 2020, Biden asks his protégé about a document authored by Ukrainian Minister of Economy Aivaras Abromavichus.[8.6] He apologizes for not being able to pronounce the minister's difficult surname. He then asks whether the document has been approved.[8.6] The document in question is draft law *No. 3062 On Amendments to Certain Legislative Acts of Ukraine Regarding the Management of State-Owned Property*, which allowed the transfer of control over state-owned companies from ministries to supervisory boards.[8.7] Biden was clearly nervous and did not even react to Poroshenko's joke that he had only learned the surname of Abromavichus, who had arrived in Kiev from Lithuania, three months earlier.

KNOWN RECORD:
Naftogaz

Naftogaz is a state-owned company of Ukraine that supports the exploration, distribution and processing of oil, natural gas and liquified gas for consumers.[8.8] Naftogaz started as Ukrgazprom in the 1990's at the end of the Cold war, rebuilding the oil industry from the ground up. In 1998, it made an agreement with the Russian gas company Gazprom to transport gas from Russia to Ukraine. In 2009, then Naftogaz took part in the EU gas investment market, which allowed gas to be traded like a commodity. In 2014, Naftogaz was a key player in the reverse gas initiative in Ukraine, which involved the transport of Russian gas to Europe then to Ukraine.[8.9]

The fact is that on February 3, 2016, the Minister of Economy resigned. Aivaras Abromavichus was one of the representatives of a group of reformist ministers who joined Prime Minister Arseniy Yatsenyuk's government after the change of power in 2014. This team was selected in the White House, and its patron was none other than Joe Biden. Therefore, he could not help but be concerned about the resignation of Abromavičius, who was responsible for expanding the powers of the National Council. However, Biden's concerns were unfounded. Bill No. 3062 was passed in its second reading in February 2016.[8.10]

Why was the adoption of this law so important for Biden? The explanation is simple. The Obama White House prepared a team of managers for subsequent deployment to the supervisory boards of Ukrainian state-owned companies. As a result, within a couple of years, foreigners became practically the owners of the Ukrainian state sector. For example, in 2020, five of the seven members of the supervisory board of the railway company Ukrzaliznytsia were foreigners. The supervisory board was headed by Sevki Acuner, a Turkish citizen and former director of the EBRD's representative office in Ukraine, a banker with many years of experience in finance. It is noteworthy that the same Turkish citizen also headed another Supervisory Board, at the company Ukrenergo, without having any connection to either the transport or energy sectors.[8.11] Many top managers were guilty of similar inconsistencies. Another well-known foreigner is Swedish economist Anders Åslund, who worked as an advisor to the Ukrainian and Russian governments in the 1990s. He and the scandalous former head of the IMF, Dominique Strauss-Kahn, joined the supervisory board of Credit Dnipro Bank, which is owned by businessman and well-known sponsor of the Democratic Party Viktor Pinchuk.[8.12]

With the help of supervisory boards, the Americans killed two birds with one stone. They rewarded their foreign agents in Ukraine with cushy jobs and also used them to build a system of shadow control over Ukraine's public sector. Biden was hardly interested in how to restore the finances of Naftogaz, where many billions of dollars of budget money had disappeared without a trace. Most likely, it was precisely this feature of Naftogaz that attracted him.

In November 2017, Joe Biden appointed long-time associate, Amos Hochstein, as independent director of the Naftogaz Supervisory Board.[8.13] Hochstein was the ideal figure to oversee the Ukrainian gas market. He had an excellent grasp of the situation in the energy sector and, importantly, was extremely cautious. For example, he advised Biden not to appoint Hunter to the Burisma board of directors, but Biden did not listen. With Hochstein's appointment, everything was ready for the reverse scheme. Poroshenko pushed

KNOWN RECORD:
Amos Hochstein

Amos worked for many years in the U.S. Congress for the Democrats and was an employee of the American lobbying firm Cassidy & Associates. In the 2000s, he tarnished his reputation by working for Teodoro Obiang Nguema Mbasogo, the president of Equatorial Guinea and one of Africa's longest-serving dictators, who has been repeatedly condemned by international human rights organizations for repression and suppression of political freedoms.[8.14] Moreover, in the pages of the Washington Post, Hochstein justified this cannibalistic regime.[8.15] In 2011, Hochstein was appointed Special Envoy for International Energy Affairs at the U.S. State Department. There, he worked closely with Biden, accompanying him on numerous tours to various countries, including Ukraine, which he has advised since 2014 on abandoning direct purchases of Russian gas.

Hochstein was always present at the vice president's negotiations with Petro Poroshenko. Amos himself said this in an interview with the *Times*, "I was at almost every single meeting that Vice President Biden had with President Poroshenko, I was on every trip, and I was present for most of the phone calls."[8.16] In the midst of the scandals surrounding Burisma, Amos Hochstein hastily left the Naftogaz Supervisory Board in 2020.[813]

Joe Biden and Amos Hochstein aboard Air Force Two

through parliament all the necessary laws that allowed gas contracts with Eastern European traders to be legalized and an American curator to be appointed to Naftogaz. Amos Hochstein was tasked with ensuring that the entire scheme ran smoothly. For example, the shell companies registered in Slovakia were handled by Andriy Favorov, a Ukrainian with a U.S. passport who eventually became also head of the Integrated Gas Business Unit of Naftogaz.[8.17] After these manipulations, official gas supplies from Russia did indeed begin to decline sharply, and supplies from the European Union began to rise rapidly. (See section titled *Known Record: Reverse Gas* for details.) Poroshenko trumpeted victory. Ukraine had supposedly finally *rid* itself of its energy dependence on Moscow.

At first glance, there is nothing criminal about Kobolev's Naftogaz scheme. If Kiev wants to pretend that it consumes European gas that does not exist in nature, then let it do so. However, that is not the point here. For example, in 2015–2018 the average price for 1,000 cubic meters of gas in Europe was $211.00 but Naftogaz purchased gas for the Ukrainian population at an average price of $245.63. *That is a difference of almost $35.00.* Or, let's say, in July 2018–April 2019, the average price of gas in Europe was almost

$238.50, while Ukraine imported it at $288.50. The difference is *$50.00 per thousand cubic meters.* So it turns out that, according to the most conservative estimates, *Ukraine overpaid almost $1.5 billion for so-called European gas over five years.*

In other words, Biden and company reached into the pockets of ordinary Ukrainians. To justify the unreasonable markup, Biden demanded that Poroshenko increase gas prices for the population by 75%.[8.18] By the way, I would like to note that the increase in gas tariffs was extremely beneficial to Burisma. After all, the more expensive gas is, the higher the profits of gas companies. Burisma supplied gas primarily to the Ukrainian population. This means that Hunter and his friends' fees increased in proportion to the increase in tariffs. In fact, this is the only explanation I can offer for the fabulous payments received by the *star-studded celebrity* board of directors of Zlochevsky's company, Burisma.

It is important to add that all this manipulation with the alleged refusal to buy Russian gas was very beneficial to traders like Zlochevsky, because the markup on *virtual European gas* led to an increase in the cost of gas, and thus to an increase in the profitability of the business. Therefore, I am convinced that behind the slogans about Ukraine's energy independence from Russia lay the personal gain of Zlochevsky and the Biden family.

Let's return to the gas scheme. Where did the difference of hundreds of millions of dollars between Russian and *European* reverse gas end up? When Amos Hochstein joined Naftogaz's supervisory board, the Ukrainian company Energy Resources of Ukraine (ERU) became among the largest gas importers.[8.19] Or rather, it would be more accurate to say that behind this brand name lies a whole group of companies with "ERU" in their names. The companies in this corrupt *umbrella* are registered in Ukraine and offshore. For example, ERU Trading, ERU Corporation, and ERU Management Services LLC, are registered in Delaware, the state from which Joe Biden was elected to the U.S. Senate.[8.20] According to some sources, the ultimate beneficiary of this *octopus* of shady companies was none other than Andrei Favorov.

Is it any surprise that this individual, Andrei Favorov, was also a direct report to Naftogaz chairman Andriy Kobolev? Of course, this is no coincidence. With Burisma being the main gas supplier of Ukraine, Favorov was involved in setting up gas imports from Europe at Zlochevsky's Burisma. Together, these two worked out all the schemes involving reverse flows and offshore companies.

Now, the U.S. Vice President's conversation with Petro Poroshenko on December 19, 2016,[8.22, 8.23] becomes very clear. As Joe Biden expressed in his comment to Poroshenko, he was very concerned about the fate of the team

KNOWN RECORD:
Andrei Favorov

Andrei Favorov is a proven and reliable manager who knows how to set up various gas schemes. He is a citizen of Russia and the U.S. but has roots in Odessa, Ukraine. He previously worked for the American energy giant AES in third world countries.

Since 2009, he has worked for AES-affiliated Contour Global in its Eastern European office. Under Viktor Yanukovych, Favorov was invited to join Rinat Akhmetov's energy holding company DTEK, which was considered larger than Burisma and was deemed the largest oil and gas company in Ukraine.[8.21] In 2013, Favorov arranged a contract for DTEK to supply natural gas from the Polish company PGNiG. This company would later become a significant partner of the ERU conglomerate of companies. In addition, he participated in the creation of the Swiss offshore company DTEK Trading SA, designed to import natural gas from Europe.[8.20] By 2016, Andriy Favorov was appointed head of the Integrated Gas Business Unit of Naftogaz.[8.17] of *committed reformers and talented managers*.[8.22, 8.23] This concern was not accidental, as the new incoming Prime Minister of Ukraine, Volodymyr Groysman, wanted to dismiss the head of Naftogaz, Andriy Kobolev.[8.22] This could have put an end to Kobolev's entire Naftogaz scheme. "In Europe, this could be seen as a problem. I hope you will ask the prime minister to slow down a little on this. This is not what we need," Biden explained to Poroshenko. Under no conditions could Poroshenko allow the dismissal of Kobolev as Naftogaz chair. [8.22, 8.23] The U.S. vice president's insistence on this issue was also explained by the fact that Donald Trump's chances of winning the presidential race had increased and Biden wanted to preserve the entire system of influence he had created, primarily in Naftogaz. In January 2017, during his farewell visit to Kiev, Biden again reminded Poroshenko of his request to appoint Hochstein as director of the Naftogaz supervisory board. According to Biden's logic, after he left the vice presidency, his protégé would control the entire reverse gas supply scheme to Ukraine. Prior to that, Biden exercised control through Kobolev, whom Biden himself had lobbied to head Naftogaz in 2014.

However, information leaked to the Ukrainian media that the corruption component of Russian gas reverse flows could amount to at least $1.5 billion USD. According to information leaked to the Ukrainian media, between 2015 and 2018, ERU Trading's revenue alone amounted to 15.6 billion hryvnia, or approximately $700 million.[8.24] Part of this money was transferred to offshore accounts. For example, between July 2016 and June 2017, almost 348 million hryvnia was transferred from ERU Trading to the account of the American company ERU Management Services LLC, and between May 2017 and July 2017, another 274 million hryvnia. In total, this amounts to more than $25 million for ERU. Perhaps someday, evidence will be made public that part of the proceeds from the reverse scheme ended up in far from random offshore accounts overseas.

CHAPTER 9:

HOW BURISMA WHITEWASHED ITS IMAGE AT THE EXPENSE OF USAID

One of the lesser-known episodes of *influence peddling* is the collaboration between Zlochevsky's Burisma company and the U.S. Agency for International Development (USAID). Beginning in 2013, USAID launched the Municipal Energy Reform Project in Ukraine (MERP) with a budget of $16.5 million, which ran until 2018.[9.1] During that time at around the end of June 2014, U.S. Senators Edward Markey, Ron Wyden, Jeanne Shaheen, and Christopher Murphy appealed to U.S. President Barack Obama to strengthen dialogue on energy efficiency and the development of Ukraine's domestic energy resources.[9.2] The U.S President supported the concept. Apparently following Obama's support calls for strengthening *dialogue in the field of energy efficiency,* Burisma signed a memorandum of understanding with the *International Resources Group* (IRG) on October 13, 2014, known as the MERP MOU.

International Resources Group (IRG) is a subsidiary of Engility Holdings Inc. In 2017, it was acquired by RTI International (https://www.rti.org/news/rti-international-acquires-international-resources-group-irg).

Headed by Paul Weisenfeld, a former USAID employee, IRG is a contractor that implements USAID programs in various countries. As a result of signing the memorandum, Burisma collaborated with USAID between 2014-2015.[9.3]

It is important to note that the MERP MOU was signed by IRG employee William [Bill] Tucker and by Andrii Kicha on behalf of Burisma Holdings.[9.4] Andrii Kicha was the Burisma's notorious lawyer, who at the time of signing the MERP MOU with USAID was a witness in a case involving Zlochevsky's money laundering in England. Kicha also became involved in an episode later in 2020 related to a transfer of a $6 million bribe to close a criminal investigation into Burisma's money laundering.[9.5]

On June 24th-25th in 2015, USAID and Burisma Holdings held a joint event as hosts of a journalism competition. The 2015 USAID report notes that Burisma sponsored the competition.[9.6] Burisma was represented at the event by Vadim Pozharskyi, an advisor to Burisma's board of directors, who was mentioned in Hunter Biden's laptop correspondence and also participated in a

Ukrainian Independence from Russian Energy Act

Prior to submitting the letter to President Obama in June of 2014, U.S. Senator Markey from Massachusetts drafted a bill entitled Ukrainian Independence from Russian Energy Act. The Bill proposed financing of the Ukrainian energy sector through USAID funds with $10 million in aid from 2015-2017. The bill aimed to help enhance Ukrainian energy infrastructure, thereby minimizing reliance of Russian gas.[9.7,9.8] The emphasis to promote changes was to alleviate Ukraine from the threat of possible Russian sanctions on oil and gas reserves, as mentioned in Senate hearing earlier in March 2014 by bill supporter Senator Wyden. Interestingly, experts appearing in that March hearing warned of corruption in the Ukrainian energy sector.[9.9] Regardless, Senator Markey's bill was passed in December 2014 with an amended $3 million total in USAID funds dedicated to this program. Details of the bill indicate the management of USAID funding arrangements through international trading organizations, like IRG.[9.10,9.11]

KNOWN RECORD:
Paul Weisenfeld

Paul Weisenfeld is currently the Senior Vice President of International Development for the now parent company of IRG, called RTI International.[9.12] However, during the Obama-Biden administration, Weisenfeld was assigned to the USAID relief team for the 2010 Haiti earthquake.[9.13] Apparently, Hunter Biden and Rosemont Seneca attempted to connect their partners to USAID programs to address the aftermath of the earthquake in Haiti in 2010. Twelve-years later, critics of the USAID response to Haiti complain that funds were paid to NGOs more often than the local Haitians.[9.14]

In 2011, Weisenfeld led USAID's Food Security Bureau and the Food for the Future initiative for food security and hunger relief. There he spoke extensively about hunger in the Horn of Africa.[9.15] Jill Biden joined the effort, campaigning in the region in support of USAID programs to address hunger, establishing a deeper tie with Wiesenfeld's USAID efforts and to Biden-related activities before his role as head of IRG in 2015.[9.15] joint meeting with Joe Biden at Café Milano in New York.[9.16] Pozharskyi was in contact with Stephen Gonyea, a career diplomat with USAID.[9.17]

Let me remind you of what I said on the first pages of the book. It is important to remember this in the context of the USAID episode. The *Daily Mail* reported that in 2014 Hunter Biden asked Vadim Pozharskyi to find someone who could help stop the prosecution of Mykola Zlochevsky.[9.18] Later, in his testimony to the Senate, George Kent claimed that Prosecutor General Vitaly Yarema had allegedly received a bribe of $7 million to close the cases against Mykola Zlochevsky (see Chapter 5).[9.18]

Interestingly, paragraph 3 of the MERP MOU states that *Burisma intends to act as a sponsor of the USAID program*.[9.4] As I already noted, the company and its management, represented by Mykola Zlochevsky and Andriy Kicha, were under investigation for money laundering in both Ukraine and the UK at the time of the contract signing. However, despite these well-known facts, *the USAID contractor IRG agreed to accept funding from a company whose beneficiaries are involved in corruption investigations*.

Therefore, as an investigator with nearly 40-years of experience, I cannot help but paint the following picture about how the USAID funds received by IRG could have been used to finance Burisma. RTI (parent

KNOWN RECORD:
FD-1023

In September 2023, Senator Chuck Grassley declassified an FBI Form 1023 report that described an agent's discussion with Pozharskyi who verified Hunter Biden's role at Burisma. The agent also described a discussion with Zlochevsky concerning a transaction having issues because it was to be processed near the time when Joe Biden threatened to withhold U.S. loan guarantees unless the Prosecutor General Shokin was fired. The Agent reported that Zlochevsky responded that Joe Biden would take care of any issues.[9.20]

According to the U.S. House Committee on Oversight and Accountability Chairman, James Comer, data in the report corroborated with activities reported by IRS whistleblowers.[9.21,9.22] Despite the stark details, the report was dismissed, especially by the Democratic majority in congress. FBI Form 1023 is a standard status report document detailing unofficial findings and activities by agents during an active investigation. Therefore, it could not be interpreted as evidence.[9.23] company of IRG) was listed as one of the top six recipients of USAID funds based on recent congressional research data, receiving over \$2.6 billion USD.[9.19] This information is also confirmed in the RTI website, which states that it has received over \$2 billion USD from USAID for the MERP program since 2013.[9.24]

Hypothetically, the money from the U.S. budget could have been used to compensate for the bribes that Zlochevsky paid to have the cases closed in 2014 and 2020, as well as compensation for the multimillion-dollar fees paid to Hunter Biden and his partners. In this light, the *FD-1023* form published by Senator Chuck Grassley alleging Zlochevsky's bribes to the Bidens, seemed very interesting to me.[9.25]

The expenditure items under MERP MOU program should have raised serious questions. According to the procurement plan, \$6,353,000 was spent on consulting and legal services. There is no strict accountability for the spending of these funds in the public domain. All thanks to Ukraine's *Resolution No. 553* that allowed special reporting exemptions for USAID, which I wrote about in Chapter 2.[9.26]

Note, the procurement plan on behalf of IRG was signed by Lithuanian citizen and USAID aide in Energy Security, Diana Korskayte, whom former President Grybauskaite of Lithuania (2009-2019) accused of lobbying for the interests of energy companies.[9.27]

It is noteworthy that the close relationship between the corrupt Burisma and USAID became a matter of concern for U.S. officials during Biden's vice presidency. The following text is an excerpt from the testimony of George Kent, the U.S. Deputy Assistant Secretary of State, which was recorded in a U.S. Senate report:

> For example, Kent raised Hunter Biden's connection to Burisma during multiple discussions over emails involving the Municipal Energy Reform Program (MERP). In those emails, Kent asked his colleagues, **"[H]ow have we traditionally treated/engaged Burisma**, given the Zlochevsky connection, **but also perhaps U.S. involvement beyond Hunter Biden**?" In another email chain, Kent also pointed out that **"[Zlochevsky] put Hunter Biden on the board of his Burisma Energy company**." When inquiring about the extent to which State Department officials researched Burisma's past, in order to determine whether to associate with the

138

company, Kent asked his colleagues whether any "'know your partner' due diligence was done" before the partnership between MERP and Burisma was established. Kent then described old news stories involving the company. "Zlochevsky as a corrupt mal actor was a 2014 story [and] his control of Burisma, and the very sticky wicket of the Hunter Biden connection on Burisma's board was circulating in 2015."[9.28]

The report on Kent's testimony continues. The report states that in an email chain, Kent voices his concern of potential reputational risk to the Obama-Biden administration.

[W]ould we want an article on the front page of the *Washington Post* (and in this case, the *Kyiv Post*, and on the FB pages of Sergiy Leshchenko and Mustafa Nayyem) commenting about this public private partnership with Burisma, the link to Hunter Biden, and the link to Zlochevsky, who almost certainly paid off the PGO in December 2014 (I had the then First

Deputy PG Danylenko tell me the bribe was $7 million) to have the case against him closed and his $23 million in assets frozen in the UK unfrozen?[9.28]

The Burisma episode is not the only time when Hunter and his partners have attempted to tap into USAID funds. As the *New York Post* reported, 34-year-old Ann Marie Person left Hunter Biden's Rosemont Seneca Partners in 2014 to join the vice president's team and maintained close contact with her former bosses. She kept them informed of visits by high-ranking officials and official events that, according to emails, might be of interest to them. She was actively involved in the Biden administration.[9.29] Her husband, Mike Muldoon also worked at Rosemont Seneca from at least December 2009 to October 2011, before he left to work for USAID, an agency that often interacted with Rosemont Seneca's clients according to emails from Hunter Biden and his partner Eric Schwerin.[9.29]

Also, according to emails on the hard drive, at least two companies Rosemont was considering investing in or taking on as clients — Aqua Sciences and Karl Storz — were seeking to profit from USAID contracts to provide aid after the 2010 earthquake in Haiti. That specific USAID program was overseen by Paul Wiesenfeld.[9.12] As I mentioned earlier in this chapter, Wiesenfeld eventually became head of the IRG and signed the MERP MOU with Burisma in 2014.[9.4]

Interestingly in 2019, John Solomon wrote in *The Hill* concerning correspondence related to USAID, which he obtained from Hunter Biden's laptop. In December 2015, Devon Archer wrote to Hunter about their joint meeting at the U.S. State Department. The text said that the meeting was about "a new USAID project that the embassy is announcing with us" and that "it would be perfect for us to move forward."[9.30]

Throughout this ordeal, George Kent continued to raise the alarm with the various federal departments during the Obama-Biden Administration about Burisma. Kent testified under oath in congress with the U.S. House of Representatives that he warned USAID about Burisma's bad reputation, which did not prevent them from working together. The following excerpt from page 102 of his congressional testimony describes one attempt to notify others:

Kent: As I said, Burisma had a reputation for being, first of all, one of the largest private producers of natural gas in Ukraine but also had a reputation for not being the sort of corporate, cleanest member of the business community.

[U.S. Congressman] Jordan: And you were so concerned about that that you advised USAID not to do any type of coordinated activity -

Kent: Correct.[9.31]

Kent also said that his views about Burisma's reputation were communicated to him from U.S. embassy staff in Kiev, as described in page 103 in his congressional testimony:

[U.S. Congressman] McCaul: Sort of following up on that question, and thank you for your service, yeah, you referred to Burisma as it had a bad reputation essentially?

Kent: That is what I was told by the members of our embassy community who focused on economic issues and had liaison with the U.S. business community, yes.[9.31]

Despite some caution in his wording, George Kent maintained a very tough stance on Zlochevsky and Burisma. For the sake of completeness, let us recall his testimony on page 82 during his 2019 interview with committee members from the U.S. House of Representatives when he directly told the Ukrainian Deputy Prosecutor General *that Zlochevsky must be arrested if he appears in Ukraine.* Kent says, "He [Kasko] did not offer the name of anyone he suspected of having taken the bribe. He did, however, say, well, I've been friends with Zlochevsky for 21 years, and he's in Dubai right now. Here's his phone number. Do you want it? And I said, no, I think you should actually arrest him next time he comes back to Ukraine."[9.31] Yet, this man, with a clearly criminal reputation dating back to the days of Ukrainian President Yanukovych's ministry, has become a respected partner of USAID—all thanks to his friendship with the Bidens.

CHAPTER 10:

LOBBYISTS RUSH TO THE RESCUE

The U.S. firm Blue Star Strategies was one among many lobbying companies that Mykola Zlochevsky hired to help *cleanse* his image and Burisma's business reputation. The founders of the Blue Star Strategies lobbying firm are Karen Tramontano, former deputy chief of staff to President Bill Clinton, and Sally Painter, another former Clinton White House staffer.[10.1] Senator Chuck Grassley is convinced that Blue Star Strategies misinformed the U.S. Department of Justice by failing to provide information about all meetings in Ukraine with U.S. officials that were held in Zlochevsky's interests. *The lobbyists met with a representative of USAID, representatives of the State Department, the U.S. ambassador in Kiev, among others.*

According to Grassley's materials, issues existed with specific government FARA reports that U.S. lobbyist engaging in foreign or international activities are required to file per U.S. law. He states, "Based on our investigative records and recently published Foreign Agents Registration Act ('FARA') forms, it appears that Blue Star Strategies' top executives, Karen Tramontano and Sally Painter, filed incomplete and misleading information with the Department of Justice ('DOJ')...Based on the senators' previous work examining the extent to which Blue Star Strategies met with Obama administration officials on behalf of Burisma and Mr. Zlochevsky, it appears that Blue Star Strategies' FARA form lacked complete and accurate information."[10.2]

Apparently, Blue Star lobbyists concealed a meeting with the hero of Chapter 8 featuring Naftogaz–Amos Hochstein. In 2015, Hochstein was Assistant Secretary of State for Energy Resources. The Blue Star lobbyists also concealed a meeting with Stephen Gonyea from USAID, who oversaw the very same USAID funded MERP program involving Burisma from Chapter 9. Why did a USAID representative need to meet with lobbyists from the U.S.? More importantly, why did Blue Star hide these meetings? This casts an additional shadow on the collaborations among Zlochevsky's company and U.S. government agencies.[10.2]

I believe that the numerous instances of communication between Zlochevsky's lobbyists and U.S. officials on topics sensitive to the Bidens should be re-investigated by the U.S. Congress. After all, if these contacts had transparent motives and no malicious intent, why was it necessary to hide them?

It must be said that Zlochevsky's legal troubles have taught him not to spare any expense in acquiring influential protégés in the West. For example, while Hunter was still working at Burisma, he hired London-based PR agency Bell Pottinger to handle media relations. The PR agency staunchly defended its clients. One of the agency's founders, Lord Timothy Bell, was an advisor to British Prime Minister Margaret Thatcher and Russian President Boris Yeltsin.[10.3] The agency's services were also used by the wife of Syrian President Bashar al-Assad and the Belarusian government.[10.4] Here's another interesting example, Hunter was joined at the Burisma board table by Joseph Cofer Black, former head of the CIA's Counterterrorism Center from 1999 to 2002.[10.5]

Under the leadership of a whole team of influential American lobbyists, Burisma successfully strengthened its business position in the Ukrainian market and defended itself against attacks from the press. Suffice it to say that in 2016 Resano Trading Ltd, a company affiliated with Burisma,

KNOWN RECORD:
Blue Star Strategies

Blue Star Strategies is an international consulting firm specializing in policy, politics, investment and resource efforts.[10.6] In 2015, Hunter Biden and Devon Archer hired Blue Star Strategies to assist with lobbying efforts for Burisma.[10.7] The company's efforts to assist in the closure of Burisma-related cases is known by members in congress, as mentioned in a 2023 letter to the company's CEO from Congressmen Jim Jordan and James Comer.[10.7] One prior investigation held in 2021 involved a FARA filing violation with Blue Star Strategies, which was rectified by and closed when the company submitted a late FARA filing in 2022 describing the work with Bursima.[10.7] In the letter dated 2023, Congressmen Jordan and Comer were summoning Blue Star Strategies to appear in impeachment inquiries for President Joe Biden, which were closed in March 2024 due to lack of evidence.[10.8]

acquired Ukrainian assets from the Canadian company Serinus Energy that were mainly gas fields in the Dnipro-Donets Basin in Ukraine. The company developed the Olgovskoye, Makeevskoye, Severo-Makeevskoye, Vergunskoye, and Krutogorskoye fields in the Luhansk region in Ukraine. Then in 2020, Mykola Zlochevsky's Cypriot company Brociti Investments Limited became the owner of 100% of the share capital of Geounit, which specializes in seismic exploration at oil and gas fields. The seemingly monopolistic deal was greenlighted by the Anti-Monopolistic Committee of Ukraine.[10.9] No one dared to accuse Zlochevsky of abusing his power, let alone of using the vice president and his son as a *shield*.

I have already mentioned John Buretta in Chapter 3. Before becoming a lobbyist, he completed his work at the Department of Justice as Deputy Assistant Attorney General.[10.10] He was an important figure in lobbying for Burisma and Zlochevsky's interests in the US, as his responsibilities included explaining the U.S. position to the Ukrainian side. Interestingly, the law firm Cravath, which hired Buretta, wrote that it was working for Zlochevsky "in connection with a possible investigation by the Federal Bureau of Investigation and/or other U.S. government agencies."[10.11] According to FARA documents dated January 4, 2024, Cravath reported receiving approximately $350,000 from clients for *professional services and advice provided* between March 2016 and August 2017.[10.12] "In January 2016, Mr. Buretta was hired to represent Mykola Zlochevsky in connection with possible investigations by government agencies in the United States," the firm's documents state. Subsequently, lobbying support for Zlochevsky expanded to include Burisma Holdings Limited's interests in the contract. In particular, in connection with "government investigations in Ukraine" against the company. According to the same 2024 FARA filing, Buretta's work on behalf of Burisma included meetings with U.S. officials "to present facts relevant to potential U.S. and Ukrainian investigations."[10.12] In September 2016, Buretta also sent a letter to Marie Yovanovitch, then U.S. ambassador to Ukraine.[10.13] Lobbying support for Zlochevsky continued until April 2017, when the first criminal cases were closed.[10.2]

Zlochevsky not only surrounded himself with Western lobbyists but also began to sponsor various events in Europe. For example, he participated in financing an energy forum in the Principality of Monaco, which was opened by Prince Albert II himself. In the summer of 2017, Mykola took a delegation of the Ukrainian government there.[10.14] In 2015, Burisma sponsored Europe's largest electric car marathon, which started in Kiev and finished in Monaco.[10.15]

How can such a *glorious guy* and his *no less glorious* American friends be subjected to persecution and criticism?

PART THREE:

A GAME OF GEOPOLITICS WITH A HINT OF PROFITEERING

"Let's return to the topic of external control over Ukraine."

—Viktor Shokin, 2025

CHAPTER 11:

HOW BIDEN BOUGHT THE POSITION OF UKRAINE'S PROSECUTOR GENERAL FOR $1 BILLION

"Hence, Joe Biden obtained what he wanted, albeit not in six hours but in five months."

—from Olivier Berruyer's film *UkraineGate – Inconvenient Facts*, 2020[11.1]

The story of my dismissal under pressure from Joe Biden made headlines around the world. What did I do to get the U.S. vice president interested in me, and with insults directed at me? The British newspaper The *Independent* investigated this issue. The publication states outright that the Burisma case was part of a widespread corruption scheme in Ukraine; accuse an oligarch, confiscate his property, agree on a bribe, and then shut down the investigation.[11.2]

Now I can't even remember the exact day and time when Petro Poroshenko first started hinting that he wanted to remove me from office.

However, it definitely started with talk about Burisma. It was something like, "Don't put pressure on the investigation, Biden is unhappy because his son is on the board of directors of this company, and we must understand Ukraine's dependence on America, and therefore its dependence on Biden's support..." and so on.

Poroshenko did not say directly, "Close the case." In fact, he would not have dared to say that to me because he knew perfectly well that it would be the height of lawlessness. I respect the law, which he understood very well. His insistent schooling, "don't put pressure on Burisma," was more of a recommendation to slow down the investigation into the company.

One of the key episodes signaling Biden's dissatisfaction with the Ukrainian Prosecutor General in connection with the Burisma case was the statement by U.S. Ambassador Geoffrey Pyatt. On September 25, 2015, during the business forum in Odessa, Ambassador Pyatt unexpectedly stated that *the results of the investigation into Burisma are unsatisfactory*. I have already cited these far-fetched claims by the ambassador at the beginning of the book (see Chapter 1).[11.3]

156

Why did Burisma feature so prominently in the ambassador's speech? The explanation is simple. Pyatt was conveying the position of Vice President Biden. Among thousands of cases, he was only interested in the Burisma case. Pyatt's words shocked the entire Ukrainian law enforcement system because everything was exactly the opposite. It was also a double shock for all diplomats because ambassadors have no right to interfere in the internal affairs of a country. Such a statement from an ambassador looked like blatant interference by an authorized representative of a foreign state in a criminal investigation conducted by a sovereign state.

Pyatt's assessment puzzled not only Ukrainian investigators and diplomats, but also the British Embassy. Within hours, Patrick Torkington, a British Embassy official in Ukraine and liaison officer for international affairs at the National Crime Agency, sent an official statement to the Main Investigation Department of the PGO, saying that "neither he nor his country understood the motives of the U.S. ambassador to Ukraine…British law enforcement agencies involved in the investigation of criminal cases against Burisma and, in accordance with a London court ruling, who blocked Mykola Zlochevsky's bank accounts worth $23 million in the spring of 2014, were, to put it mildly, surprised by this assessment of the U.S. ambassador."[11.4]

To be honest, Burisma was not my priority at work. Of course, I was well informed about the progress of the investigation and personally kept it under control. I was aware of everything the investigators had uncovered and what new facts they had discovered. However, my main focus was on the events in Maidan, the crimes committed by Yanukovych and his officials, and the rescue of Ukrainian prisoners of war captured in Donbas. There was an incredible amount of work to be done, and I worked 24/7, with almost no days off.

Since the fall of 2015, President Poroshenko reminded me about Burisma more and more often. He was getting annoyed, and the tension between us was growing. Around the same time, the first media attacks against me began. What's more, there was even an attempt on my life. On November 2, 2015, an unknown assailant fired shots at the windows of the PGO on Rylnytska Street. I was saved by bulletproof glass, which had been installed as a precaution by Viktor Pshonka, the prosecutor general during Ukrainian President Yanukovych's time. I didn't even know that the windows in my office were bulletproof.[11.5]

I will tell you the story of the assassination attempt very briefly. By the way, as far as I know, the investigation into this incident is not yet complete. It was late in the evening. My assistant Vladimir Stetsenko and I were planning our work for the coming weeks. The phone rang—it was Foreign Minister Pavlo Klimkin.

Suddenly, in the middle of the conversation, Klimkin asked anxiously, "Is everything okay there? Are they shooting?"

At that moment, my assistant grabbed me by the arm and shouted, "Let's get out of here!" and pushed me out of the office.

It all happened in a matter of seconds. I didn't even have time to understand what was going on. The building's security guards arrived immediately, followed by a group of SBU special forces. After the shooting, law enforcement officers found three bullet holes in the window frame.

I told investigators that if they really wanted to kill me, first they would have killed me. Secondly, they would have done it somewhere else—definitely not in my office. Incidentally, shortly before the assassination attempt a hidden pistol was found in the corridor near my reception room, but it had no bullets.

Now, ten years later, I still don't understand what it was. Was it an assassination attempt? A threat? A warning? If it was a warning, then from whom? There are more questions than answers. However, it is evident that there was a real threat to my life. You will understand why later.

So in the fall of 2015, my official relationship with Petro Poroshenko became strained. It was becoming increasingly clear that the Ukrainian president no longer needed a strong and independent prosecutor general. It seems that Poroshenko had made the decision to dismiss me long before we had our fundamental and heated conversation on the subject. According to my information, the decision was made about three months before the conversation. I heard rumors that in November 2015 Yuriy Lutsenko begged Poroshenko on his knees to appoint him Prosecutor General. I was told about this scene by a person who saw it with his own eyes. It happened when the President of Ukraine and Lutsenko were on a visit to Japan. I have no reason not to trust this information, because I know Yuriy Vitalievich well and know a lot about him in all his guises.

In any case, according to records of telephone conversations between President Petro Poroshenko and U.S. Secretary of State John Kerry, they discussed my resignation in early December 2015. "I just wanted to try to urge you to see if there is a way to resolve this issue - to replace the Prosecutor General of Ukraine - you know who - Shokin. I know the vice

160

president is very concerned about this. And I think
it would be good to try to find a solution to the
problem," Mr. Kerry said at the time.[11.6]

Here's an interesting fact. Hunter Biden's business partner and
Burisma board member Devon Archer met with John Kerry just a few weeks
before I was fired.[11.7] As mentioned earlier, Archer was a friend of Chris Heinz,
who is also John Kerry's stepson. Why was this meeting necessary?

Be that as it may, Petro Oleksiyovych Poroshenko found the *solution
to the problem* that the Secretary of State and Joe Biden demanded of him.
Poroshenko did this in a very *original* way. He called me and tried to intimidate
me. "Biden is coming to Kiev and will bring information
about your corruption."

I shrugged, "Well, let him come." Although I understood that
if desired, a corruption story could be fabricated, even about me.

On December 15, 2015, Joe Biden arrived in Kiev on a visit. Both
politicians and political analysts were left guessing about the purpose of this
trip. It is now clear that Biden's visit had no other purpose than to cover up the
financial payments from Burisma to his son Hunter. The U.S. Vice President
gave an eloquent speech in the Verkhovna Rada. He spoke about the fight

against corruption. However, he did not say a word about my mythical *corrupt activities*. Meanwhile, publicly, before his arrival in Ukraine, he accused me of corruption. I said directly to Poroshenko, "Petro Oleksiyovych, Joe Biden is the second most powerful man in one of the most influential countries in the world. He has the FBI, the CIA, and other special services at his disposal. If he has not brought any evidence of my alleged corruption, then there is no such evidence. Am I correct?"

Poroshenko remained silent in response because he had nothing to say. Biden blackmailed him, stating that Ukraine would not receive a $1 billion loan tranche unless the president dismissed me. On August 22, 2016, Joe Biden repeated this in an interview with The *Atlantic*.[11.8]

"Petro, you're not getting the billion," Biden reminded President Poroshenko. "All right. You can keep the prosecutor general. Just remember one thing. If you keep him, we won't pay."[11.8]

Later, on January 23, 2018, Joe Biden confirmed his words while speaking at the Council on Foreign Relations in Washington. "Petro, you won't get your billion...unless you fire that son of a bitch...Well, okay. You can keep the prosecutor general. But in that case, keep in mind that we won't pay."[119]

**Joe Biden During His Legendary Speech at the
Council on Foreign Relations**

The fact that Joe Biden directly interfered in the internal affairs of Ukraine, and particularly illegally secured my dismissal from the post of Attorney General is objectively confirmed by the findings of investigations. Further evidence can be found in the four-part documentary film *UkraineGate – Inconvenient Facts* with part two of the film titled *Joe Biden: A Friend or an Enemy of Corruption?*[11.1] The film is directed and edited by the aforementioned French journalist Olivier Berruyer, founder of the website www.les-crises.fr, which specializes in geopolitics and the global economy. Part one of the film series is called *Not Such a Reliable Prosecutor*[11.1] It is about the scandal surrounding my resignation, provoked by Biden because of his defense of Burisma. I was interested to hear the comment by Colin Kahl, Joe Biden's personal advisor in 2014-2017:

> The general opinion, not only in the U.S. but also in the IMF, was that Shokin had become a kind of stumbling block. In December 2015, Vice President Joe Biden flew to Kiev. We discussed his speech and loan guarantees for Ukraine on the plane. The vice president then received instructions from his advisers, as well as from Victoria Nuland, who was with us on board. After landing in Kiev, he was also briefed by the ambassador to Ukraine, Geoffrey Pyatt. But after consultations, the vice president told us, "Listen, I'll just tell Poroshenko that he won't get the money unless he forces Shokin to resign." He said this in a very commanding tone. Because I was convinced that we would never have such a strong lever.[11.1]

Later, this story was supplemented by statements from George Kent that he had raised concerns about Hunter Biden's work in Ukraine, but his concerns were ignored.[11.10]

Incidentally, I tried to find out where the money went—the billion dollars guaranteed by the U.S. that Ukraine received in exchange for my dismissal. I wanted to believe that my resignation had at least benefited the country's budget and economy. In open financial sources, I found only scant information that the funds were allegedly *directed to social assistance for low-income citizens of Ukraine affected by gas price increases.*[11.11] Once again, Burisma came out on top, because higher gas prices mean more money for Zlochevsky's company. So, a piece of the ill-fated *Shokin billion* ended up in Hunter Biden's pocket.

However, let's return to the episode of my resignation. One way or another, when negotiations were taking place behind the scenes between Biden and the President of Ukraine from mid-December 2015 until mid-February 2016, Poroshenko did not speak to me about my resignation. Of course, I understood that clouds were gathering over me. However, no offer to resign was ever made.

Meanwhile, investigators came to certain conclusions in the Burisma case. On February 4, 2016, at the request of the GPU [an arm of Ukraine's national police], the court again arrested Mykola Zlochevsky's property. Among other things, two of his estates, measuring 1,000 and 2,300 square meters, as well as a Rolls-Royce Phantom, were seized. I think Zlochevsky immediately ran to Joe Biden. or conveyed his indignation through Hunter.

Then Joe Biden called Petro Poroshenko, who called me. `What are you doing again?` he growled. `Why are you pushing this investigation?`

I believe Poroshenko promised Biden that everything would be *OK*. However, it didn't turn out quite *OK* for them. So, the *vice-king of Ukraine* was very angry.

Around that time, I ran into an old acquaintance who worked in the government. He said that while talking to the president the other day, he mentioned me in passing, to which Petro Poroshenko waved his hand and advised, `Forget about Shokin, he's already gone.` In other words, before talking to me *about my* resignation, Poroshenko *had already discussed it with other people as a fait accompli.* However, the day for the difficult conversation about my resignation finally arrived. It took place on February 16, 2016.

"Viktor Nikolaevich, you have to leave," the president said calmly. Then he began to think aloud about what kind of far-fetched excuse to use to justify me leaving, since he himself repeatedly acknowledged that I was doing a good job. Also, he had no complaints about me. "Write that you are leaving for health reasons," he advised.

"But I am healthy!" I interrupted him.

"Well, then write that it is of your own volition!" he replied.

To say that it was annoying would be an understatement. The bitter taste of injustice that I felt at that moment still lingers with me to this day. That same day, February 16, 2016, President Poroshenko, succumbing to pressure from Biden and without even waiting for my resignation statement, made a televised address to the Ukrainian people in which he announced my dismissal.[11,12] He said, "Viktor Shokin implemented reforms that the Prosecutor General's Office had sabotaged for decades, depriving the prosecutor's office of general oversight, creating the National Anti-Corruption Bureau and the State Bureau of Investigations, etc.. I was praised on behalf of the

President of Ukraine on his official website. On the one hand, this was progress, but on the other hand, the Prosecutor General's Office, unfortunately, failed to win the trust of society, and that is why the question of the resignation of the Prosecutor General is on the agenda."[11.1]

Understanding how much my war-torn country needed the money promised by Biden, I was forced to agree with the decision of the President of Ukraine. On February 19, 2016, I submitted my resignation. So, to sum up, the only reason for the resignation of the Prosecutor General of independent Ukraine was the desire of a very influential American, Joe Biden!

Petro Poroshenko himself acknowledged that there were no other reasons for the dismissal in a telephone conversation with Biden. "Despite the fact that we have no allegations of corruption against him [Shokin], we have no information about his wrongdoing...I asked him to resign," Poroshenko said to Biden. "Shokin held a government position and, despite having the support of parliament, at the end of our meeting with him, he promised to submit his resignation. An hour ago, he brought me his resignation letter." Then the fifth president of Ukraine added, "This is my second step in fulfilling my promise." We can only guess what the first step was. Or wait for the investigation to establish this one day.[11.13]

I cannot help but recall that there was one high-ranking witness in the story of my resignation, Kurt Volker who was the U.S. State Department's special representative for Ukraine. In his testimony to the U.S. House of Representatives Intelligence Committee, he confirmed that pressure had been exerted on Kiev and on me. "There is clear evidence that Biden asked the Ukrainian president to fire Shokin." According to Volker, the motivation behind this request had nothing to do with Biden's business dealings. *Instead, it was related to the fact that the prosecutor general was corrupt and obstructing the reform of the prosecutor's office.*[11.14]

However, Petro Poroshenko disagreed with Volker's statement, saying to Biden in a recording dated February 18, 2016, "Yesterday I met with Prosecutor General Shokin…and despite the fact that there are no allegations of corruption or wrongdoing against him…I especially asked him to resign…And an hour ago, he brought me his letter of resignation."[11.14]

Listening to the telephone conversations between Petro Oleksiyovych and *Uncle Joe*, I recalled a statement by U.S. President Lyndon Johnson that illustrates the asymmetry of their relationship, "When I need your opinion, I'll let you know."

On February 19, President Poroshenko submitted a draft resolution to the Verkhovna Rada on my dismissal from the post of Prosecutor General. The vote in the parliament took place almost two months later, on March 29, in violation of constitutional procedure. At least four deputies were absent from the chamber when the issue of my dismissal was considered, but their cards were counted as votes in favor. As I later pointed out in an administrative lawsuit seeking reinstatement as Prosecutor General of Ukraine, "...the roll call vote indicates that MPs Dubinin O.I., Kuzmenko A.I., Moskalenko Yu.M., and Svyatash D.V. allegedly participated in the vote on the aforementioned resolution, but did not confirm their presence in the Verkhovna Rada on that day with their personal signatures on the registration card, and did not undergo either written or electronic registration."[11.15]

However, the shortage of *button-pushing* within the Rada due to the absence of four members during the vote on my resignation is not the most interesting of these alleged violations. I am convinced that a significant portion of the deputies' votes were bought. Journalists and political analysts spoke about this at the time proposing that it was no secret that the resignation of Prosecutor General Shokin was accompanied by more than one violation of Ukrainian law. These sentiments are reflected in the following excerpt from Ukrainian political scientist Ruslan Bornik.

It is no secret that last year's resignation of Prosecutor General Viktor Shokin was accompanied by more than one violation of Ukrainian law, and the «silencing» of deputies in the council during the vote for his dismissal is not the most interesting of them, said on his Facebook page the political scientist, director of the Ukrainian Institute of Analysis and policy management Ruslan Bortnik.

There is also an extremely resonant and underestimated (by anti-corruption authorities) statement of the person involved in the «gas case», People's Deputy Alexander Onishchenko, about bribery of these very deputies, which no one has denied to this day.

Excerpt from Ruslan Bornik's Facebook Post

According to Onyshchenko, parliament not only appointed Yuriy Lutsenko as the new head of the PGO they did so for money. In a news article Onyshchenko claimed "$3 million had been disbursed for the vote to approve the appointment of Prosecutor General Viktor Shokin in 2015."[11.16] According to political analysts, *between $2 million and $3 million* were spent on a media campaign to discredit me. "A very serious and expensive information campaign has

171

been going on for at least six months. I have seen several such waves of information. According to the most modest estimates, 2-3 million U.S. dollars were invested in such a campaign against Shokin," political analyst Andriy Zolotarev commented on Channel 24.[11.16]

I can only imagine how much it cost to *motivate* the deputies to agree to Lutsenko's appointment, because my successor didn't even have a law degree! His candidacy was *pushed through* in parliament for more than two months.[11.1,11.17] All this lawlessness was in essence *dedicated* to Joe Biden's whims.

The presidential decree on my dismissal was finally signed on April 3, 2016. It is difficult to convey my emotions due to all this dirty political game. What hurt me the most was that an American gentleman from across the ocean who was taking advantage of the extremely difficult situation in Ukraine could play with the fate of my country, could remove and appoint senior government officials at his whim. I was saddened by such humiliation of my country.

On December 22, 2016, I appealed to the High Administrative Court of Ukraine (HACU) demanding that my dismissal be declared unlawful and that the decree and the resolution of the Verkhovna Rada legalizing my dismissal be revoked. Later, the court dismissed my claim.[11.18] On March 28, 2017, I filed an application with the Supreme Court of Ukraine requesting that it consider my reinstatement as Prosecutor General. However, the court rejected my request without justification.[11.19] Then, on October 25, 2017, I filed a lawsuit with the European Court of Human Rights. However, all my attempts to achieve justice have been in vain.[11.20]

I believe that everything that has happened to me in recent years—the blackmail and pressure from Joe Biden, the coercion of Ukrainian President Petro Poroshenko to force me to resign as Prosecutor General, the bribery of MPs to secure my dismissal, and the attempts on my life—will one day be investigated and those who are responsible will be punished.

It is also worth adding an important comment regarding the international context of my dismissal and responding to the criticism of the *good/bad Shokin*. I categorically reject the allegations that *broad international circles* demanded my dismissal. This was stated, for example, by former U.S. Ambassador Geoffrey Pyatt. I am convinced that the pressure came specifically from Joe Biden. Do the restrictions on the supply of long-range weapons to Ukraine, introduced by him in the last years of his presidency, not confirm the extent of his influence? Biden influenced the geopolitical picture of the world, which prevented him from putting pressure on some ambassador.

To reaffirm my international support, I declare that during my time in office no ambassador has ever expressed any complaints or grievances to me personally. In February 2016, when the issue of my dismissal became public knowledge, I received calls of support from ambassadors from numerous countries.[11.21] Reports of my meetings with ambassadors and their positive feedback were published on the official website of the PGO of Ukraine. I am confident that all these materials are available or can be restored. I am ready to help you find them.

Though, it would be better to ask these diplomats themselves, what exactly did I do wrong? Make a list and ask each of them directly. I am sure that in response you will hear roughly what Biden said in the Verkhovna Rada about *Shokin's corruption* or you will hear nothing, silence.

I also reject Pyatt's completely unfounded claims regarding the freezing of Zlochevsky's assets in the UK. These events took place before I took office as Prosecutor General in February 2015.[11.22] I had nothing to do with them. Nothing.

Joe Biden could not have failed to understand that in accusing me of corruption and blackmailing Poroshenko with a billion dollars, he needed something to back it up. That is how the *Diamond Case* came into being in June 2015. The deputy prosecutor of the Kiev region was involved in this case. I dismissed him immediately. Some of Joe Biden's buddies in our law

KNOWN RECORD:
The Diamond Prosecutor's Case

The Diamond Prosecutor's Case refers to a criminal case involving Oleksandr Korniets, who was formerly the head of the Kiev Oblast prosecutor's office. Korniets was charged with bribery related to him acquiring 12 hectares of land in Kiev Oblast, which was more value than his salary could afford. When Korniets was arrested in early July 2015, several cut diamonds were discovered in his residence, publicly labeling the criminal case the *Diamond Prosecutor's Case*. Yet, Korniets was released within weeks of his arrest after his lawyer paid 3.2 million Hryvnia bail, sparking outrage.[11.23]

The seriousness of PGO's reforms to end corruption were questioned, which spurred more investigations to determine who was responsible. An internal fight in the PGO's office arose, creating conflict among the NABU and SBU.[11.24] The scandal questioned Shokin's efforts without reason. Requiring no further discovery, Shokin tried to shut down the investigations but was accused of hiding departmental corruption.[11.23] enforcement agencies decided to link me to this scandal, saying that I was covering up the scam of the former deputy prosecutor of the Kiev region. The case was opened 10-years ago and is still ongoing. It has never been brought to court because there is no evidence linking me to the dismissed deputy prosecutor of the Kiev region.

I have carefully studied this case. There are a lot of fake expert reports. These reports were fabricated by Democrats appointed to the prosecutor's office: Vitaly Kasko, David Sakvarelidze, and others. The case was cobbled together in a hurry to support Biden's accusations of corruption against me. He was supposed to present a fake case against Poroshenko. It was all done so clumsily that they just shouted about it in the media but were afraid to take the case to court. That's why Biden flew in empty-handed. He had no choice but to twist Poroshenko's arm and demand my resignation. Poroshenko himself did not dare to mention the *Diamond Prosecutor's Case* in conversations about my resignation. As I wrote earlier, he admitted that there was nothing on me. Neither he nor Biden had anything.

Thus, the attempt to discredit me failed miserably. As the saying goes, "the spoons were found, but the sediment remained." I am confident that the ugly truth about this case will come out and justice will prevail. I have no doubt that a large-scale campaign was launched to discredit me. The person behind it was none other than Joe Biden.

CHAPTER 12:

POCKET PROSECUTOR GENERAL AND HOW LUTSENKO CLOSED THE BURISMA CASES

Paradoxically, the louder American politicians talked about building a system of rule of law in Ukraine, the deeper the country sank into the swamp of corruption. After my resignation, nothing stood in the way of Poroshenko's desire to turn the prosecutor's office into his own personal fiefdom. And why not? Joe Biden himself taught him how to use prosecutors to his advantage.

One of the most striking stories about how the system of external governance of Ukraine built by the Democrats gave rise to large-scale corruption is the scandalous episode involving the *bribe of the century* worth $50 million for closing all criminal cases against Burisma. In fact, it wasn't just the cases against Burisma that were closed. Everything that could in any way compromise the Biden family in Ukraine was swept under the rug.

As I mentioned earlier, Biden demanded that Poroshenko remove all references to his son and, of course, to himself from all cases. Poroshenko promised to do everything to ensure that the heavyweight of American politics had nothing to worry about. That was how they parted ways. However, as soon as Donald Trump entered the White House in 2016, his lawyer Giuliani began digging up all the Bidens' dirty deeds in Ukraine.

Joe was right to be worried. My dismissal in April 2016 wasn't enough.[12.1] The criminal cases against Burisma couldn't be hushed up right away. Some of the cases were closed by my replacement, Prosecutor General Yuriy Lutsenko from 2016-2017. According to Giuliani, this was done under pressure from the U.S. "I can't believe how blind our media is. They are blindly using a prosecutor who corruptly closed cases against Biden's son and his corrupt company. There was no investigation at all. Where is the report? Use common sense — those of you who haven't lost it. Analyze it...," Giuliani wrote on Twitter on September 30, 2019.[12.2]

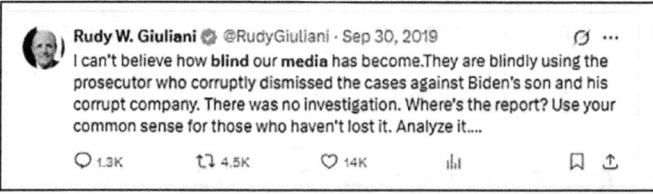

Rudy Giuliani's X post on September 30, 2019

KNOWN RECORD:
Rudy Giuliani

Rudolph Giuliani is a former Mayor of New York City and U.S. Attorney General for the Southern District of New York where he masted prosecution of organized crime.[12.2a] While serving as attorney general in 1985, Giuliani became the first attorney to ever prosecute a case under the federal Racketeer Influenced and Corrupt Organizations Act, or RICO(passed in the U.S. Congress in 1970), which resulted in the imprisonment of multiple mob family leaders. He later became mayor of New York City, where he made sweeping changes to reduce corruption in a law enforcement. He also reduced crime by 50%, while helping to restore the city from the 9/11 attacks.[12.3]

Guiliani served as President Trump's personal attorney during Trump's first term in office.[12.4] Giuliani made several visits to Ukraine during 2019 in support of Trump's America First agenda with a promise to reduce and clean up U.S. foreign aid.[12.5] Trump's aspirations sent Giuliani to Ukraine to investigate claims of corruption in relation to U.S. foreign aid with the cooperation of newly elected president, Volodymyr Zelenskyy. Zelenskyy, having expressed his approval of these activities in the infamous 2019 phone call with President Trump, allowed Giuliani to collaborate with different Ukrainian heads of state, such as Ukrainian Deputy to the Office of the President, Andrew Yermak, and Parliamentary Member Derkach, among others.[12.6-12.8] His probes brought him to discover various corrupt activities in Ukraine, such as Burisma, Biden's influence, 2016 election-related actions, and possible obstruction from the U.S. embassy. These topics were openly discussed during Trump's first impeachment trials in 2019.[12.9-12.11]

Amid immense political turmoil in the United States, Guiliani became subject to multiple suits against him simultaneously in what appeared to be politicized lawfare, stemming from work he performed while servicing as President Trump's personal attorney. His law licenses in both Washington D.C. and New York were banned.[12.12] In December 2023, Guiliani was forced to file for bankruptcy due to legal costs related to the court cases filed against him.[12.4,12.12]

On the day Yuriy Lutsenko was confirmed by the Verkhovna Rada as Prosecutor General of Ukraine, President Poroshenko called me and asked me to come to Bankova Street where the presidential administration is located (now called the Office of the President). It was a bit unexpected because it happened in the evening, and I had to arrive after 10 p.m.

Poroshenko and Lutsenko were sitting at the president's desk, which was covered with all kinds of snacks and alcoholic beverages. "Well, say hello to the Prosecutor General," Poroshenko said, pointing to Yuriy and inviting me to the table.

"Who?" I asked ironically. "There is only one Prosecutor General now, and that's me, the former one."

Yura shifted in his chair. Lutsenko said, "Come on, Viktor Nikolaevich, what are you talking about?"

"Vitya, help Yura, teach him what to do as Prosecutor General," Poroshenko asked me in a friendly manner.

"In what sense?" I asked.

"You know he doesn't understand these things. Tell him what the Prosecutor General should do first, and then... give him some advice." Poroshenko answered.

I replied, "If Yura saw himself as the country's chief prosecutor, he should do it himself." In the end, we drank some whiskey, talked, and Lutsenko promised to ask my advice, including on personnel issues. Yet, he never called.

It should be noted that about three months passed between the day Poroshenko *asked* me to resign and the day of Lutsenko's appointment as Prosecutor General. This delay was not because the president was considering the wisdom of such a move, but because the Verkhovna Rada had been searching for votes in support of Lutsenko's candidacy for all those months.[12.13] In order to push through the parliament's decision in favor of this man, amendments were made to the law, according to which the country's Prosecutor General is not required *to have a law degree or relevant work experience.*[12.14]

The speed with which the Verkhovna Rada amended the law on the Prosecutor's Office for the sake of Yuriy Lutsenko impressed everyone. May 12, 2016, can be considered the day when a sad record was set. For the first time in the history of Ukrainian parliamentarism, the process began with the submission of a bill named *No. 4389 "On Amendments to Certain Legislative Acts of Ukraine Regarding the Activities of the Prosecutor's Office,* followed by its adoption, next signing by the Speaker of the Verkhovna Rada, then by the President, and finally publication in *Holos Ukrainy*. This entire process *took only 2 hours and 15 minutes*. Never before in the history of the Ukrainian Verkhovna Rada has a law in Ukraine been *brought to its knees* in such a short time![12.15, 12.16]

Incidentally, Lutsenko was the only candidate for the post of Prosecutor General. When asked in parliament why he was the only candidate, one of the deputies from Poroshenko's BPP faction apparently said, "It's not for nothing that he spent a year and a half behind bars!"[12.17]

"I am convinced that Yuriy Lutsenko has more moral right to demand justice. He faced the gallows for his beliefs, while some MPs essentially collaborated with the previous regime," said President Poroshenko, supporting the dubious logic behind the appointment in his speech to the Verkhovna Rada. "He did not betray his beliefs. Now we need a heavyweight in the PGO who will not be guided by revenge, who will not be guided by a desire to settle scores. This will be a prosecutor who will be guided only by a sense of justice." The speaker did not add one nuance—he did not indicate that the new appointee would establish *Biden-style justice*.

Thus, with the humiliating appointment of Lutsenko as head of the PGO, the collapse of the entire prosecution system began. As the collapse of the prosecutor's office accelerated under Prosecutors General such as *Yuriy Lutsenko, Ruslan Ryaboshapka*, and *Iryna Venediktova,* I feared that we would soon see the Verkhovna Rada churning out prosecutors without legal education like a mad conveyor belt. You know, in the legal world, there are sacred rules that cannot be disregarded, even if the country is undergoing serious reform.

The basic code of legal affairs is the so-called *Bordeaux Declaration* (a.k.a. Judges and Prosecutors in a Democratic Society). The spirit and letter of this document indicate that the figure of the Prosecutor General should remain key in the fight against crime.[12.18] However, in the case of the new Prosecutor General, the word *fight* seemed superfluous.

> The *Bordeaux Declaration* is a legal opinion adopted by the European Council (EC), which is an older but similar governing body like the European Union made up of a consortium of European countries. Members of the EC, like Ukraine, agree to follow the *Bordeaux Declaration* which is a protocol for practicing law that considers the roles, responsibilities, and rights of legal professionals (i.e., lawyers, judges), and their clients.[12.18,12.19]

I was not the only one who felt that Lutsenko had come to the prosecutor's office as an outsider. Colleagues from the PGO said at the time that the new prosecutor general signed official documents without even reading them because he did not understand the professional terminology and found it difficult to understand their content. All the prosecutors quietly laughed at him, and rumors about this spread throughout Kiev. In such cases, a smart leader usually relies on his deputies. But Lutsenko couldn't even do that. He completely lost his way in personnel matters. He fired almost all the competent deputies who worked with me, replacing them with people with low competence and sometimes questionable reputations.[12.20]

Yuriy Lutsenko was focused on several tasks that he had received from Biden via Poroshenko. In fact, their completion was a prerequisite for his appointment to the position he had begged for on his knees. Yuriy successfully and quickly completed all the tasks assigned to him.

First of all, he had to stop the money laundering case against Mykola Zlochevsky and close all cases related to Burisma. The next task was to close the case on the disappearance of U.S. state funds allocated for the reform of the GPU. Around this time, there was also a case against David Sakvarelidze.

In addition, it was necessary to *close the issue* of Vitaly Kasko's apartment. Yes, this is the same Kasko who, in 2014, allegedly missed the deadline for submitting materials from the GPU to British investigators, as a

KNOWN RECORD:
Yuri Lutsenko Sentenced

Yuriy Lutsenko was Minister of Internal Affairs from 2005-2006. During those same years, according to the newspaper *Zerkalo Nedeli*, a huge amount of weapons and military equipment were written off the balance sheet of the Interior Ministry's internal troops.[12.21,12.22] A single government decision in 2006 indicated the write-off of 93 armored personnel carriers, 5,765 automatic weapons, 100 guns, 81 Igla man-portable air defense systems, and 183 million rounds of ammunition.

Lutsenko was eventually tied to these embezzlement activities, and in 2012 Lutsenko was sentenced to jail.[12.23] Notably, these items were never transferred to the Armed Forces of Ukraine but simply written off. Where did these weapons go? There is still no answer to this question.

KNOWN RECORD:
Case Against Vitaly Kasko

So, in March 2014, thanks to forged documents, Kasko took possession of a property that was on the GPU's balance sheet—a spacious apartment with an area of 155 square meters.[12.24] Additionally, the investigation later revealed that in 2015 Kasko used his personal electronic key to access the unified register of information on investigative and procedural actions of the GPU. He used his access to obtain data on persons who had committed serious crimes, including those related to politicians and party organizations.[12.25] Additional details about activities like this one are discussed in Chapter 20.

Result of which a court in London lifted the arrest of $23.5 million in Zlochevsky's accounts.

As soon as Yuriy Lutsenko took office as Prosecutor General, his first act was to signal to U.S. officials that they had nothing to worry about regarding the reputation of Hunter Biden, whom the investigators from the PGO planned to question in connection with numerous Burisma cases. "Hunter Biden has not violated any Ukrainian laws — at least not yet, and we have not found any violations on his part. The company can pay its board members as much as it wants,"Lutsenko said in an interview with Bloomberg at the end of May 2016, just two weeks after his appointment.[12.26]

By the end of the year, he will close all cases involving Zlochevsky and Burisma, which were investigated by the GPU. However, the story of the closure of the cases did not end there.

CHAPTER 13:

LESSONS FROM BIDEN FOR UKRAINE ON HOW TO FLEECE THE OLIGARCHS

I think readers of my book will be interested to learn how Poroshenko managed to amass a personal fortune of a billion dollars. Mykola Zlochevsky also contributed to Poroshenko's rise to wealth. I don't know the details of the personal relationship between Petro Poroshenko and Mykola Zlochevsky, but I do know that they have known each other since the 2000s, when they both entered politics. They then worked together in Mykola Azarov's government. Petro Poroshenko was Minister of Foreign Affairs (2009-2010) and Minister of Economy (2012), while Mykola Zlochevsky headed the Ministry of Environmental Protection (2010-2012). In short, over the years Petro Oleksiyovych Poroshenko managed to form the opinion that *Kolya is a good guy*.

However, at Joe Biden's instigation Poroshenko saw Zlochevsky not only as a *good guy* but also as a *cash cow*. After all, by carrying out Biden's orders to increase gas tariffs, the Ukrainian president did Kolya a big favor.

Burisma received additional income. For such a gift, Poroshenko expected generous gratitude from Zlochevsky.

I must say that Poroshenko always closely followed the investigation of cases against the owner of Burisma. In the first years after the Revolution of Dignity in Ukraine, people liked to quote Lee Kuan Yew. He advised the leaders of countries embarking on reforms to start by putting three of their friends who were embezzling state funds in prison. Poroshenko was advised to use this recipe from the author of the Singapore Miracle. He did not fail to take advantage of this advice. The opportunity presented itself very quickly. When Joseph Biden made it clear that Burisma should be treated favorably, Poroshenko apparently rubbed his hands with satisfaction. This allowed him to kill two birds with one stone by pleasing his Washington curator and at the same time getting money from Zlochevsky for closing the cases.

According to open sources, Igor Kononenko, met several times in 2016 with the owner of Burisma in Spain, Vienna and Dubai.[13.1-13.3] Kononenko was a close associate of the Ukrainian president and deputy chairman of the parliamentary faction of the presidential party named the Petro Poroshenko Bloc (BPP).

After my dismissal in 2016, the frequency with which cases collapsed, or courts unfroze the assets of former ministers proves the likelihood of those meetings. High-ranking extortionists gradually withdrew funds from the gas trader, and the longer the negotiations lasted, the higher the *price of the issue* became. In other words, *it was profitable to keep Zlochevsky's case in limbo.*[13.4]

The new Prosecutor General, Yuriy Lutsenko, successfully accomplished this task. In the fall of 2016, the Ministry of Internal Affairs removed the corrupt ex-minister from the state investigation department's records based on a resolution sent by the Department of the PGO for the Investigation of Particularly Important Economic Cases.[13.5] Moreover, six months later, in January 2017, Yuriy Lutsenko's PGO dropped all its claims against Zlochevsky.[13.6]

Meanwhile, Zlochevsky's business ran like clockwork, even after he fled abroad in 2014. Everything functioned almost as smoothly as it had during Viktor Yanukovych's presidency. Burisma bought new gas companies and obtained new licenses to develop Ukrainian mineral resources. Poroshenko decided to take advantage of this, especially since the oligarch's *disgraced* position was particularly tempting.

According to Oleksandr Onyshchenko in his book *Peter the Fifth*, in 2015-2016, Zlochevsky supplied gas worth more than $10 million to companies owned by people in Poroshenko's team. The only nuance is that

KNOWN RECORD:
Igor Kononenko

Igor Kononenko is a Ukrainian businessman, former politician, and an old friend of Petro Poroshenko. The two met between 1984-1986 when both men served in the Soviet Army. The two developed a deep business relationship, with Kononenko serving as member of the supervisory board in Poroshenko's companies. After entering politics in 2006, he was the people's deputy on the Petro Poroshenko Bloc a political party aligned with President Poroshenko in 2014.[13.7] After Yuriy Lutsenko was appointed to the PGO, a report filed by the U.S. congress stated Kononenko worked closely with Lutsenko and even helped supervise special cases.[13.8-13.10]

these supplies were free of charge.[13.7] So much for Poroshenko not including Yanukovych's former minister on any sanction lists. According to Onyshchenko, Zlochevsky was not happy with this situation, and at the end of 2015, he asked Onyshchenko to talk to Poroshenko to put an end to this *exploitation.* [13.11] According to his information, Igor Kononenko conducted secret negotiations with Mykola Zlochevsky on behalf of Petro Poroshenko, extorting a large sum of *compensation* from him for the final and irrevocable closure of criminal cases.[13.11]

Lutsenko also had his own role to play in this game. He loudly announced new cases against Zlochevsky in the media. Lutsenko's *moment of glory* came in 2019, when a large-scale scandal broke out involving the largest bribe in Ukrainian history.

If earlier Zlochevsky had given some *small change* for the closure of criminal cases ($7 million) and did not get the desired result, with the coming to power *of Vladimir Zelensky*, he decided to get rid of all his problems at once with the help of the *bribe of the century*. In 2019, the gas oligarch decided to bribe investigators from the PGO and NABU with *$50 million* to finally resolve the issue and cover up the *feeding trough* of his blackmailers.

195

This episode was recounted in June 2020 at a press conference by Konstantin Kulik, a former employee of the PGO of Ukraine and senior member of the office's group of prosecutors investigating economic crimes in 2016-2019.[13.12] Here is what the New York Times wrote about Kulik, "Kulik oversaw cases related to Burisma Holdings. He told The New York Times that he analyzed millions of dollars in payments from Burisma to a company that paid Hunter Biden [Rosemont Seneca Bohai LLC]."[13.13]

According to Kulik, in 2019, Burisma representatives decided to start negotiations with prosecutors from the Ukrainian PGO to close criminal case *No. 42014000000001590* (hereinafter referred to as case *No. 1590*). The case concerned Zlochevsky's involvement in the legalization of Burisma's funds through accounts belonging to Rosemont Seneca Bohai, owned by Devon Archer and Hunter Biden. Case *No. 1590* is the latest in a long list of ten criminal proceedings opened around Burisma, the threads of which led to the Bidens.

I have always been amazed by the cynicism with which many Western media outlets have stubbornly whitewashed Hunter and his father, saying that the vice president's son was just doing business and there was nothing criminal about it. Except, of course, that Burisma was owned by someone close to

KNOWN RECORD:
Konstantin Kulik

Konstantin Kulik is a former Ukrainian prosecutor who claims to have initiated a legal case against Hunter Biden within Ukraine in 2019 prior to the Ukrainian presidential elections. Termed by some social media as a Biden Dossier, Kulik was tasked as the lead prosecutor for criminal investigations against the Bidens. Per Kulik's testimony, the case was filed in court, but no hearings were ever scheduled due to alleged obstruction. Since that time, Kulik was dismissed from his position in the PGO. Corruption charges were issued against him in 2019, which he was cleared of in 2020.[13.14] In 2021, under President Joe Biden's administration, Kulik was placed on the U.S. sanctions list after being aligned with Andriy Derkach. Derkach was the former Ukrainian member of Parliament who leaked the tapes of Joe Biden to the U.S. media, including the recording of Biden's speech at the Council for Foreign Affairs, known in the U.S. as the Derkach Tapes.[13.15] Like Derkach, Kulik was labeled violating U.S. election interference laws.[13.15]

Yanukovych. Zlochevsky also had a string of a dozen criminal cases behind him, including international ones.[13,16] If the media working for the Democratic Party saw nothing wrong with this story, Biden clearly understood that this string of corruption scandals *could seriously damage his career.*

According to Konstantin Kulik, in 2019, Burisma lawyer Andriy Kicha began negotiations with the PGO to close case *No. 1590* in exchange for a hefty sum. At that time, Kicha was helping Mykola *distribute* millions stolen to Cypriot accounts. To better understand what kind of person Zlochevsky is, here is an excerpt from the British court documents on his 2014 criminal case.

> Mr. Andrii Kicha is a Ukrainian commercial lawyer, the chief legal officer of Burisma and other companies owned by the defendant. He was the sole authorized signatory on the BNP accounts that are the subject to the restraint order. On March 11 and 25, 2014, he instructed BNP to transfer the balance of some $23 million held in the accounts to other accounts of the companies held in Cyprus. In his witness statement of June 18, 2014, made for the purpose of these proceedings,

he states that the reason for the transfer was that BNP had wanted, since October 2013, to close the accounts and an end date of April 4, 2014, had been agreed in order to do so.[13.17]

Let's return to Kulik. He said that as soon as Kicha got involved in the decision to close the cases, pressure began to be exerted on his group of prosecutors by the Deputy Prosecutor General of Ukraine, Yevgeny Enin. Apparently, there were motives for the pressure. Back in August 2019, Kulik had information that Zlochevsky had allocated 50 million to close the Burisma criminal cases. "I prepared a report and informed the Prosecutor General of the need to document the attempt to give a bribe," Kulik said, as quoted by Censor.net.[13.18] He also described how the PGO and the Security Service of Ukraine planned a special operation to catch the Burisma bribe-takers red-handed. "The key question is how such a large amount of money could be transferred. Can you imagine the volume of banknotes worth $50 million? It is clear that such a bribe could not have been paid in cash. Therefore, we asked the Security Service of Ukraine to help us create a front company to which the funds would be transferred," Kulik said.[13.18]

However, Kulik's special operation was thwarted due to a change in the leadership of the PGO. After Vladimir Zelensky came to power and Yuriy Lutsenko resigned, Ruslan Ryaboshapka took over as Prosecutor General. "After that, the recording of the $50 million bribe stopped, and Ryaboshapka stated that there was no case against Burisma," Kulik said.[13.19] Afterwards, the information about payments to Hunter Biden also disappeared from the criminal case. Zlochevsky still managed to pull off a scam to close the cases—much to Joe Biden's delight.

However, something did not go according to plan. On June 12, 2020, several officials and representatives of Burisma were detained while handing over a *$6 million* bribe to an agent of the National Anti-Corruption Bureau (NABU).[13.20] Among those detained was Zlochevsky's lawyer and negotiator, Andriy Kicha. However, Ukrainian investigators were also quick to hush up this scandal. At a press conference on the bribe to the NABU employee, bureau chief Artem Sytnik stated that U.S. presidential candidate Joseph Biden and his son Hunter were not involved in this episode and had nothing to do with it.[13.21] Finally, he added that there was no need to interfere in international political processes. The funny thing about his statement is that it was Sytnik who interfered in the 2016 U.S. presidential election, using fake news from the so-called *Barnyard Book (a.k.a. Black Ledger)* in the case of Trump's chief of staff, Paul Manafort. This episode will be described in more detail in Chapter 18.

The final chapter in the *Burisma bribery* case was written on August 1, 2023. On this *momentous day*, the High Anti-Corruption Court (HACC) approved an agreement on the admission of guilt by former Minister of Ecology of Ukraine Mykola Zlochevsky in receiving bribes *and sentenced him to a fine of 68,000 hryvnia ($1,644.24 USD).*[13.22]

Zlochevsky concluded an agreement with the investigation, in which he admitted his guilt in the case of a $6 million bribe to the head of the SAP, Nazar Kholodnitsky, and the director of the NABU, Artem Sytnik, for closing criminal proceedings against him. In other words, the multimillion-dollar bribes were acknowledged as fact, which also confirms the motive for the bribes, which was the closure of cases involving Burisma that were dangerous for the Bidens. However, Zlochevsky, who is suspected of bribery, got off with a laughable fine of a couple thousand dollars. That's all there is to it!

In the U.S., all loose ends of these investigations were also tied up. With Joe Biden's victory in the 2020 election, the elimination of all witnesses and those who investigated his schemes in Ukraine became one of the main

KNOWN RECORD:
Artem Sytnik

Artem Sytnik worked at the PGO from 2001-2011, then left the agency due to personal conflicts with the Yanukovych administration. After obtaining his law license, Sytnik opened a private legal practice in 2011 where he worked until 2015. Sytnik became the first to lead the newly created National Anti-Corruption Bureau of Ukraine (NABU) in 2015, after winning a contest for the position. Later he became the Deputy Head of the National Agency on Corruption Prevention NACP) from 2022-2024.[13.23] Sytnik now serves as the deputy director of the Defense Procurement Agency.[13.24]

Vadim Pozharskyi

Vadim Pozharskyi was a Burisma Board advisor and the Director for International Cooperation and Strategic Development of Burisma Group. In 2018, he was also the Chairman of the Board of the Association of Gas Producers of Ukraine.[13.25] He drew attention when Pozharskyi's records suggested that Joe Biden was aware and involved in Hunter's role at Burisma.[13.26,13.27] priorities of Joe Biden's administration. I have already written about this in detail above. A striking example of this cover-up is the persecution of Trump's lawyer, Rudolph Giuliani. In April 2021, investigators came to Giuliani's home with a search warrant. As many experts noted at the time, the search warrant was an extraordinary step taken by the prosecutor's office against the lawyer of the then former president.[13.28] Giuliani's lawyer, Robert J. Costello, called the searches unnecessary, as his client had offered to answer questions from the U.S. Department of Justice, except those relating to his confidential communications with the former president. "What they did today was legal thuggery," Costello said.[13.29]

Federal authorities explained the harsh measures by saying that Giuliani allegedly lobbied for business projects of Ukrainian officials and oligarchs, who at the same time helped him find dirt on Trump's political rivals, primarily Biden, who was then the Democratic presidential candidate. The oligarch in question is Igor Kolomoisky, who has long been hunted by the FBI.[13.30] These harsh measures appear primarily motivated by the newly elected administration's attempts to silence Biden's critics in the US.

Investigators dug not only into Giuliani's business ties. They also looked into his role in the removal of U.S. Ambassador to Ukraine Marie Yovanovitch, who sabotaged Giuliani's mission to find compromising information in every way possible. For example, she refused to issue visas to a group of Ukrainian witnesses to testify in the Hunter Biden case.[13.31] Giuliani was accused of attempting to remove Ambassador Yovanovitch from her post.[13.32] All this was presented as evidence that Giuliani could have been working on behalf of Ukrainian officials or business representatives who were interested in the U.S. ambassador's resignation. Under the U.S. Foreign Agents Registration Act (FARA), attempts to influence the U.S. government or lobby on its behalf at the request or direction of a foreign official without notifying the Department of Justice are a federal crime.[13.33] In this light, one can suggest that in his an attempt to play *for the winning team*, Yuriy Lutsenko initially helped Giuliani in his search for compromising material on the Biden family.

However, no one is concerned about the unfavorable facts gathered about the Bidens. Everything has been turned upside down. The investigation made no secret of its intention to bring criminal charges against Trump's lawyer, claiming that he had dug up dirt and brought about the removal of the ambassador who was standing in his way. A month before the U.S. elections, on November 3, 2020, Giuliani handed over to journalists at the *New York Post* materials on Hunter Biden. The information given detailed Hunter introducing his father, the U.S. vice president, to businessmen from Ukraine, particularly Vadim Pozharskyi.[13.34] The scandalous article was immediately blocked on social media, with Twitter and Facebook explaining their decisions by saying that the material needed to be verified for accuracy.

After the Democrats returned to the White House, all the scandalous facts about the Bidens' *leftist* earnings were presented as a *witch hunt against respectable members of American society for dirty political purposes*. With such harsh administrative and judicial pressure, the Democrats tried to protect the reputation of the Biden family.

You are unlikely to find any of these facts in the American or European press. Outwardly, the press *appears* to be free of censorship in the EU and the U.S., and that correspondents from leading European and American media outlets work in Ukraine. However, for the most part, they have ignored all the scandalous facts that have come to light over the past ten years. I am not saying that the Biden family should be branded with shame and that we should believe everything his detractors say. The thing is, why is the media, which are so stubborn in other cases, in no hurry to dig up or refute such scandalous facts? I am convinced that this whole issue is so painful for the Democratic Party leadership that a taboo has been imposed from above.

CHAPTER 14:

CREDIT GUARANTEES ARE LIKE A CARROT DANGLED IN FRONT OF UKRAINE

Let's return to the topic of external control over Ukraine. Natalya Yaresko, a U.S. citizen of Ukrainian origin, played an important role in establishing this control over Ukrainian state institutions.[14.1] She became a real conduit and lobbyist for the interests of foreign corporations and investment funds that drove Ukraine into a debt trap for decades.

Yaresko was fluent in Ukrainian and was on friendly terms with representatives of the financial world in both the U.S. and other countries. Natalia Yaresko headed the Ministry of Finance of Ukraine from December 2014 to April 2016. She ended up in this position thanks to Joe Biden's patronage. She is remembered in Ukraine for her involvement in the issuance of $3 billion in Eurobonds guaranteed by the U.S., and then in the spectacular restructuring of the external debt that drove Ukraine into a debt trap.

Natalia Yaresko worked for many years at the U.S. Agency for International Development (USAID). Prior to that she worked at the U.S. State

Department. From 1992 to 1995, she was the first head of the economic department at the U.S. Embassy in Ukraine. From 1995, she worked as a regional investment manager at the Western NIS Enterprises Fund (WNISEF), a direct investment fund established by the U.S. Congress and financed by USAID. In 2001, Yaresko became head of WNISEF. Later, she became co-founder and head of the management company Horizon Capital in 2006.[14.2] Under the auspices of Horizon Capital, the Americans launched a program called the Emerging Europe Growth Fund (EEGF), which was allocated $132 million. The program's goal was to finance investment projects in Ukraine. In 2008, a second program, EEGF II, was launched with a budget of $370 million, followed by EEGF III with a budget of $200 million.[14.3] All of these programs were financed primarily with American money.[14.4] However, these funds never published regular reports on the use of USAID money. Moreover, for example, the *2006 Horizon Capital Report* recorded a loss of $5.3 million.[14.5]

However, the losses of her funds did not affect Natalya Yaresko's wealth in any way. In her 2014 declaration, the minister reported a solid income of $2 million.[14.6] In addition, during her first year as finance minister, Yaresko acquired an apartment in Kiev. The scandalous details of Yaresko's sudden enrichment came to light during her divorce proceedings with her husband, Igor Figlus. Ukrainian court gathered information about all

Yaresko's assets. It turned out that the American woman owned expensive real estate, valuable property, and a substantial amount of money. However, this money was not just sitting in a bank; *it was in the accounts of the Horizon Capital fund, which was financed by USAID.* This is confirmed by an official document—the decision of the Shevchenkivskyi District Court dated February 19, 2013 (Case No. 2-9816/11), which recognized Natalya Yaresko's ownership of a share in the Emerging Europe Growth Fund LP in the amount of USD $777,815.[14.7] The dispute over the former spouses' money then continued in a U.S. court in Delaware.[14.8, 14.9] In general, there have always been numerous allegations against Yaresko regarding financial matters during her years of work in various structures.[14.10]

However, Biden did not make a mistake in his choice. As soon as Natalia Yaresko took office as finance minister, her first task was to prepare loan guarantees. In paragraph 3 of the Credit Guarantee Agreement of May 18, 2015, the Ministry of Finance of Ukraine committed to amend the gas market legislation and the management structure of Naftogaz of Ukraine.[14.11] In fact, these were the very changes that allowed the supervisory board to expand its powers to establish control over the most lucrative parts of Ukrainian state property. First and foremost, this concerned Ukraine's oil and gas sector. In addition, the agreement on guarantees contained in paragraph 4 of the treaty, another unprecedented requirement, which I have already mentioned. Ukraine had to provide USAID with a schedule for increasing energy tariffs by 75% by 2017.[14.11] However, Petro Poroshenko exceeded his commitment and reported to Biden that he had increased tariffs by 100%.[14.12]

To obtain loan guarantees, Poroshenko and Biden reached into the wallets of Ukrainian citizens, and some of the money taken from there went back to Zlochevsky's accounts in the form of profits, and from there to Hunter's accounts in the form of fees. The recordings of Poroshenko's conversations with Biden also include this episode, "In the last three weeks, we have demonstrated significant progress in the area of reforms. We voted for 100 percent on tariffs, even though the IMF was only expecting 75 percent," Poroshenko reported to Biden.[14.12] The latter welcomed this decision because it was necessary to justify the markup on *reverse gas*.[14.12]

The crowning achievement of Natalya Yaresko's career was the famous restructuring of Ukraine's external debt. In August 2015, with Yaresko playing an active role, Ukraine concluded an agreement with its creditors to restructure its external debt of $15 billion.[14.13] Incidentally, among the creditors was the American fund Franklin Templeton, the largest holder of

Ukrainian government debt. The fund was notorious for being used by Yanukovych to launder money stolen from Ukraine. In January 2013, Ukraine's First Deputy Prime Minister Sergei Arbuzov and Finance Minister Yuriy Kolobov paid an *unofficial visit* to the U.S. They met with representatives of the Franklin Templeton investment fund, which then began actively buying up Ukrainian Eurobonds.[14.14,14.15] As a result, the fund concentrated a third of Ukraine's debt obligations. Franklin Templeton bought the largest package, worth $5 billion, in early November 2013, just before the Maidan.[14.16] According reports, Kolobov and Arbuzov agreed to place money belonging to the *family* that had been laundered in the UAE, Hong Kong, Uruguay, and Cyprus in the fund. Then they offered to purchase Ukrainian Eurobonds at a 50% discount.[14.17] The tragic irony is that the country's citizens paid for the restructuring of the Yanukovych family's shadow capital, among other things, at the behest of Joe Biden, the *godfather* of post-Maidan Ukraine.

Let's return to the agreement. It provided for a 20% reduction in external debt (i.e., $3.6 billion), which was presented by the Ukrainian and foreign press as a phenomenal victory for Yaresko, a *master of financial diplomacy*. In reality, there was no debt forgiveness. Instead, Ukraine issued special securities for its creditors, known as GDP warrants or *Value Recovery*

Instruments, the income from which was linked to the country's economic growth.[14.18]

Thus, with GDP growth of up to 3%, payments are zero percent, with economic growth of 3% to 4%, payments are 15% of one percent of GDP growth. And if growth exceeds 4%, Ukraine will have to pay 40% of each additional percentage point of economic growth. The condition imposed by Yaresko linking debt payments to economic growth is unprecedented. The term of the *Yaresko* GDP warrants is almost two decades, from 2021 to 2040. The holders of the debt securities were satisfied with this agreement. However, Sergei Marchenko, who became Ukraine's finance minister after Yaresko, did not hide his pessimism, "Potential payments on government derivatives by 2040, with moderate GDP growth, could exceed $22 billion. And we have Natalya Yaresko to thank for that."[14.18]

To express gratitude for resolving the debt crisis in Ukraine in such a way that was so beneficial to the U.S., Yaresko was sent to carry out economic reforms in Puerto Rico. This assignment turned into an economic crisis there. According to the annual reports of the government watchdog Open Spaces, during the five years that Natalia Yaresko was executive director of the Financial

Oversight and Management Board of Puerto Rico (FOMB), this body spent $1.2 billion on consultants.[14.19] This figure is more than three times the budget that was planned for 10 years.

In addition, Open Spaces has repeatedly pointed out the lack of transparency in FOMB's work, including the absence of adequate details on expenditures and any control over conflicts of interest among board members.[14.20] It is noteworthy that the debts that Yaresko drove Puerto Rico into by spending hundreds of billions on consulting were proposed to be paid off through increases in electricity tariffs.[14.21]

Therefore, reading about the *Puerto Rican page* in Yaresko's biography, I was overcome by déjà vu. The budget had huge spending on consulting services, opaque reporting, possible tariff increases—all of this is directly parallel to Ukraine. The painfully familiar recipe for *reform* of the system always ends in the same way—national debt and billions of dollars squandered.

Chapter 15:

How Biden Tried to Appoint Yaresko as Prime Minister

In 2016, following the resignation of Ukrainian Prime Minister Arseniy Yatsenyuk, Biden even tried to promote Ukrainian Minister of Finance Natalya Yaresko to the post of prime minister. It was the perfect move, because her U.S. citizenship exempted her from any criminal prosecution for any wrongdoing. Here is where President Petro Poroshenko came into play. He quickly granted Yaresko Ukrainian citizenship. Yaresko promised to begin the process of renouncing her U.S. citizenship, as required by Ukrainian law but she never did. It's clear why. As a U.S. citizen, Yaresko could avoid responsibility for any manipulations in Ukrainian jurisdiction. Incidentally, this was one of the reasons why Biden lobbied for foreigners with U.S., Lithuanian, and Georgian passports to be appointed to the National Security Council.

It must be said that the system of governance built by Biden often took on caricatured forms. For example, in one conversation, U.S. Vice President Biden defended Yatsenyuk, who was threatened with dismissal due to his disagreements with the Samopomich party faction in the Ukrainian Parliament. In the spring of 2016, the political crisis in parliament escalated. Not only Samopomich, but also Batkivshchyna and Lyashko's Radical Party left the coalition. According to the law, Poroshenko was obliged to dissolve parliament and call new elections. Yet, he did not do so at Biden's request, in order to keep Yatsenyuk in office as prime minister. Here is an excerpt from this curious conversation:[15.1]

> <u>Petro Poroshenko</u>: As I expected, the Batkivshchyna and Samopomich factions have left the coalition. The coalition now has fewer than 226 votes, so we no longer have a majority. I personally, together with the prime minister, invited Lyashko's Radical Party to join the majority so that we could formally maintain legitimacy. But we have no formal power in parliament or support in society.
>
> <u>Joe Biden</u>: So, if I understand correctly, the no-confidence motion against the government did not pass; you blocked it? Arsen is still there. But then there was a vote on the package of

reforms proposed by the government, and 247 votes were against it. So in terms of moving forward and implementing additional reforms, you don't have a majority in parliament, you don't have a coalition for that, is that right? Is that what you're saying?

Poroshenko: No, not exactly. First, parliament had to evaluate the government's work, and it gave the Cabinet an unsatisfactory assessment. That was the first event. It does not mean the immediate resignation of the government; it is simply a political assessment of its actions. Then, when the no-confidence motion was put to a vote, I arranged for there to be insufficient votes in my faction and in other factions. The prime minister also played a role in this, of course, but I personally blocked the government's resignation **because I promised you that I would** [emphasis added]. But now that two of the four factions have left the coalition, we no longer have a majority in parliament.[151]

Judging by this dialogue, Biden was well versed in the intricacies of Ukrainian politics and was trying to keep Yatsenyuk in the post of prime minister. He recommended that Poroshenko form an alliance with Lyashko's Radical Party in the Parliament. However, Poroshenko explained to the vice president that Lyashko's votes would not be enough to preserve the coalition and hinted at the possibility of buying votes from deputies. Then, out of the blue, Natalya Yaresko pops up.

> Biden: Just recently, on her Facebook page, Yaresko said she was ready to be prime minister and head a government of technocrats. And I know that in any case you need 226 votes. Tell me what's going on, if you can?[15.1]

Poroshenko agreed with Biden's idea and said that he had discussed her candidacy with the Samopomich faction. However, the faction has set too many political conditions, and Poroshenko asked Biden to influence the faction to compromise. Poroshenko then begged Biden to use his leverage not only on Samopomich but also on other parties. Here is how the discussion went verbatim.[15.1]

> Poroshenko: This is exactly what I am asking you.

U.S. Ambassador Pyatt: Please do not give grants to Samopomich. Do not give them money because this is not funding for an opposition party, but funding for a completely irresponsible political leader who is doing very bad things for the future of my country, for Ukraine, and for security and stability.

In fact, Poroshenko is throwing the question of forming a coalition under Yaresko's premiership into Biden's lap like a hot potato, forcing *Papa Joe* to perform the duties of the Ukrainian president and delve into the political crisis down to the smallest details. In general, the situation became absurd. Poroshenko proposed that the U.S. vice president form a coalition in support of his own creation. Petro himself was unable to cope with the situation. There is no clearer example of external control over Ukraine. It is no coincidence that the recordings of Biden and Poroshenko's conversations provoked such an angry reaction from the Democrats that, upon arriving at the White House, they declared a vendetta against Republican investigators of *Biden corruption*. What was secret became clear. The recordings of the talks paint an impressive picture of Ukraine being controlled from across the ocean, with very earthly financial interests looming behind it all. The U.S. embassy, as the *tapes* revealed, was also involved in the plundering of American taxpayers' money.

CHAPTER 16:

THE EMBASSY OCTOPUS AND HOW USAID MONEY WAS STOLEN

"The story of how the Ukrainian authorities, under the wing of American officials and diplomats, mastered international financial aid is worthy of a film by a master of *crime drama* such as Martin Scorsese."

—Viktor Shokin, 2025

In Chapter 2, we discussed that after the Maidan Joe Biden's protégés, Parliament Speaker Groysman and Prime Minister Yatsenyuk, approved *Resolution No. 553*, which legalized the lack of control and audit of foreign aid spending.[16.1] The issue of potential corruption in the use of Western aid was widely reported in the Ukrainian media at the time. In particular, the National Police entered a case into the Unified Register of Pre-trial Investigations concerning the possible embezzlement of international technical assistance involving the Anti-Corruption Center.[16.2] Here is what was stated in the police materials, "...they [Shabunin and

221

Sherembei] organized a scheme to embezzle international technical assistance funds through a charitable organization created by Sherembei called the All-Ukrainian Network of People Living with HIV/AIDS. Between 2015 and 2017, USD $142.9 million passed through this network of organizations." It was noted that Sherembey and Shabunin lobbied for the interests of commercial companies in the procurement of medical equipment and medicines. Importantly, some of these companies showed signs of being fictitious and had a negative business reputation.

The scheme for embezzling international financial aid was very simple. Large sums (ranging from $33,324 to $7,821,215) were transferred to front companies. The companies drew fake reports on the use of the funds received. The Ukrainian investigation uncovered a whole series of similar companies and organizations. Moreover, many of them previously specialized in embezzling international financial aid and have even been involved in criminal cases.

According to the information at my disposal, the company FarmaCo received $2,721,279 from the Shabunin-Sherembey Fund for the supply of

KNOWN RECORD:
Vitaly Shabunin and Dmitry Sherembey

Vitaly Shabunin is the head of the Anti-Corruption Action Center, and Dmitry Sherembey is the founder of that same organization.[16.3] This pair was very effective in *carving up* international financial aid. Both are close friends. Notably, Sherembei, the *chief anti-corruption activist of Ukraine*, was in close contact with the acting U.S. Ambassador to Ukraine, Kristina Kvien, on issues related to the use of U.S. grants. The diplomat was not at all embarrassed by the fact that Sherembey was convicted three times for theft.[16.4]

Nevertheless in 2015, they organized a charitable organization called the All-Ukrainian Network of People Living with HIV/AIDS. From 2015-2017, their main donor was the Global Fund to Fight AIDS, which is financed in part by USAID.[16.5] It was this fund that transferred $133,881,757 to the organization's accounts. During those years, the U.S. ambassadors to Ukraine were Geoffrey Pyatt (until August 18, 2016) and Marie Yovanovitch (until May 20, 2019).[16.2] Both oversaw this *charitable project*.

certain equipment. This company is involved in a criminal case concerning the misappropriation of funds from the International Charitable Foundation *International Alliance with HIV/AIDS in Ukraine*. The firm also carried out operations to legalize funds obtained by criminal means. It was the perfect *money laundering machine,* but it was exposed. However, this did not bother Sherembeya and Shabunin.[16.2]

Incidentally, Shabunin recently resurfaced in connection with a criminal case against him. The Financial Times wrote about this in July 2025. However, the case did not concern his collusions with American money, but rather his evasion of military service. Therefore, I would recommend revisiting these pages of his biography, since there is now a reason to take an interest in him.[16.6]Another example of a scheme to squander USAID funds is the company Optima Farm Ltd , which received $942,139. At the same time, the firm was repeatedly involved in criminal cases related to the *creation of shadow and corruption schemes to conceal the real value of medicines.*[16.7] Another charitable organization, Svet Nadezhdy (Light of Hope), received $5,399,355 for its program. This *charitable organization* is well known to Ukrainian law enforcement agencies. Its representatives *appropriated* a European Union grant in the amount of €1,000,040. The funds were allegedly allocated to aid *internal migrants* (i.e., refugees from Donbas). However, the investigation found that not a single euro reached the migrants. The Poltava Regional State Administration also participated in the scheme. While news of this incident is unknown among U.S. media, information confirming Light of Hope's project in the Poltava Region as well as the organization's involvement in issues related to unfulfilled charitable funds can be found.[16.8, 16.9]

I know that Kristina Kvien, who served as U.S. Ambassador to Kiev, personally selected and approved the lists of organizations that received USAID grants and financial assistance. In addition, the reform of the Ukrainian PGO was supervised by the embassy. In April 2020, criminal case *No. 12020800000000444* was even registered. The case was opened on the grounds of embezzlement of international technical assistance funds by officials of the International Development Law Organization (IDLO) representative office in Ukraine and the company Saitemix-Ukraine LLC during the reform of the prosecutor's office. IDLO is an international organization for the development of law. I will tell you more about it later.

According to the procurement plan for the reform of the prosecutor's office, $7.38 million was allocated specifically for the project *Support for the Reform of Criminal Justice in Ukraine*. Of this substantial amount, $744,000

KNOWN RECORD:
Polina Chizh

Polina Chizh is known for her involvement in the scandal with NABU as head of the patronage service of the first deputy director of the Bureau, Gizo Uglava. Uglava and Chizh leaked secret criminal cases to the U.S. Embassy, in particular information on the Burisma case involving Zlochevsky. Read about this in extra special Chapter 20.

was spent by the *reformers* on hotels, receptions, advertisements, *seeking new prosecutors*, and other items *essential* to the reform.

Those responsible for carrying out the reform of the GPU were Deputy Prosecutor General Vitaliy Kasko (from Chapter 5) and the head of the GPU's international cooperation department, Polina Chizh. So, these two worked with the International Development Law Organization (IDLO), whose Ukrainian office was headed by Levan Duchidze. Together, Kasko and Chizh decided that IDLO would be the executor of the program to re-certify GPU employees as part of the reform. The IDLO organization is registered in Rome, has a branch in The Hague, and is embroiled in scandals around the world. In each case, there were three key complaints against IDLO: inefficient use of funds, lack of real results, and *window dressing* for presentations.[16.10]

Here is a striking example of IDLO's activities. On January 24, 2014, the Special Inspector General for Afghanistan Reconstruction (SIGAR) published an audit report. The report stated that IDLO, under a $47.8 million contract to provide assistance to the Afghan justice system, was supposed to establish a specialized electronic case management system in all 34 provinces of the country. However, the system was only deployed in seven regions. The terms of the contract were then changed to make it appear as if it had only ever covered seven regions. In other words, they received money for work that was actually five times less than what was contracted.[16.11]

This scandalous organization was chosen to implement the programs for *reforming* the PGO. IDLO entrusted this task to a subcontractor, Symetrix-Ukraine LLC. The subject of the contract was anonymous testing of prosecutors within the PGO, which was something like a professional aptitude test. Logically, such an exam could only be entrusted to an authoritative, certified organization with extensive experience. Because the quality of the personnel of the PGO, the country's main law enforcement agency, would depend on it. Symetrix-Ukraine was, of course, not such an organization. The firm was established in 2018, with no experience in such activities. It was selected for a single contract, which was to dismantle the personnel structure of the PGO. As soon as the tests were conducted, Prosecutor General Ryaboshapka destroyed all the documentation. The company then changed owners and started trading bananas in the markets of the Kiev region.[16.12]

Another program authorized by the U.S. Embassy, called *Improving Public Trust*, received nearly $52 million. Another empty promise, the *Ukrainian Confidence Building Initiative*, cost $36 million. What kind of confidence this is supposed to build and who is supposed to be confident in its reliability remains a mystery. The millions these programs received have also

228

disappeared. Another program with the grandiose name *Democratic Rescue of Eastern Europe* cost even more—$57 million. It is also worth mentioning the Municipal Energy Reform Project in Ukraine (MERP), whose grant money may have gone to Burisma, as I wrote about in Chapter 9.

One of the problems was that the project was registered immediately after the memorandum was signed with the Ministry of Education and Science (MES), which was a procedural violation. The electronic document management system was created without analyzing the needs of the MES. In addition, the development of the financial reporting system for universities was started without agreeing on the format with the MES. *Some $274,700 from the project budget was spent on conferences, seminars, accommodation, and meals for contractors.* This is one of the most common ways of wasting funds. Tens of millions of dollars were spent on useless PR, seminars, conferences, and coffee breaks that benefited no one except the contractors providing these services. Needless to say, the estimates for these services were greatly inflated.[16.13]

Violations such as the implementation of USAID projects that were not properly registered were also practiced.[16.14] For example, the State Property Fund (SPF) implemented five projects without registering them with the Ministry of Economic Development. One example is the *Privatization of Fuel and Energy Complex Facilities* project (supported by the UK Foreign Office and USAID). Finally, American taxpayers' money was used to create ineffective IT systems.[16.13] For example, the e-declaration system did not meet technical specifications and had critical failures. As a result, the system was deemed inoperable, and its replacement was estimated to cost between $8.5 million and $12.8 million.[16.13] The consequence of this oversight was a complete lack of control over the targeted use of the program budget.[16.14] There were huge gaps in the legislation. For example, there was no law on international technical assistance.[16.13] The draft laws from 1999 and 2013 were rejected.

In addition, the results of project monitoring and control were not systematically tracked.[16.14] For example, the Ministry of Economic Development did not receive monitoring results from project beneficiaries for *170 international technical assistance projects*, which is 43.6% of the total number of projects operating in the first half of 2017. There were *39 projects where no reports were received at all*, which was 10% of the total number of funded projects.[16.14] The ministry has not received a single report in the proper form on any of these loudly proclaimed programs. According to some estimates based on data from the Accounting Chamber of Ukraine, *more than $5 billion* could have simply disappeared with the connivance of Biden's *team of reformers*. Or, hypothetically, this money was channeled through foreign *intermediary funds, such as those of Natalia Yaresko* or dozens of other similar structures of dubious origin.

Such programs instantly received funds through USAID, while the U.S. Embassy in Kiev turned a blind eye to dubious contractors and completely opaque results of spending tens of millions of dollars. In turn, Kristina Kvien sent laudatory reports to the U.S. State Department about Ukraine's confident progress on the path of reform, although this hardly corresponded to reality.[16.14]

I would also like to say that after Russia's invasion, the situation with transparency of international aid has become even worse. This happened despite the fact that since 2022, Ukraine has received amounts that are many times greater than the aid provided in 2014-2021. Over the years of the war, I have read many publications in the American press describing cases of ineffective spending of military aid. Most recently, I heard accusations from Congresswoman Victoria Spartz that the Ukrainian authorities are involved in *shadow* trade in weapons from Western military aid packages. Well, such things do not surprise me. I saw this when I worked in the prosecutor's office, and I continue to observe it today.

Unfortunately, there is only one conclusion. Under Joe Biden, a system emerged in which billions of U.S. taxpayers' dollars sent to Ukraine are not subject to any control. It is clear why. Since Biden's vice presidency, taxpayer funds were used in part as a kind of bribe to local elites in exchange for their loyalty, as I discussed in the chapters of my book. That is why various kinds of *front companies* in the form of Ukrainian volunteer organizations and all kinds of foundations through which huge sums of money passed were so much in demand.

I could go on and on about the episodes of looting of American aid. You could write a whole book about the abuses in the use of these funds. I think that if the DOGE team were to investigate how these funds were used in Ukraine, Elon Musk and American taxpayers would be horrified by the scale of the misuse.

PART FOUR

HOW BIDEN BUILT EXTERNAL CONTROL OVER UKRAINE FOR HIS OWN GAIN

"I am outraged when my country is not offered but rather forced to accept a matrix of decisions and actions on issues that it is capable of resolving on its own and could even advise other countries on."

—Viktor Shokin, 2025

CHAPTER 17:

REFORMS WITHOUT REFORMS AND HOW NABU IS BIDEN'S PERSONAL SUPERVISORY AGENCY IN UKRAINE

"Biden's surveillance agency for Ukraine—that's how I interpret the abbreviation NABU (National Anti-Corruption Bureau of Ukraine)."

—Viktor Shokin, 2025

Undoubtedly, Ukraine had to actively fight corruption, which had reached alarming levels by 2014. I believe that this threat has not disappeared to this day. This situation is largely because the anti-corruption agencies, artificially created under Biden's dictates, have failed to cope with their primary task.

NABU is Mr. Biden's whim. The purpose of creating this structure was to control all serious criminal cases against top Ukrainian politicians and businessmen. NABU serves to keep them *on the hook* and to promote U.S.

interests, especially the business interests of individual corporations and investment funds.

Understanding this flip side of the coin, I was initially a staunch opponent of the creation of NABU. First, it is a fictitious *new entity* that has no analogues in any Western country. Secondly, I am outraged when my country is not offered but rather forced to accept a *matrix* of decisions and actions on issues that it is capable of resolving on its own and could even advise other countries on. Finally, the main reason for my negative attitude toward this format of oversight is that these *artificial bodies*, implanted into the existing justice system, duplicate the functions of other law enforcement agencies. Thereby, it confuses the legal field and creates unnecessary competition in the fight against corruption, which, in the absence of a proper legal culture, looks extremely pathetic.

The Criminal Procedure Code of Ukraine (CPC) was adopted by the Verkhovna Rada in 2012 and incidentally, considered the recommendations of the Venice Commission and commitments to the Council of Europe. The CPC provided for the creation of a State Bureau of Investigations (GBR) for a three-year term to investigate corruption in the highest echelons of power.[17.1] This was a purely Ukrainian-project. Unlike the NABU, it was clearly embedded in Ukraine's legal framework. Looking back at the recent past, I would note that the only, albeit questionable, advantage of NABU was that it was created faster than the SBI. The reason for the delay was because the SBI was deliberately blocked by the Ukrainian Criminal Procedure Code until the very last day of its formation.[17.2]

The *Biden Agency for Oversight of Ukraine* was literally forced into our reality. The law establishing the NABU was rushed through the Ukrainian parliament on October 14, 2014. Just six months later, on April 16, 2015, the Bureau announced that it was ready to begin work.[17.3] Ten years have passed, and the results of this hastily created organization, as we can see, are close to zero. President Poroshenko did not care whether the new anti-corruption body would have any effect. He was eager to please Biden, so he pushed and forced the creation of NABU in every way possible.

When I was head of the PGO, a competition was announced for the position of head of the bureau. Two candidates made it to the final selection. They were Mykola Syriy, a well-known lawyer and lecturer at the Institute of State and Law, and Artem Sytnik. I supported Syriy because I knew Sytnik well from his work in the 1990s as head of the investigative department of the Kiev region prosecutor's office. At that time, hundreds of shares in hundreds of hectares of land were being illegally re-registered in the capital region.[17.4] Criminal proceedings were even initiated in connection with these incidents.

It is also known that in 2008 Sytnik, using his official position, put pressure on a developer. As a result, he obtained an apartment in a new building in Brovary. He paid only a fraction of the cost, with the rest being *donated* to him by the Volna Hromada Charitable Foundation. Eventually, the Rivne court found Sytnyk guilty of corruption. Basically, the court said the future head of NABU was corrupt and ordered him to pay a fine and give the *gift* to the state. Based on this decision, *Sytnik was added to Ukraine's register of corrupt officials.*[17.5] Where else have you seen a corrupt official appointed to head an agency responsible for fighting corruption?

In short, I was very surprised when it became clear the next morning that it was not Mykola Syriy who had been appointed director of NABU, but Mr. Sytnik after all.[17.6] Later, on August 28, 2020, the Constitutional Court of Ukraine (CCU) ruled that the decree of Ukrainian President Petro Poroshenko o*n the appointment of A. Sytnik as Director of the National Anti-Corruption Bureau of Ukraine* dated April 16, 2015, was unconstitutional.[17.7] Despite this, Artem Sytnik remained in office as head of NABU until April 16, 2022.[17.8]

Following this, on September 16, 2020, the Constitutional Court of Ukraine declared unconstitutional the provisions of the Law *on the National Anti-Corruption Bureau of Ukraine*. The judgement focused particularly on the provisions concerning the powers of the President of Ukraine to establish this body.[17.9] This proves once again that to please U.S. Vice President Biden, an unconstitutional body with excessively broad powers has been operating in Ukraine for 10-years. Such things as the unconstitutional formation of the NABU and the unconstitutional appointment of its head seriously undermine the legitimacy of our legal system.[17.9] However, Mr. Biden and Poroshenko, who hastily *cooked up* this structure, did not care about such nuances.

But let's get back to the story. From the very beginning, Joe Biden sent his people to NABU, first and foremost Gizo Uglava, who was appointed first deputy director.[17.10] Two freelance FBI agents who were Biden's people were constantly present at the Bureau under the guise of consultants. Thanks to them, the U.S. Embassy kept its finger on the pulse of all events at NABU—not a single case left its walls without the approval of Biden's people.

As I mentioned, the heads of the new anti-corruption agencies were selected through competitive procedures, but the final approval of the candidates remained with Joe Biden. Yes, few people know that the competition for the position of head of the Specialized Anti-Corruption Prosecutor's Office (SAPO) was won by Roman Govda, then deputy head of the General Prosecutor's Office.[17.11] However, his appointment was blocked by Biden, who preferred to see Vitaliy Kasko at the helm of the SAPO. The message was clear, either appoint Kasko or remove Govda.

An irritated Petro Poroshenko called me. "What are we going to do? We can't appoint Govda, even though he won the competition."

"But how can we appoint Kasko," I asked, "if he failed the competition?"

Then a compromise was reached. Both Govda and Kasko were removed from the competition. In the end, the choice was between Nazar Kholodnytskyi and Maksym Hryshchuk. After talking to both of them, I was struck by Hryshchuk's unprofessionalism. Apparently, he managed to pass the competition mainly thanks to his status as a participant in the ATO (anti-terrorist operation). Before the war, Hryshchuk worked as an assistant prosecutor in the Lviv region and dealt with juvenile justice. In other words, he had no experience in anti-corruption investigations and was a complete novice in these matters.

Against the backdrop of Hryshchuk, Nazar Kholodnytskyi stood out because he had real work experience, which is why he became the head of the SAPO.[17.12] Thanks to a massive media campaign, anti-corruption agencies were presented to Ukrainians as *the best experience in the democratic world*. However, no Western country has such agencies, except in scenarios where they are created for a specific period to solve specific tasks. In Ukraine, however, the NABU and SAPO have *settled in* for an indefinite period. Instead of positive results, they are engaged in power struggles with other law enforcement agencies, monitoring each other, conducting illegal surveillance, and wiretapping people. As a result, this mutual competition has escalated into serious inter-agency conflicts.

It seems that by now, NABU and SAPO have not only discredited themselves in the eyes of the Ukrainian public but have also been burned in the *fire of civil war*, forgetting their very purpose—the fight against corruption and its results. Incidentally, there is a real gap in our legislation. There is no clear indication of who should perform the duties of the head of the SAPO in the event of the removal of the head from office, his death, or serious illness. Apparently, even in their worst nightmares, they could not imagine that someone could replace the specially selected and completely controlled leaders of these bodies.

Meanwhile, Ukrainian taxpayers continue to finance an ineffective structure that does not bring any significant benefit to the Ukrainian people. Moreover, my worst fears, which I voiced from the very first days of the creation of NABU and SAPO, were confirmed then and continue to be confirmed to this day.

But first things first.

CHAPTER 18:
THE MANAFORT CASE

One of the sensations of the summer of 2025 was the report by CIA Director John Ratcliffe on *serious violations* in the investigation of Russian interference in the 2016 U.S. elections. I read about this with interest in The *Washington Examiner*.[18.1] The new CIA report mentions a document declassified at the initiative of Director Ratcliffe. It concerns another report prepared during the Obama administration. It claimed that *Putin sought to help Donald Trump win*. However, Ratcliffe said that American *intelligence analysts* made this conclusion *with procedural violations in too short a time frame, with limited access to classified information, with the exclusion of the National Intelligence Community, and with excessive involvement of senior intelligence officials*. According to the authors of the CIA report, this *undermined the analytical standards* of the intelligence service. The CIA's analytical reports that launched *Russiagate* also excluded information contradicting the version of Putin's support for Trump. Finally, leaks to the media were allowed even before the assessment was completed, which could also have influenced the final conclusions of the intelligence services.[18.1]

Thus, Trump managed to return to the topic he had tried to launch an investigation into back in 2020. At that time, he demanded that Attorney General William Barr conduct an objective investigation into *Russiagate*.[18.2]

Donald Trump and Attorney General William Barr

Screenshot from Donald Trump's Twitter[18.3]

Be that as it may, Ratcliffe's new report reminded me of a long-standing scandal involving American political strategist Paul Manafort. There were so many *procedural violations* and *interference* by interested parties in this story that the CIA should take another look at this episode, which was one of the key elements in the accusation of Trump's *collusion with Russia.*

I will make a small lyrical digression on the topic of *Russian interference.* Of course, I know what real Russian interference is. My knowledge is not from the press, but I have experienced it *firsthand* as they say. Russian interference means 3.5 years of bloody war [as of summer 2025] and constant shelling of Ukrainian cities, including Kiev. All these years we have been living on a schedule—from one air raid siren to another.

However, the Manafort story has many sides. Russian interference in the U.S. elections is just one version of events, which has not been proven or properly investigated, as the new CIA documents show.[18.1] The notorious *Steele Dossier* that launched *Russiagate* did not stand up to *fact-checking*, as modern journalists like to say. Even before the release of the latest CIA materials, FBI Director Kash Patel concluded the following on this subject in his book, "By linking the Steele dossier to the Clinton campaign and the Democratic National Committee, we have exposed the Russia collusion hoax as nothing more than a political hit job."[18.4]

In the midst of the U.S. presidential campaign, on August 19, 2016, Donald Trump's campaign manager, Paul Manafort, suddenly resigned.[18.5] The reason was the hysteria unleashed in the leading American media over allegations that he had received money from Ukrainian President Yanukovych for working as his personal political strategist. The first to fire shots at Paul Manafort on August 2, 2016, was Pulitzer Prize winner and columnist for the American newspaper The *Washington Post*, Anne Applebaum.[18.6] In an interview with Ukrainian television channel Hromadske, she raised the issue of Trump's ties to Russia and claimed that Manafort was the link between them.[18.7]

Applebaum's interview heated up the information space before the main blow was dealt to Manafort. On August 14, 2016, the *New York Times* published a report by the newspaper's correspondents in Kiev. The article, citing anonymous NABU representatives, claimed that "handwritten notes were found indicating confidential cash payments totaling $12.7 million to Manafort from Yanukovych's pro-Russian political party (the Party of Regions) between 2007 and 2012." In confirmation of the *Russian trace*, the article also mentioned Manafort's partnership agreement with Russian oligarch Oleg Deripaska for $18 million (referring to Deripaska's investments in a Ukrainian cable TV provider).[18.8]

The next day, August 15, 2016, the *Washington Post* also published a lengthy article about Manafort and his ties to Russians. It also referred to his connections with Deripaska.[18.9] Following the lead of the American press giants, a similar publication appeared in the Ukrainian edition of the *Kyiv Post*.[18.10] Three days later, an article in *Politico* finished off Manafort. They went further and wrote about Manafort's possible connection to Russian intelligence and the hacker attack on the Democrats' server. The article mentions Konstantin Kilimnik, Manafort's translator, who is portrayed as a Russian intelligence agent and Manafort's liaison.[18.11]

The coordinated attack in the American media was preceded by the publication on July 18, 2016, on the NABU website of 22 excerpts from the so-called shadow cash book of Viktor Yanukovych and the Party of Regions, also known as the *Barn Book or black ledger*. The explanation accompanying the excerpts on the NABU website stated the information was about confidential cash payments *totaling $12.7 million* to Paul Manafort, for which he allegedly signed the *black ledger* between 2007 and 2012.[18.12]

So, how did Yanukovych's secret accounting records end up in the hands of NABU? And why did they *explode* after Paul Manafort was appointed

KNOWN RECORD:
NABU and the Democratic Party

As I wrote earlier, the National Anti-Corruption Bureau of Ukraine (NABU) was created by Democrats under loud slogans of fighting oligarchs and corruption. The NABU became the first link in a chain of anti-corruption agencies that were supposed to bring Ukraine into the family of civilized Western nations. However in reality, the bureau became a tool for establishing control over Ukraine's political system and its law enforcement agencies. Instead of fighting for their stated goals, the Democrats and their Ukrainian agents used NABU to create a system of external control over Ukraine in the interests of the U.S. Democratic Party.

head of Trump's election campaign? Some pretty famous and influential people got mixed up in this shady story. Among them were Artem Sytnik, head of NABU; Serhiy Leshchenko, a member of the Ukrainian parliament; Gizo Uglava, first deputy director of NABU; Serhiy Horbatyuk, head of SAPO; and Viktor Trepak, former deputy head of the Security Service of Ukraine (SBU). It was Viktor Trepak who was the initiator of the high-profile scandal that led to Manafort's resignation and launched a campaign to discredit Donald Trump.

In April 2016, Viktor Trepak resigned from his position as first deputy director of the SBU and went to teach at the SBU Academy. However, it was precisely into the handsof this modest teacher that documents of devastating power suddenly fell—585 handwritten A4 pages containing tables with columns labeled *Date, Name*, and *Purpose*. These papers were the *black ledger* of the Party of Regions in the Ukrainian Parliament, which exposed dozens of politicians and journalists. All of them signed their names in the column opposite the amounts of money they had received. Paul Manafort became the star of Trepak's *documents*, allegedly signing his name dozens of times opposite the amounts of money he had received.[18.13]

Viktor Trepak had to publicly explain how these *destructive* documents ended up in his hands. The explanations given by the former deputy head of the SBU did not sound very coherent or plausible. According to the

249

general's version, *an unknown person entered* his apartment building *and left a thick envelope with documents for him*. This individual did not introduce himself to the concierge and immediately left. However, the resourceful general did not lose his composure. He immediately ran with the bundle of documents he had received from the stranger. For some reason, he did not go to his *home* SBU, but to the newly created NABU. There, he quickly wrote a statement about the materials that had come into his possession. NABU detectives immediately went to the scene—to Trepak's house. However, the concierge, where the retired officer lived, was unable to describe the stranger in detail and admitted that he would not be able to identify him if he saw him again. The CCTV footage did not show any visitors with an envelope. However, for some reason, NABU did not attach any significance to this fact. There were no other witnesses who could confirm that the documents had been received. Wait, the miracles did not end there. NABU decided to open a criminal case based on handwritten notebooks of unknown origin that mysteriously found their way into Trepak's hands.[18.14] However, to open a criminal case, the source of the documents must be established. In fact, the materials were obtained by the investigative authorities in gross violation of the Criminal Procedure Code and other laws of Ukraine, which already precluded the lawful use of these materials in court.

Regardless, the deed was done. On May 27, 2016, former SBU employee Viktor Trepak wrote a statement to the NABU reception desk saying that the materials he had received allowed him to accuse politicians from the Party of Regions and individuals who collaborated with it of crimes totaling more than 10 billion hryvnia (about $400 million at the time). Trepak attached his *notebooks* to the statement, which also mentioned Paul Manafort. The handwritten documents recorded payments ranging from $2 to several million dollars.[18.14] This could not fail to alarm an experienced investigator like me. It is suspicious when millions in payments and expenses for office supplies are lumped together.

However, all these oddities did not stop NABU. on May 30, 2016, following Trepak's statement, detectives from the bureau headed by Roman Yegizarov registered criminal case No. 52016000000000166 in the Unified Register of Pre-trial Investigations regarding the possible commission of a crime under Part 4 of Article 369 of the Criminal Code of Ukraine, and began a pre-trial investigation.[18.14] The misunderstandings began immediately. According to Part 1 of Article 214 of the Criminal Procedure Code of Ukraine, the registration of the application in the Register should have been carried out no later than 5:00 p.m. on May 28, 2016. Such a strict requirement of criminal law is intended to prevent the falsification of submitted documents and to exclude the possibility of access to them from third parties. However, the fact is that registration took place only on May 30, 2016.

To create the appearance of investigative action, NABU investigators, acting on the orders of investigating Judge Andriy Makukha of the Solomensky District Court of Kiev, conducted a search of the housing company's premises, the concierge's room, and Trepak's apartment, but were unable to establish the authenticity of the transfer of documents to the concierge.[18.14] Thus, the main and only evidence against Manafort, which ruined his career, literally came out of nowhere. Plus the dubious *notes* were given credence without any legal basis. At NABU, the case was immediately taken under control by the bureau's first deputy head, Gizo Uglava. Having obtained General Trepak's *notes*, Uglava set about the key task of legalizing them. NABU detectives began searching for evidence to support their own version of events, according to which the Party of Regions' *secret black ledger* was allegedly kept in the Party of Regions' office in Kiev at 10 Lipska Street. It should be noted that after the Maidan, the party's office was almost completely burned down. So, by some miracle, the surviving manuscripts ended up in the hands of a well-wisher, who immediately took them to former security officer Trepak *with home delivery.* Strangely enough, investigators never once looked inside the building, which was stormed by protesters in

KNOWN RECORD:
Gizo Uglava

The story of this Georgian who settled in Kiev is as full of mysteries as the appearance of Trepak's "records." Uglava arrived in Ukraine in 2015 on the recommendation of former Georgian President Mikheil Saakashvili, with whom he worked in his homeland. To confirm Uglava's appointment, the MPs Yegor Sobolev and Sergei Leshchenko specifically amended the law *On the National Anti-Corruption Bureau of Ukraine* in February that same year. The change exempted deputy directors of NABUI from competitive selection. This amendment was necessary because Uglava was still a Georgian citizen at that time, making him ineligible to meet the requirements for competitive selection. Particularly, he did not know the Ukrainian language or local legislation. After Uglava's appointment, NABU chief Artem Sytnik admitted that the Georgian candidate had been lobbied for by the U.S., Canadian, German, and French embassies. And Gizo Uglava instantly became the all-seeing eye of the U.S. embassy in NABU.

February 2014 in search of compromising evidence against Yanukovych's party. The office was set on fire, but after the fire was extinguished, the security forces, for some reason, did not find any papers there.[18.15]

According to another version, the *records* could have been fabricated by Trepak himself, who has experience working in the operational units of the SBU. Or by another organization with experience in creating forgeries. Which one? It's not hard to guess. Likely, it's a very *deep* one.

Be that as it may, Trepak's materials did not gather dust for long. That's not why they ended up in the hands of a retired general. On May 28, 2016, the Kiev newspaper *Zerkalo Nedeli* published a lengthy interview with Trepak about his discovery. The publication, funded by billionaire George Soros, has close ties to the U.S. Embassy. It is not surprising that the first article about the scandalous records of the Party of Regions' *black ledger* appeared in this newspaper. According to the editorial office, the general visited them on May 26, apparently impressed by the ledger. Only the next day, on May 27, did he rush to report his finding to the NABU. Journalists who knew Trepak well said that the general is not known for his eloquence. Then, suddenly, a detailed interview appeared with attacks on Paul Manafort.[18.16]

After warming up the topic, well-known journalist Sergei Leshchenko, joined in promoting the *notebook*. He wrote in detail about the discovery of the Regionals' *black ledger* and its *sensational* contents in an article for *Ukrainska Pravda*.[18.17] It is noteworthy that based solely on Leshchenko's article, NABU issued search warrants for Trepak's apartment and the concierge's room. As already noted, the searches yielded nothing, but they gave the investigation the appearance of being genuine.

Meanwhile, Leshchenko, the deputy and journalist, did not stop at the article. On the day of May 31, 2016, he held a large briefing for journalists in parliament on the *black ledger*. Thus, General Trepak's *notes* took on a life of their own. But this was not enough for NABU and those who were promoting the scandal. A decision was made to publish excerpts from the *black ledger* on Paul Manafort on the NABU website.[18.18] On July 18, 2016, 22 fragments of Viktor Yanukovych's *black ledger* appeared on the bureau's website.

It is characteristic that NABU confirmed the unsubstantiated basis of the accusations against Manafort. After the publication of Manafort's alleged signatures in the Regionals' *black ledger*, NABU commented, "We emphasize that the presence of P. Manafort's surname in the 'lists' does not mean that he actually received these funds, since the column of recipients contains the signatures of other persons. The pre-trial investigation in this case is ongoing."[18.19]

KNOWN RECORD:
Sergei Leshchenko

Sergei Leshchenko is a renowned investigative journalist who started his work on Ukrainian TV channel *Novyi Kanal* and a correspondent for *Ukrainska Pravda*.[18.20] He worked in the team of presidential administration head Sergei Levochkin during Yanukovych's time.

At Levochkin's behest, he wrote an exposé on Yulia Tymoshenko's gas scams.[18.21] Leshchenko actively supported the Maidan. Later, he joined George Soros'team and became a member of the Verkhovna Rada of Ukraine.[18.20]

With this statement, NABU decided to cover its own ass, realizing the complete lack of evidence in Trepak's hastily made *notes*. However, newspaper publications and links to the NABU website were immediately picked up by the U.S. democratic press. These publications seemed to be waiting for the signal and immediately launched a *killing salvo* at Trump's campaign manager. It is evident that the public would not have believed in the existence of the Regionals' *black ledger* records if they had been presented by an ordinary person. To lend credibility, an alliance was formed between a former high-ranking SBU official and a well-known journalist, Leshchenko, to give at least some legitimacy to the general's *archives*. It didn't matter that former first deputy head of the SBU Viktor Trepak, without any grounds or authority, took it upon himself to act as an operative agent to collect and obtain evidence that goes beyond the scope of operational and investigative activities. Incidentally, Ukrainian President Poroshenko would later publicly reprimand General Trepak for this violation. Purely for show.

As you may have noticed, the topic of Manafort's involvement in secret payments began in a *friendly circle* of interconnected people. All of this may be a coincidence, but the development of the story with the Party of Regions' *black* accounting suggests something else entirely. Realistically, it all looks like a well-rehearsed play in which everyone had their own role to play, and the overall goal was *to link Trump's campaign team to the Russians*, either through Manafort or through other scandalous actions. Despite the lack of evidence, the NABU investigation continued, and the American and Ukrainian media kept the scandal surrounding Manafort alive. All of this dealt a huge blow to Donald Trump's reputation.

However, not everyone supported the U.S. Democratic Party's version of events in the Manafort case. Skeptics clearly saw this as an attempt by Ukraine to interfere in the U.S. elections on the side of Hillary Clinton. Thus, in August 2017, a criminal case was opened in Ukraine.[18.13] A statement was sent to the Prosecutor General's Office proposing to investigate all the circumstances surrounding the emergence of the *black ledger* of the Party of Regions. The case involved MP Sergei Leshchenko, who helped inflate the scandal with Manafort, four high-ranking officials of the U.S. Embassy in Ukraine, Ukrainian Ambassador to the U.S. Valery Chaly, former deputy head of the Security Service of Ukraine Viktor Trepak, who leaked Leshchenko Manafort's records, and a number of Ukrainian security service employees.

Republicans at the time welcomed the PGO's initiative. In fact, the opening of the case by the PGO was preceded by a tweet from Donald Trump, in which he called for an investigation into possible Ukrainian interference in the U.S. election. Trump and his allies suspected at the time that Ukrainian

258

officials were trying to help Hillary Clinton by fabricating evidence against Trump's former campaign manager Paul Manafort.

Screenshot from Donald Trump's Twitter[18.22]

It is noteworthy that *Politico*, one of the first publications to attack Manafort in 2016, published an article in November 2017 in which they were forced to write about an alternative version of the story with Manafort. "Ukrainian officials tried to help Democratic candidate Hillary Clinton undermine Trump's position, in particular by distributing documents about the involvement of Paul Manafort, Trump's chief aide, in corruption."[18.23]

On November 26, 2019, Secretary of State Mike Pompeo appeared to acknowledge the legitimacy of the idea that Ukraine was behind the interference in the 2016 U.S. election. A reporter asked him, "Do you think the U.S. and Ukraine should investigate the theory that it was Ukraine, not Russia, that hacked the DNC emails in 2016?"

Pompeo replied, "Whenever information comes to light indicating that a country has interfered in U.S. elections, we not only have the right, but the obligation to make sure we investigate it." He added, "To protect our elections, America must leave no stone unturned."[18.24]

After this statement, the officials at NABU became nervous, and not without reason. The GPU responded to Leshchenko's parliamentary inquiry by opening a criminal case against NABU head Artem Sytnik and his deputies.[18.25]

That's not all the scandals surrounding this case. In 2018, MP Boryslav Rosenblat filed a lawsuit with the Kiev District Administrative Court.[18.26] On December 11, 2018, by court decision No. 826/12998/17, it was finally recognized that NABU head Artem Sytnik and MP journalist Sergei Leshchenko had no right to publish unsubstantiated allegations and materials related to the *Manafort case*, **which constituted interference in the U.S. elections**.[18.27]

This did not end the *war of criminal cases* between supporters of the Democrats and those who exposed their plots. The criminal investigation into abuses in the *Manafort case* was closed in January 2019 by senior investigator for particularly important cases Mykhailo Nechitalyuk. The U.S. Embassy was involved in this as well. However, in March 2019 an audio recording of a conversation between NABU head Sytnik was published, in which he admitted *that he had helped Hillary Clinton in the 2016 election.*[18.28] Suspicions of abuse in the Manafort scandal proved to be true, but Ukraine did not investigate Sytnik's role in the Manafort case. It is clear why. Sytnik, who is *in the pocket* of those in power, would not dare to challenge his *creators* led by Joe Biden.

Be that as it may, after Donald Trump's election victory, the Ukrainian authorities refused to investigate the Manafort scandal and tried in every way to hush up the high-profile story, which had been blown up in the hope of a victory for Democratic candidate Hillary Clinton. On June 29, 2017, Sytnik's agency stated that NABU had not conducted an official investigation into Manafort because Manafort *is not a Ukrainian official.*[18.29] This was very strange to hear, considering that NABU had published Manafort's receipts from the *black ledger* on its website, completely forgetting that Manafort is not a Ukrainian citizen. It's completely double standard. What can you say?

The most serious blow to Manafort's *notes* was dealt by none other than the former head of the Central Election Commission, Mikhail

Okhendovsky. No one expected such a turn of events. The fact is that in order to legalize Yanukovych's *black ledger*, Trepak's *materials* also included the name of the former head of the Central Election Commission, Mikhail Okhendovsky. Why was it necessary to conduct a high-profile trial for receiving bribes from the *black ledger*? In this case, all questions about Trepak's *records* would disappear. So, NABU immediately opened a criminal case against Okhendovsky on suspicion of illegal enrichment.[18.30]

In June 2016, it became clear that Okhendovsky had been chosen as the first victim of the NABU's attempts to legalize Trepak's *notebooks*. As part of the criminal case, he was questioned on June 13, 2016. During the first interrogation, Okhendovsky voluntarily handed over samples of his handwriting to NABU detectives. In the summer of 2016, the Bureau conducted a series of fruitless searches at the premises of the Central Election Commission (CEC). At the same time, leaks about all procedural actions involving Okhendovsky were leaked to the press, including the publication of court decisions that gave detectives access to his bank accounts.

The wife of the CEC head, who works as a private notary, also came under the investigators' scrutiny. In December 2016, NABU officially charged Okhendovsky with receiving unjustified benefits in the form of cash, allegedly at the Party of Regions office on Lipskaya Street in 2012 "worth $161,000 from Yanukovych's Party of Regions."[18.31] That same evening, NABU detectives illegally searched Okhendovsky's home. No evidence of the alleged crime was found.

The entire charge boiled down to a ridiculous argument. The head of the CEC allegedly received his *travel expenses* illegally from a *slush fund*. They were aiming for millions, but it turned out to be restaurant tips.[18.30, 18.31] The investigation against the head of the CEC in NABU was supervised by the Georgian Gizo Uglava, whom we already know. When he realized that Okhendovsky would defend himself against the attacks, militants controlled by him were brought in. Thus, the head of this gang, a certain Vano Nadiridze, was specially summoned from Georgia. The task of his group, called the *Civil Corps of Donbas*, was to use force and intimidation against individuals against whom NABU had opened criminal cases. On February 2, 2017, Vano Nadiridze and five other gangsters attacked Okhendovsky's wife on the steps of her office in central Kiev. She had been summoned to the office by a text message from the Ukrainian Ministry of Justice. They were met by gangsters threatening physical violence. Prior to that, in December 2016 and January 2017, gangsters from the *Civil Corps of Donbas* demonstratively visited the school where Okhendovsky's three daughters studied. They were interested in the classroom and the lesson schedule.

KNOWN RECORD:
Mykhailo Okhendivsky

Mykhailo Okhendivsky was elected chairman of the Central Election Commission (CEC) in July 2013. He is fluent in English. He has regularly participated in international forums and events related to elections.[18.32] I would like to note that the head of the CEC was often received at the U.S. Embassy when Geoffrey Pyatt was ambassador. However, immediately after Pyatt's departure, relations cooled sharply. The new ambassador to Kiev, Yovanovitch, and the deputy ambassador for political affairs, George Kent, began to avoid contact with the CEC chairman.

The trial that began fully exonerated Okhendovsky. The court found that the preliminary investigation authorities, NABU and the Specialized Anti-Corruption Prosecutor's Office (SAPO), had violated the defendant's rights under Article 6 of the Convention on Human Rights. Moreover, an independent expert from the Kiev Scientific Research Institute of Forensic Expertise, which is controlled by the Ministry of Justice, acknowledged that it was impossible to reliably determine the authenticity of Okhendovsky's handwriting in Trepak's *notebooks*. An urgently organized re-examination at the expert center of the Ministry of Internal Affairs of Ukraine also failed to help.[18.33, 18.34]

I recall that after the trial, in an interview with the publication *Strana* in December 2018, Okhendovsky laid everything out on the table, "It became clear to everyone that this case was purely political, fabricated and false. In addition to the well-known foreign policy goals related to the 2016 U.S. presidential election, there's evidence of collusion involving our diplomats in Washington, as reported by foreign media. The NABU was probably told to come up with something against a high-ranking official. My rank is sufficient. They were probably just afraid

to go any higher. So, everything came together...
They tried to achieve several goals with one
action."[18.35]

The ruling of the Kiev Court of Appeal dated February 9, 2017, which has entered into force and cannot be appealed, explicitly stated that the NABU's charges in the black ledger case *are unfounded due to lack of evidence*. I recall that in the interview with the publication *Strana*, Okhendovsky noted that NABU Director Artem Sytnik was strictly forbidden from apologizing to Okhendovsky "...through the actual head of NABU... and obviously an official from a foreign embassy. Mr. Kent or Mr. Smith, what's the difference?"[18.35] Incidentally, this is the same Kent who served as head of the political department of the Ukrainian Embassy in Kiev, whom I have written about previously.

After the trial, the Prosecutor General's Office launched criminal investigation No. 42017000000000102 into the fabrication of Trepak's *notebooks* and abuse of power by NABU and SAPO employees, as well as *pressure on a public official* and illegal disclosure of investigation secrets. It would seem that after such a high-profile fiasco, NABU should have closed the case on the *black ledger* and apologized to all those involved. However, that was not the case. In the spring of 2017, a decision was made to transfer the scandalous case from NABU to the PGO, to the Special Investigations Department headed by Sergei Gorbatyuk. The department was investigating the circumstances of the mass killings on the Maidan. However, no progress was made in the case. In the fall of 2019, Gorbatyuk was dismissed, in part because the investigation had reached a dead end. It was decided to transfer the case of the *black ledger* of the Regionals to this hapless investigator. At the same time, they wanted to distract the public from the failure of the NABU. Gorbatyuk did not disappoint. He tried to fabricate another case against Manafort. The journalist and MP Sergei Leshchenko, whom we already know, accused Manafort of receiving kickbacks of $750,000. Leshchenko presented allegedly *substantial evidence* of this scam. Gorbatyuk took on the investigation of this case.

However, like the investigation into Maidan, this new case also fell apart. Leshchenko's *substantial facts* could not be confirmed. None of the witnesses gave any testimony confirming the payment of $750,000 to Manafort. Nevertheless, the Special Investigations Department of the PGO, now without Gorbatyuk, never closed the case on the Maidan shootings or the case on Yanukovych's *black ledger*. The cases exist, but there is still no evidence. *It seems that while Trump was in power, this dubious case was not allowed to die*. The main task of the investigators and prosecutors in Gorbatyuk's department was to find a way to link the entries in the *black ledger* to Paul Manafort. Why? *To justify the illegal interference of Ukrainian <u>Biden agents</u> in the U.S. election process in August 2016 on the side of Hillary Clinton.*

Incidentally, Biden was well aware of the situation surrounding Manafort because his trusted informant Petro regularly reported on everything that was happening *in the domain of Vice President Joseph*, as reflected in the following excerpt from the Biden tapes:[18.36]

> Petro Poroshenko: And one more thing, just as a joke. We have published documents from the former Party of Regions. As I understand it, one of Mr. Trump's key advisers, Paul Manafort, resigned today.
>
> Joe Biden: Yes. I think he'll go back to Russia, I don't know...
>
> Petro Poroshenko: In my opinion, it was a bad idea to take Yanukovych's advisor into Trump's team.

Joe Biden: I agree. But there are many other bad decisions that he [probably Trump] is making.

Petro Poroshenko: Yes.

Joe Biden: Great. We'll talk at the beginning of the week, okay?

Petro Poroshenko: Okay, Joe. Thank you very much. And let me know about the outcome of your lunch with Obama, and I can share with you the information from Berlin. We could do that tomorrow, or whenever you are ready. Let me know. [18.36]

The fabricated Manafort case was the best proof of the Democrats' policy of using all their connections in Ukraine to cover up corruption and use the country to discredit their opponents, led by Donald Trump.

CHAPTER 19:

BIDEN'S GEORGIAN LANDING PARTY OF SAAKASHVILI, SAKVARELIDZE, AND THE MISSING MILLIONS FOR REFORMS

Let me say right away. I did not welcome and do not welcome the appointment of foreigners to important and, even more so, key positions in the Ukrainian government or state-owned companies. In my opinion, even those foreigners who have successful experience in transforming their own countries can only serve as advisors or consultants in another country, but not as ministers, prosecutors, or judges.

I would like to note that in 2014-2015, almost all personnel proposals for the Ukrainian government were coordinated with Biden. Law enforcement agencies were forced to hire exclusively people from Georgia. It was Biden who was behind the *invasion* of Georgian officials who flooded Kiev in the first years after the Maidan. They were personally indebted to him and were under his political patronage, dating back to the presidency of Mikheil Saakashvili in Georgia.

KNOWN RECORD:
Mikheil Saakashvili

A poser and a windbag, Mikheil Saakashvili managed to win over ordinary Ukrainians with his fiery revolutionary rhetoric. I'll share one episode from Saakashvili's activities, hidden from public view to clarify what really lies behind his thirst for reform. Recall that in 2015, when Saakashvili headed the Odessa Regional State Administration (ORA). At that time, he leveled baseless accusations at the PGO. After that, Poroshenko decided to introduce us so that we could talk in person and understand each other. The meeting took place on Bankova Street, in the president's office. Poroshenko gave Saakashvili the first word, and he began to rant long and pompously. It was unpleasant he addressed me familiarly, without respect, despite the 15-year age difference. I listened carefully to our Georgian guest, then clearly explained to him what violating Ukrainian law would lead to and left. Afterward, the negativity from Saakashvili stopped. He understood me correctly.

In fact, the most prominent and well-known of the Georgian reformers selected was Mikheil Saakashvili, the former president of Georgia. In the same year, Biden imposed another pseudo-reformer on Ukraine. He was former Deputy Prosecutor General of Georgia David Sakvarelidze. In my early days as Prosecutor General, Poroshenko suggested that I "talk to the Georgians who have come to U.S. to carry out reforms," who were waiting for an audience in the office of Boris Lozhkin, then head of the Presidential Administration (now called the Office of the President). "We need to take some of them to the Prosecutor General's Office. The Americans consider these people progressive; they will help us," Poroshenko explained.

I pointed out that foreigners should not be allowed into law enforcement, as they know neither the Ukrainian language nor our legislation. Even with all their possible professional merits, this alone is enough to cast serious doubt on their qualifications. Moreover, Georgia is incomparable to Ukraine. For example, its population is only slightly larger than that of Kiev. However, Poroshenko did not want to listen to any arguments. I later understood that Poroshenko's dismissal of my arguments was because Sakvarelidze's employment in the GPU had already been agreed with Joe Biden.

When we arrived at Bankova street, Boris Lozhkin met me at the entrance to his office and immediately stunned me. "The Americans have an idea to appoint one of these Georgians as your deputy," he said.

"I have professional deputies," I replied, adding, "and I don't intend to replace anyone."

"Then create a new position of deputy for reforms," Boris suggested. I had to agree, but I demanded that the visitors outline their vision for these reforms and explain exactly what they wanted to reform, describing the expected results in detail.

David Sakvarelidze spoke the most out of the group of Georgian prosecutors, from which I concluded that it was him whom his American friends saw as my *deputy for reforms*. David began his *presentation* of reforms with the idea of removing the turnstiles at the entrance to the GPU building and replacing them with glass doors to symbolize the transparency of the renewed PGO.

I even got a little angry. "Do you understand what you're saying? Special investigators work here. Anyone could come in at any moment and 'take them out.' We are a country at war. It's not for nothing that we are guarded by the police and even the State Security Service."

"We will install bulletproof glass," David reassured me. That was the extent of his understanding of the reforms.

I asked where the money would come from for the *glazing* of the GPU and other similar *whims*.

"Eh," Sakvarelidze waved his hand, "the money will be found... We are very well received in America."

We agreed that he would provide me with a draft plan for the *renovation*, which would show what the entrance to the GPU would look like and how the security of employees would be ensured. However, when the door closed behind our Georgian comrades, I directly expressed my thoughts to Boris Lozhkin, "I don't see any of these Georgians in any role in the GPU."

They took this to Poroshenko, but he insisted. This was a requirement of the International Monetary Fund (IMF). What did the IMF have to do with internal reshuffles in the GPU?

KNOWN RECORD:
David Sakvarelidze

Born in Georgia, David Sakvarelidze was Deputy Chief Prosecutor of the country of Georgia from 2008-2012 before serving in the Parliament form 2012-2015. He then migrated to Ukraine where he was appointed the Deputy Prosecutor General of Ukraine in February 2015. While there, Sakvarelidze headed the division of Reforms. Sakvarelidze remained in that position until he was removed in 2016 by Prosecutor General Shokin.[19.1]

"You see, if we don't follow their instructions, we won't get any money," Poroshenko argued.

"Prosecutorial reform and personnel issues are internal matters," I objected. "Besides, I have not heard that the activities of the national prosecutor's office are part of the IMF's responsibilities."

However, I was unable to convince the president, so I was forced to accept Sakvarelidze into the PGO and create a position specifically for him called *Deputy for Reforms*. He was appointed to this position on February 16, 2015, just six days after my appointment.

I soon realized that *David Sakvarelidze was much more familiar with the U.S. Embassy than with his colleagues at the GPU.* Sometime in March, during a working meeting with Ambassador Geoffrey Pyatt, Sakvarelidze entered the office, shook the ambassador's hand, and chatted casually, like a good friend. Turning to me and pointing to Sakvarelidze, the ambassador said grandly, "This is a man who is highly respected by the American people."

I couldn't help asking, "What has he done for the American people?" adding, "He had to flee his own country." Pyatt seemed a little offended by my skepticism about Sakvarelidze's *authority*.

Incidentally, it is interesting that the SBU did not grant Sakvarelidze access to state secrets. He did not receive such access in the future either. I noticed that the Georgian reformer cannot read or speak Ukrainian. I do not understand how he familiarized himself with laws and official documents that were exclusively in the state language. It seems that Sakvarelidze was either unable or unwilling to learn Ukrainian. However, why would a *seasonal worker* bother? Today you are working in Ukraine, tomorrow in another country.

Despite all this, the new *Deputy for Reforms* sought not only to initiate vigorous activity, but also to influence and demonstrate his exceptional importance in every way possible. Therefore, he made up a story about a bribe of 10 million hryvnia, which was allegedly offered to him by a certain man when Sakvarelidze was jogging in the Botanical Garden in the morning. I laughed, "Seriously? Why would anyone give you a bribe, David? You can't do anything, and you have no influence." However, a case was opened based on his statement. It has probably closed long ago due to lack of evidence.

Soon, Petro Poroshenko asked me to *keep David busy* and come up with some special area for him to work in. I already had plans to set up a General Inspectorate to oversee internal security at the GPU and fight corruption within the agency. I appointed a professional as head of the inspectorate and entrusted David Sakvarelidze with overseeing its work. It was a serious structure with extensive operational capabilities and access to materials that ordinary prosecutors did not have. In particular, the inspectorate had access to the databases of the Security Service of Ukraine and the Ministry of Internal Affairs. Soon, we began to identify and detain unscrupulous prosecutors in the PGO. These cases resulted in court convictions. However, Sakvarelidze had nothing to do with this.

I didn't get along with David. It was impossible, because I didn't see his real value, especially after Sakvarelidze failed to organize the competitive selection process for local prosecutors. I then proposed an option that everyone happily supported. Roman Govda, the prosecutor of the Odessa region, would return to Kiev as my deputy, and David would take his place while retaining his position as Deputy for Reforms. This option seemed comfortable for David, not least because the regional administration was headed by his friend Mikheil Saakashvili. In September, we found out that the funds allocated by the U.S. government for preparing tests for the local prosecutor competition had disappeared. What's more, millions of dollars for reforming the prosecutor's office had also disappeared. I will tell you everything in order.

The new law on the prosecutor's office provided for a comprehensive reform of the prosecutor's office system, including testing and open competitive selection of candidates for local positions. I instructed Sakvarelidze to develop test assignments and software for the qualification exam. The tests were to be ready by August 15, 2015. As I have already written, analyzing some programs under the auspices of USAID, the U.S. government allocated significant funds from its taxpayers to the program for testing employees of the PGO.

The test questions, supposedly developed by Sakvarelidze and his team and sent to the National Academy of Prosecutors for review, were shocking: 1,171 out of 5,235 questions—*almost a third*—contained significant errors. It seemed as if Sakvarelidze and his team had taken a questionnaire tested in Georgia, slightly reworked it, translated it into Ukrainian, and passed it off as their own intellectual product. Among the questions rejected by experts were gems such as, "What is the distance from Tbilisi [the capital of Georgia] to Moscow?"

Naturally, the Academy returned the tests for revision. A month later, they received the updated version and concluded that the defects had either not been corrected or had been corrected unsatisfactorily. Despite the tests failing professional review, Sakvarelidze posted them on the GPU website. Presumably, he then reported to donors that the work was complete. Prosecutors were indignant and laughed.

However, we could not announce the competition without a professional set of theoretical and practical tasks. Therefore, specialists from the National Academy of Public Prosecutors subsequently developed new tests. As it turned out later, not everything was in order with the testing software, specifically with the developer PJSC Finport Technologies Inc. The contracts with the company were not properly drawn up. At the end of the financial year, the GPU accountant submitted a report to me in which she emphasized that the funds for the tests *had not passed through our accounts.*

We launched an internal investigation to try to get to the bottom of the situation. Representatives of the organizations tasked by the Georgian reformer with developing the tests included the EU project *Support to Justice Reform in Ukraine* and the Organization for Economic Cooperation and Development (OECD). However, they stated that they had only been partially involved in developing the tests. Because they were unable to reach an agreement, they did not actually carry out the work. As a result, it was not possible to identify the developer of the tests.

However, this telling episode is not limited to the story of the money that the U.S. government allocated to reform Ukraine's law enforcement agencies, which could well have ended up in the pockets of Georgian *comrades* and their Ukrainian colleagues. In the summer of 2015, the U.S. Embassy website reported that the U.S. government was allocating *$2 million* to the GPU *for reform*. An action plan for reform was even approved, signed by Deputy Prosecutor General David Sakvarelidze and Ambassador Pyatt.

David shared this joyful news on his Facebook page. However, it is unclear why he did not inform the leadership of the PGO. During the investigation, which began in March of the following year, Sakvarelidze denied signing such a framework document and was unable to explain why he had shared information on social media about the U.S. providing $2 million in aid.

It turned out that this amount was indeed allocated as part of international technical assistance for the project *Support for Criminal Justice Reform in Ukraine*. The donor was the U.S. government; the recipients were the GPU. And...Attention Please!...And, also included the Odessa Regional State Administration, the Anti-Corruption Center, plus other public organizations. It remains unclear why the regional administration headed by

282

Saakashvili was singled out for such generosity by the U.S. government. Why is Odessa so important for reforms, and not any other region of Ukraine?

This is something that American politicians and officials should probably think about. They should also consider why the NGO *Center for Combating Corruption* receives funds for reforming government agencies when it has no connection to this work. In addition, between 2014 and 2016, the U.S. government provided *$4,436,129* in assistance for personnel selection, including the development of special tests for the Ukrainian prosecutor's office. The recipients under the agreement were the GPU and, once again, the *Odessa administration!*

In 2013-2016, the European Union allocated a significant amount in the sum of *€8,547,885* to the project *Support for Justice Reform in Ukraine*." The project required that Ministry of Justice and the PGO were supposed to participate. However, our agency did not receive a single penny for this project or any of the above-mentioned projects.

In March 2016 all these facts, including Sakvarelidze's involvement in the disappearance of funds allocated for the reform of the prosecutor's office, formed the basis of criminal proceedings. The case was initiated by Acting Prosecutor General Yuriy Sevruk.[19.2] I was on vacation at the time. An annoyed Petro Poroshenko immediately called me, "What are you doing on vacation?! Close the case! Biden is angry."

"But how did Biden find out?" I asked.

"Saakashvili told him," Petro replied.

I regret that our investigators did not have time to conduct a full investigation at the time. It is unknown who we would have found. Of course, no one can be accused without facts, but I will allow myself a personal assumption. I have no doubt that some of the American taxpayers' money was *sawed off* by Georgian reformers and grant seekers right here in Ukraine. Some of it probably never even left the United States. Nineteen days after his appointment as Prosecutor General of Ukraine, Yuriy Lutsenko, without conducting all the necessary investigative actions, put an end to this criminal case.[19.3]

I remember that in 2020, one of Ukraine's MPs appealed to the Prosecutor General to open a criminal case on the embezzlement of U.S. financial aid for reforming the PGO. However, this story came to nothing, and all the sins of the reformers were swept under the carpet according to the principle that "war will write all sins dead."

HOW GIZO UGLAVA FROM NABU LEAKED INFORMATION ON CRIMINAL CASES TO THE U.S. EMBASSY

It should be noted that information for Joe Biden's personal interests was gathered not only through unofficial channels and through his proxies in Ukraine, but also through state bodies. During 2014-2015 a total of 56 working meetings among the heads of the investigative departments of the PGO and representatives of the FBI took place in the office of the Prosecutor General. The meetings were initiated by both the Ukrainian and American sides.

The main topic of discussion was cooperation in the investigation of criminal proceedings against high-ranking Yanukovych officials for embezzlement, illegal enrichment, abuse of office, and so on. The Americans were particularly interested in whether such officials and their relatives had real estate, financial assets, and related companies in foreign jurisdictions.

The Americans also expressed a desire to gain access to all materials related to the criminal proceedings, including those classified as restricted and even secret. At the same time, when the Ukrainian side requested assistance in compiling or verifying specific classified data, these requests were ignored, or formal responses or completely outdated information was sent.

We always provided the FBI with detailed information about the fugitive Ukrainian president, Viktor Yanukovych, his son Alexander, and the young oligarch Kurchenko, as well as information about the SEPEK group of companies he created through which money was transferred out of Ukraine. We shared complete information about the head of the NABU, former Ukrainian Prime Minister Arbuzov, Prime Minister Azarov, the head of Yanukovych's administration, the head of the tax inspectorate Klimenko, the head of Naftogaz Kobolev, and many other corrupt officials. Information was also provided about Mykola Zlochevsky. As for the cases against the latter, four working meetings between our investigators and representatives of the FBI took place at the PGO. As I wrote in Chapter 5, the FBI spent a lot of money investigating Zlochevsky's illicit activities.

However, there is one episode involving Gizo Uglava that I would like to discuss separately. This prominent *Biden paratrooper* has repeatedly appeared in the episode involving the *Paul Manafort case*, which was supervised by this brave lawyer from Georgia.

NABU, represented by its first deputy director Uglava and his assistant Polina Chizh, not only manipulated the investigation into the Barn

Book (a.k.a. black ledger) episode, but also passed on information about the progress of the investigation to third parties, *which is a criminal offense*. At the request of third parties, including U.S. citizens, NABU passed on information about the progress of the investigation with the NABU detectives in charge of various cases, and also influenced the course of the investigation. I have documents in front of me that reliably confirm that various information which should not have left the walls of NABU was sent from Polina Chizh's email during 2016-2018.

These documents confirm that personal data was collected on a number of individuals. Among them are myself, *former Prosecutor General of Ukraine V.M. Shokin, and my wife, O.V. Grinevich.* In addition, data was collected on the former chairman of the Central Election Commission, M.V. Okhendovsky, and his wife, as well as on the People's Deputy of Ukraine of the VIII convocation, S.I. Berezenko. A report was made on the close relationship between the head of the SAP, H.I. Kholodnytsky, and the oligarch I.B. Kolomoisky.

This information was sent to the email address of Anna Emelyanova, a legal expert on the anti-corruption program of the U.S. Department of Justice at the U.S. Embassy in Ukraine. Confidential materials from the NABU investigation were also sent to her, including a list of criminal cases being investigated by NABU detectives. In addition, Emelyanova requested information on six ongoing criminal investigations, in particular those concerning the former Ukrainian Minister of Ecology, and owner of Burisma Group, Mykola Zlochevsky.

Chizh also sent numerous emails to Alena Kustova, an employee of the law enforcement department of the U.S. Embassy in Ukraine. She was sent information on the audit of the NABU's activities, as well as a list of criminal proceedings being investigated by NABU detectives. The *hottest information was the transfer of information on individuals who are to be charged with crimes*. In particular, the head of the Tax Service of Ukraine, R.M. Hatsirov, is suspected of crimes.

On October 23, 2018, a letter was sent from Chizh's email address to the email address of Alexander Tiguy, an employee of the U.S. Embassy in Ukraine, requesting approval of the draft suspicion in criminal case *No. 52016000000000319* against Pavlovsky I.B., Deputy Minister of Defense of Ukraine.

On January 5, 2016, and February 22, 2016, Chizh sent an email to Svetlana Berleva, assistant to the police attaché at the Austrian Embassy in Ukraine, with information on criminal proceedings against N.V. Martynenko, a member of the Ukrainian Parliament of the VII convocation. A request was made to organize an investigation into this criminal case and to collect information from Austrian law enforcement agencies on other individuals. Finally, on July 10, 2017, FBI agent Michael T. Solari sent a request to Chizh's email address asking for the names of the detectives investigating criminal case *No. 52016000000000005.*

For those who did not fully understand the text above, NABU employee Polina Chizh forwarded information about the progress of the investigation to unauthorized people who had no legal grounds to receive such information. Even if they were U.S. embassy employees or FBI agents. Such information is confidential and falls under the jurisdiction of the Ukrainian state. For Ukrainian law enforcement agencies to consider the possibility of transferring such information, an official request from the interested party is required. Of course, no such requests were received, because the whole point was to keep these manipulations *secret.*

The head of the agency, on whose initiative the transfer of classified information was carried out, cemented his reputation as a scandalous and unreliable official in the years that followed. His activities are riddled with scandals and intrigue. In April 2022, he became acting head of NABU, but on March 6, 2023, Uglava was fired, believe it or not, *for leaking information about the investigation.* The press reported that Uglava put pressure on detectives who reported leaks of information to a person involved in the NABU investigation. This probably refers to leaks in the NABU case on corruption schemes in the *Big Construction* project in favor of Yuriy Golik, a person involved in the case.[20.1]

Thus, through his *agents of influence*, Joseph Biden became the master of all Ukraine, both secretly and openly. He brazenly meddled in our domestic and foreign policy, including the law enforcement system.

CHAPTER 21:

POISONING IN GREECE...WHO TRIED TO ELIMINATE ME AND WHY?

In 2015, I followed the Bidens' money. Unraveling this web of intrigue led me to results I never expected. First, there was a smear campaign in the media puppeteering rhetoric about the *corrupt Shokin*. Let me remind you that even U.S. Vice President Biden could not find any dirt on me. When attempts to discredit me and bring me to justice failed, they tried to *take me out*. It was in the style of the Kiev gangsters of the 1990s, whose black humor said, "The best witness is a dead witness."

In October 2019, I found myself in the private clinic Rudolfinerhaus in Vienna. I looked at my blood test: *mercury content – 9.7 μg/L*, with a normal range of 0-2 μg/L. My doctor was Professor Mykola Korpan. On that day, Dr. Korpan whispered to me, "This is no accident. This is how professionals are killed."

Dr. Mykola Korpan was the one who treated Viktor Yushchenko after he was poisoned with dioxin in 2004 during the presidential campaign. This

291

same doctor helped nurse Yushchenko back to health. Later, in an interview with *Ukrainski Novosti* Dr. Korpan recalls the incident, involving me, "Viktor Nikolayevich came to us with complaints, and we began to investigate their cause. When we conducted extensive tests, in particular for heavy metals, we found that the mercury levels in his blood were very high. At first, we didn't believe it, because the levels indicated a lethal dose. We initially thought it was some kind of technical error, but after double-checking, it was confirmed that Viktor Shokin's blood mercury levels were at 9.7, and we began intensive treatment....we diagnosed [him with] acute mercury poisoning, which is fatal, and we had to resort to special treatment with special antidotes."[21.1]

I was poisoned with mercury. The level of mercury in my body was almost five times higher than normal. My heart stopped twice, and I miraculously survived. I had to learn to walk and talk again, perhaps so that I could tell you this story.

So, on September 8, 2019, I flew to Greece, to the island of Crete, for a vacation. On September 10th, I went to Rethymno with my Greek friend

Thomas Kyriakidis. My friend was driving. We stopped for a coffee. I felt ill, got out of the car, and collapsed. The metaphor *fell like a tree* is no exaggeration here, because I woke up in the hospital. As the doctors later reported, I had two cardiac arrests. They used a defibrillator and brought me back to life. They say I must have been born under a lucky star, because a few minutes delay would have been fatal. Thank God my friend was not a tourist but a local Greek, and he took me straight to the hospital.

I spent five days in intensive care in Rethymno. The local doctors were puzzled by the inability to diagnose me. High blood pressure, elevated potassium levels, and reduced kidney function. Yet, none of the symptoms they recorded gave them a complete picture of my illness or its nature. My condition was so critical that I was transferred to the intensive care unit of the main hospital in Heraklion. Over the next three days, the local doctors were also unable to determine the cause of my illness.

On September 20, half dead, I was discharged from the hospital in Heraklion. Friends helped me get to Kiev. However, my health continued to deteriorate. Therefore, in early October, I decided to undergo a thorough examination and treatment at the Rudolfinerhaus clinic in Vienna where I was treated by Dr. Mykola Korpan.

After dozens of complex tests, the Viennese specialists concluded that the cause of my mysterious illness was mercury. The mercury concentration was 9.7 µg/L. The normal level for the human body is no higher than 2 µg/L. This was clear evidence of an attempted murder. Toxicologists I spoke to later said that, unfortunately, it was impossible to determine how long ago and how the mercury had entered the body. It could have happened three days or two months ago, through food or drink. However, the experts had no doubt that it was not a natural occurrence.

I spent a whole month being brought back to life at the Rudolfinerhaus clinic. The blow to my body was very powerful. These were not days of rest and relaxation. To give the reader an idea, I will just say that the IVs started at 9 a.m. and ended at 9 p.m. I lay there and just thought, and thought, and thought.

My thoughts inevitably returned to one person. I have no proof that Joseph Biden initiated my, fortunately unsuccessful, assassination. However, I rule out the possibility that someone else could have organized the heavy metal poisoning because I have no other obvious enemies who would want me dead. The fact remains that it was Biden who pursued me with blatant malice over the Burisma case. In any case, the investigation should confirm or refute my assumptions.

Upon my return to Kiev, I filed a statement through my lawyer with the Rethymno police. On November 12, 2019, Greek law enforcement authorities opened a case of poisoning, classifying it as an attempt on my life. In early 2020, Greek investigators sent a request to Ukraine for international legal assistance in this criminal case. According to this international request, Ukrainian law enforcement officials were to question me here in Kiev as the victim and were to also provide the opportunity to attach any documents and question any persons I might identify.

I participated in a one-and-a-half-hour interrogation conducted on June 16, 2020, by an investigator for particularly important cases of the Investigative Department of the National Police of the Capital. I gave a detailed account of everything that happened to me in Greece and then in the Vienna clinic. I provided numerous medical certificates and other documents.

I also petitioned Greek law enforcement authorities to question Joseph Biden, John Kerry, and others who, in my opinion, may be involved in the case. However, our investigators were in no hurry to send the materials they received to their Greek colleagues. I understand the reason for their lack of motivation delay. It is obvious that they received instructions from above to *drag out the investigation* because if the Greek police obtain evidence of poisoning, they will immediately send a request to the U.S. to question Biden and Kerry. Then the case will gain international publicity. However, the Ukrainian government does not seem interested in this investigation.

AFTERWORD

When the circumstances surrounding U.S. President Donald Trump's phone call to Ukrainian President Volodymyr Zelensky became public in September 2019, a huge scandal was already brewing on Capitol Hill. Democrats were *calling for blood* from Donald Trump, accusing him of using his office to undermine his political rival Joe Biden in the upcoming 2020 presidential election.

I carefully read the transcript of the conversation between the two leaders and was shocked. I was deeply outraged by the *bacchanalia* that the Democrats staged in the U.S. Congress. A perfectly businesslike and specific conversation requesting an investigation into the financial plots of the Biden family was presented in a tragic light. Trump must be crucified for pressuring Zelensky and interfering in Ukraine's affairs. Read this transcript carefully. Zelensky himself admits that he would like to *drain the swamp* in Ukraine. He was talking about the swamp of corruption, the large-scale corruption that the Democrats had created in the country under Obama. And yet, Special Counsel Robert Mueller, encouraged by the Democrats, seriously tried to prove that Trump was being controlled by the Kremlin. In the end, even the special counsel himself acknowledged the absurdity of these accusations.

I will emphasize this key point. In his conversation with Trump, Zelensky promised him that all investigations into the Bidens *would be conducted openly and honestly*. It was a real tragedy for Ukraine that Zelensky, under pressure from the Democrats, did not comply with Trump's request. Instead, he refused to investigate the Biden family's corruption schemes. Even in 2019, the colossal *corruption swamp* into which the Democrats had dragged Ukraine could have been exposed.

Just imagine how events could have unfolded after that phone call. Republicans could have brought me in as a consultant to the Justice Department and the FBI on corruption schemes involving not only the Bidens, but also high-ranking American and Ukrainian corrupt officials, whose exposure I have dedicated this book to. I am confident that if investigations had been done properly, Biden would be in prison instead of the White House.

I am still ready to give all the necessary testimony and provide incriminating documents revealing the extent of corruption among Democrats in Ukraine.

We have wasted ten years. Billions of U.S. taxpayers' dollars have disappeared and been lost in the steppes of Ukraine. My country has been turned into a giant money laundering operation. Amid the clamor of declarations about fighting corruption and building a democratic state, all reasonable ideas about creating anti-corruption mechanisms in the law enforcement system have been neutered. In the hands of the Democrats, such ideas have become a means of profiteering and plundering not only my country but also the American treasury.

If we want to build a free and democratic Ukraine today, we cannot do without *draining the swamp of corruption* in both Washington and Kiev. The sooner we start this work, the better it will be for the future of our two countries.

GLOSSARY

Cap-Intro – also knowns as capital introduction, it is a brokerage company that introduces hedge fund clients to hedge fund investors.

FINCEN - U.S. Financial Crimes Enforcement Network, a bureau of the U.S. Department of the Treasury that oversees prevention, monitoring, and investigations of financial crimes.

FIU - Financial Intelligence Unit of Latvia, the investigative law enforcement body who questioned Burima's financial transactions during 2016.

GPU – Arm of the national police in Ukraine (pronounced phonetically as Gosudarstvennoe politicheskoe upravlenie).

Holos Ukrayiny – The publication dedicated to the members of Ukraine's Parliament, the Verkhovna Rada. Per Ukrainian regulations, each party in parliament must be provided equal print space. It is one of the official publications authorized to public legislation.

Maidan – Term used to refer to the events occurring during the 2014 Revolution of Dignity (see Chapter 1 for details).

MPs – Members of the Ukrainian Parliament, the Verkhovna Rada.

Orange Revolution – A political uprising occurring in Ukraine between November 2004 January 2005, also referred to as one of the color revolutions funded by George Soros. The event forced a runoff race for the Ukrainian presidential office involving Yanukovych and Yashenko, leading to Yashenko's win.

PGO – Prosecutor General's Office of Ukraine, governmental office equivalent to the U.S. Attorney General and the U.S. Department of Justice.

President (of Ukraine) – Person elected by the people of Ukraine to be the leader of the state (country), who oversees foreign policy and appoints the Prime Minster of Ukraine, Minister of Defense and Minister of Foreign Affairs with the approval of the Parliament.

Prime Minister – Person appointed by the president with the approval of the Parliament to be head of the domestic government of Ukraine, overseeing the cabinet of ministers and the executive branch of the government.

Quid Pro Quo – Greek term meaning a favor for a favor. It is at term used by then U.S. Congressman Adam Schiff to describe the 2019 phone call between President Trump and President Zelenskyy, based upon a Schiff's version of the conversation presented to the U.S. media, which led to the first impeachment trials against President Trump in 2020.

Revolution of Dignity – Term used to refer to the event occurring during 2014 referred to as Maidan or the Euromaidan (see Chapter 1 for details).

Subsoil – Natural resources that are underneath the earth, such as minerals, natural gas, oil, etc.

Verkhovna Rada – Ukrainian Parliament, which is the legislative body of the Ukrainian government.

NOTES

CHAPTER 1 NOTES

1.1) "Jan Tombinski: Several Ukrainian Ministries Have Already Shifted from
Short-Term to Long-Term Thinking on the European Integration Process |
UACRISIS.ORG." 2015. Uacrisis.org. July 21, 2015.
https://uacrisis.org/en/29467-yan-tombinski. Accessed in September 2025.

1.2) Young, Cathy. n.d. "What Really Happened in Ukraine in 2014—and since
Then." Www.thebulwark.com. https://www.thebulwark.com/p/what-really-
happened-in-ukraine-in-2014-and-since-then. Accessed in September 2025.

1.3) Weir, Fred. 2013. "Russia Cries Foul over Western Embrace of Ukraine's
Demonstrators." The Christian Science Monitor. December 13, 2013.
https://www.csmonitor.com/World/Europe/2013/1213/Russia-cries-foul-
over-Western-embrace-of-Ukraine-s-demonstrators. Accessed in September
2025.

1.4) Open Society Foundation. 2019. Open Society in Ukraine.
opensocietyfoundations.org. September 30, 2019.
https://www.opensocietyfoundations.org/uploads/5febed12-a6b1-47da-881a-
1620cf685b77/fact-sheet-open-society-in-ukraine-eng-20190930.pdf.
Accessed in September 2025.

1.5) Ray, Michael. 2020. "Viktor Yanukovych | Facts, Biography, & Flight to
Russia | Britannica." In Encyclopædia Britannica.
https://www.britannica.com/biography/Viktor-Yanukovych. Accessed in
September 2025.

1. 6) U.S. Deputy Secretary of State Victoria Newland to Prosecutor General of
Ukraine Viktor Shokin, letter, 2015.

1.7) Pyatt, Geoffrey. "U.S. Embassy Kyiv Ukraine." 2022. Facebook.com. 2022.
https://www.facebook.com/usdos.ukraine/posts/10153248488506936?paipv=
0&eav=AfYSlmcnKZxNQNqBMpWqyaYBnDJ7C_ByEsTsm4bWUajo-
FWfymfxHqEkWCtLC4fnPkY&_rdr. Accessed on September 2025.

1.8) "Petro Poroshenko | Facts & Biography." n.d. Encyclopedia Britannica.
https://www.britannica.com/biography/Petro-Poroshenko. Accessed in
September 2025.

1.9) NATO. 2025. "Statement of the NATO-Ukraine Commission." NATO. 2025.
https://www.nato.int/cps/en/natohq/news_108499.htm. Accessed in
September 2025.

1.10)   The Associated Press. 2025. "What to Know about Crimea and How It Factors
          into the Russia-Ukraine War." AP News. August 18, 2025.
          https://apnews.com/article/crimea-ukraine-russia-war-putin-
          d6c9d21427844a0aae9253e94ea055c4. Accessed in September 2025.

1.11)   Ap Correspondent. 2025. "Why Crimea Is Coveted by Both Russia and
          Ukraine - and the Role It Plays in the War." The Independent. March 20,
          2025. https://www.independent.co.uk/news/world/europe/crimea-russia-
          ukraine-war-history-b2718503.html. Accessed in September 2025.

1.12)   Blog, IACL-AIDC. 2020. "NATO'S Aspirations in the Constitutional Preamble
          of Ukraine: Distorting Historical Roots of the Constitution or Reflecting
          Societal Changes?" IACL-IADC Blog. June 30, 2020. https://blog-iacl-
          aidc.org/2020-posts/2020/6/30/natos-aspirations-in-the-constitutional-
          preamble-of-ukraine-distorting-historical-roots-of-the-constitution-or-
          reflecting-societal-changes. Accessed in September 2025.

1.13)   "Would Ukraine Breach Its Own Constitution If It Dropped Its NATO Bid?"
          n.d. Verfassungsblog. https://verfassungsblog.de/would-ukraine-breach-its-
          own-constitution-if-it-dropped-its-nato-bid/. Accessed in September 2025.

1.14)   Wikipedia Contributors. 2025. "Mykola Zlochevsky." Wikipedia. Wikimedia
          Foundation. July 27, 2025.
          https://en.wikipedia.org/wiki/Mykola_Zlochevsky. Accessed in September
          2025.

1.15)   "The largest bribe in the history of Ukraine. The VAKS approved the
          agreement between ex-Minister of Ecology Zlochevsky and the
          investigation." 2023. New Voice Ukraine. August 1, 2023.
          https://nv.ua/ukraine/events/delo-zlochevskogo-vaks-utverdil-soglashenie-so-
          sledstviem-o-priznanii-vinovnosti-50343196.html. Accessed in September
          2025.

1.16)   Burisma. 2014. "Burisma Announces Hunter Biden's Appointment to the
          Board (May 12, 2014) | DocumentCloud." Documentcloud.org. 2019.
          https://embed.documentcloud.org/documents/5980032-Burisma-Announces-
          Hunter-Biden-s-Appointment-to/?embed=1. Accessed in September 2025.

1.17)   Gisonna, Kelly. 2024. "Hunter Biden | Biography, Addiction, Legal Issues, &
          Facts | Britannica." Www.britannica.com. January 31, 2024.
          https://www.britannica.com/biography/Hunter-Biden. Accessed in September
          2025.

1.18)   "Ukraine to Investigate Leaked Tapes with Ex-President, Biden." 2020. AP
          News. May 20, 2020.
          https://apnews.com/article/02895b0ffce2b6c6f11c20333fe7ba3d. Accessed in
          September 2025.

1.19) "TREATIES AND OTHER INTERNATIONAL ACTS SERIES 15-526 Loan
       Guarrantee," Agreement Between the UNITED STATES OF AMERICA and
       UKRAINE with Annexes, signed May 18, 2015. https://www.state.gov/wp-
       content/uploads/2019/02/15-526-Ukraine-Loan-Guarantee.pdf. Accessed in
       September 2025.

1.20) "Opinion: Joe Biden Forced Ukraine to Fire Prosecutor for Aid Money." n.d.
       WSJ. https://www.wsj.com/video/opinion-joe-biden-forced-ukraine-to-fire-
       prosecutor-for-aid-money/C1C51BB8-3988-4070-869F-CAD3CA0E81D8.
       Accessed in September 2025.

1.21) Pavel Polityuk, and Matthias Williams. 2016. "Ukrainian Chief Prosecutor
       Back at Work despite Resignation." Reuters, March 16, 2016.
       https://www.reuters.com/article/world/ukrainian-chief-prosecutor-back-at-
       work-despite-resignation-idUSKCN0WI1UA/. Accessed in September 2025.

1.22) Wikipedia contributors. "Devon Archer" 2025. wikipedia.com. September 13,
       2025. https://en.wikipedia.org/wiki/Devon_Archer. Accessed in September
       2025.

1.23) Dorn, Sara. 2023. "Who Is Devon Archer? Hunter Biden's Ex-Business Partner
       Says He Never Saw President Talk Business with Son's Associates." Forbes,
       August 2, 2023. https://www.forbes.com/sites/saradorn/2023/08/02/who-is-
       devon-archer-hunter-bidens-ex-business-partner-says-he-never-saw-
       president-talk-business-with-sons-associates/. Accessed in September 2025.

1.24) United States Attorney's Office. "Devon Archer Sentenced to a Year and a Day
       in Prison for the Fraudulent Issuance and Sale of More than $60 Million of
       Tribal Bonds." 2022. Www.justice.gov. February 28, 2022.
       https://www.justice.gov/usao-sdny/pr/devon-archer-sentenced-year-and-day-
       prison-fraudulent-issuance-and-sale-more-60-million. Accessed in September
       2025.

1.25) Zelenskyy, Vlodymyr (President of Ukraine) "telephone conversation with"
       Trump, Donald J. (President of the United States). July 25, 2019.
       https://www.documentcloud.org/documents/6429020-Ukraine-
       Transcript/?mode=document#document/p2/a526697. Accessed in September
       2025.

1.26) Cohen, Marshall, and Annie Grayer. 2023. "US Attorney Who Initially Vetted
       Biden Bribery Tip Explains Why It Deserved Further Scrutiny." CNN.
       October 28, 2023. https://edition.cnn.com/2023/10/27/politics/us-attorney-
       biden-bribery-tip-scrutiny. Accessed in September 2025.

1.27) PBS NewsHour. 2023. "WATCH LIVE: House Begins Debate for Vote on
       GOP Resolution Authorizing Biden Impeachment Inquiry." YouTube.
       December 13, 2023. https://www.youtube.com/watch?v=6m8N3-nqN0w.
       Accessed in September 2025.

1.28) Michail Bulgakov. 1967. The Master and Margarita. Penguin Classics.

CHAPTER 2 NOTES

2.1)   The New York Post. "Recording of calls between Joe Biden and ex-Ukraine President Poroshenko leaked." YouTube. May 20, 2020. News video, 1:51. https://youtu.be/7lA3oOo1oZc?si=_5YHqkja-WNWlm2l. Accessed in September 2025.

2.2)   United States Committee on Oversight and Government Reform. December 4, 2020. "The Bidens' Influence Peddling Timeline." https://oversight.house.gov/the-bidens-influence-peddling-timeline/. Accessed in September 2025.

2.3)   Georgi Gotev. 2016. "Court of Auditors Unable to Say How EU Money Was Spent in Ukraine." Euractiv. EURACTIV. December 7, 2016. https://www.euractiv.com/section/global-europe/news/court-of-auditors-unable-to-say-how-eu-money-was-spent-in-ukraine/. Accessed in September 2025.

2.4)   Cabinet of Ministers of Ukraine. August 5, 2015. "Resolution No. 553: On Amendments to the Procedure for Attracting, Using and Monitoring International Technical Assistance." https://zakon.rada.gov.ua/laws/show/553-2015-%D0%BF#n2. Accessed in September 2025.

2.5)   Wikipedia Contributors. 2022. "Arseniy Yatsenyuk." Wikipedia. October 10, 2022. https://en.wikipedia.org/wiki/Arseniy_Yatsenyuk. Accessed in September 2025.

2.6)   andrewfp. 2025. "Interview - Volodymyr Groysman, Prime Minister of Ukraine." Foreign Policy. September 11, 2025. https://foreignpolicy.com/sponsored/volodymyr-groysman-prime-minister/. Accessed in September 2025. Accessed in September 2025.

2.7)   Wikipedia Contributors. 2025. "Volodymyr Groysman." Wikipedia. Wikimedia Foundation. August 30, 2025. https://en.wikipedia.org/wiki/Volodymyr_Groysman. Accessed in September 2025.

2.8)   United States Committee on Oversight and Government Reform. July 31, 2023. "Comer Statement on Devon Archer's Testimony." https://oversight.house.gov/release/comer-statement-on-devon-archers-testimony%EF%BF%BC/. Accessed on September 2025.

2.9)   Vincent, Isabel. 2025. "How the 'Biden Brand' Was Used to Rake in $30 Million for Joe and the First Family, Detailed in James Comer's Book." New York Post. January 9, 2025. https://nypost.com/2025/01/09/us-news/biden-brand-raked-in-30m-for-joe-and-family-comer-book/. Accessed in September 2025.

2.10) United States Committee on Oversight and Government Reform. November 17, 2022. "A President Compromised: The Biden Family Investigation." https://oversight.house.gov/wp-content/uploads/2022/11/Interim-Staff-Report-A-President-Compromised-The-Biden-Family-Investigation-1.pdf. Accessed in September 2025.

2.11) No-Principle-2071. September 2024. "What is the deal with hunter bidens laptop?" reddit. https://www.reddit.com/r/TooAfraidToAsk/comments/1bjrjdw/what_is_the_deal_with_hunter_bidens_laptop/. Accessed in September 2025.

2.12) Wikipedia Contributors. 2022. "Hunter Biden Laptop Controversy." Wikipedia. September 21, 2022. https://en.wikipedia.org/wiki/Hunter_Biden_laptop_controversy. Accessed in September 2025.

2.13) Nelson, Steven. 2023. "FBI 'Verified' Authenticity of Hunter Biden's Abandoned Laptop in November 2019: IRS Whistleblower Gary Shapley." June 22, 2023. https://nypost.com/2023/06/22/fbi-verified-authenticity-of-hunter-bidens-abandoned-laptop-in-november-2019-irs-whistleblower-gary-shapley/. Accessed in September 2025.

2.14) Cuebas-Fantauzzi, Brian Flood,Alba. 2024. "Hunter Biden 'Laptop from Hell' Scandal Turns 4: How Media, Intelligence Community Misled Americans." Fox News. October 14, 2024. https://www.foxnews.com/media/hunter-biden-laptop-from-hell-scandal-turns-4-how-media-intelligence-community-mislead-americans?msockid=1ea70dc7d9d56bd918071874d83b6a30. Accessed in September 2025.

2.15) Nelson, Steven. 2024. "Facebook Execs Suppressed Hunter Biden Laptop Scandal to Curry Favor with Biden-Harris Admin: Bombshell Report." House Judiciary Committee Republicans. October 30, 2024. https://judiciary.house.gov/media/in-the-news/facebook-execs-suppressed-hunter-biden-laptop-scandal-curry-favor-biden-harris. Accessed in September 2025.

2.16) Herridge, Catherine and Graham Kates. 2022. "Copy of What's Believed to Be Hunter Biden's Laptop Data Turned over by Repair Shop to FBI Showed No Tampering, Analysis Says." November 21, 2022. Www.cbsnews.com. https://www.cbsnews.com/news/hunter-biden-laptop-data-analysis/. Accessed in September 2025.

2.17) Singman, Brooke. 2023. "Biden Campaign, Blinken Orchestrated Intel Letter to Discredit Hunter Biden Laptop Story, Ex-CIA Official Says." House Judiciary Committee Republicans. April 21, 2023. https://judiciary.house.gov/media/in-the-news/biden-campaign-blinken-orchestrated-intel-letter-discredit-hunter-biden-laptop. Accessed in September 2025.

2.18)   Washington, District of Columbia 1800 I. Street NW, and Dc 20006. n.d.
         "PolitiFact - Poll on Voters' Opinion of Biden Laptop Story Doesn't Tell
         Whole Story." @Politifact.
         https://www.politifact.com/factchecks/2023/feb/25/elise-stefanik/poll-on-
         voters-opinion-of-biden-laptop-story-needs/. Accessed in September 2025.

2.19)   Grassley, Chuck (U.S. Senator) "Letter to" Patel, Kash (Director of the U.S.
         Federal Bureau of Investigations). Washington D.C. April 9, 2025.
         https://www.grassley.senate.gov/imo/media/doc/johnson_grassley_to_fbi_-
         _hunter_biden_laptop_fbi_messages.pdf. Accessed in September 2025.

2.20)   Accounting Chamber Supreme Audit Institution of Ukraine. August, 2025.
         "Annual Reports – Accounting Chamber." Annual reports - The Accounting
         Chamber. https://rp.gov.ua/Activity/Reports/?lang=eng. Accessed in
         September 2025.

2.21)   "About." 2012. Congressman James Comer. December 3, 2012.
         https://comer.house.gov/about. Accessed in September 2025.

2.22)   Diaz, Jaclyn. 2023. "House Republicans Will Soon Begin the First
         Impeachment Inquiry Hearing into Biden." NPR. September 28, 2023.
         https://www.npr.org/2023/09/28/1202010186/biden-impeachment-inquiry-
         hearing. Accessed in September 2025.

2.23)   United States House Committee on Oversight and Government Reforms. 2023.
         "Comer Releases Third Bank Memo Detailing Payments to the Bidens from
         Russia, Kazakhstan, and Ukraine - United States House Committee on
         Oversight and Government Reform." United States House Committee on
         Oversight and Government Reform. October 2, 2023.
         https://oversight.house.gov/release/comer-releases-third-bank-memo-
         detailing-payments-to-the-bidens-from-russia-kazakhstan-and-
         ukraine%ef%bf%bc/. Accessed in September 2025.

2.24)   Yilek, Caitlin. 2024. "House Oversight Chairman Invites Biden to Testify as
         GOP Impeachment Inquiry Stalls - CBS News." Www.cbsnews.com. March
         28, 2024. https://www.cbsnews.com/news/james-comer-biden-impeachment-
         hunter-biden/. Accessed in September 2025.

2.25)   Otten, T., Otten, T., Houghtaling, E. Q., Otten, T., Otten, T., Houghtaling, E.
         Q., Houghtaling, E. Q., Houghtaling, E. Q., Otten, T., & Otten, T. (2024,
         March 26). James Comer Finally Admits Defeat in His Biden Impeachment
         Crusade. The New Republic. https://newrepublic.com/post/180126/james-
         comer-admits-defeat-biden-impeachment . Accessed on September 2025.

2.26)   United States Government Accountability Office. 2024. "Ukraine: DOD
         Should Improve Data for Both Defense Article Delivery and End-Use
         Monitoring." Gao.gov. March 13, 2024. https://www.gao.gov/products/gao-
         24-106289. Accessed in September 2025.

3.1)   United States Committee on Oversight and Government Reform. September 13, 2023. "Evidence of Joe Biden's Involvement in His Family's Influence Peddling Schemes." https://oversight.house.gov/blog/evidence-of-joe-bidens-involvement-in-his-familys-influence-peddling-schemes/. Accessed in September 2025.

3.2)   Gera, Vanessa. "AP Interview: Ex-Polish President Defends Biden and Burisma." 2019. AP News. November 28, 2019. https://apnews.com/article/37424b8a0a994c1a935c5831643a84e3. Accessed in September 2025.

3.3)   The Hill. 2023. "READ: Devon Archer Interview Transcript Released by House Oversight Panel." The Hill. August 3, 2023. https://thehill.com/homenews/house/4135288-read-devon-archer-interview-transcript-released-by-house-oversight-panel/. Accessed in September 2025.

3.4)   Hudson, J., Bade, R., & Viser, M. (2019, October 18). Diplomat tells investigators he raised alarms in 2015 about Hunter Biden's Ukraine work but was rebuffed. The Washington Post. https://www.washingtonpost.com/politics/diplomat-tells-investigators-he-raised-alarms-in-2015-about-hunter-bidens-ukraine-work-but-was-rebuffed/2019/10/18/81e35be9-4f5a-4048-8520-0baabb18ab63_story.html. Accessed in September 2025.

3.5)   Nelson, Steven. 2023. "Joe Biden Boosted Ukraine Gas Industry as Hunter Took Burisma Role." New York Post. April 12, 2023. https://nypost.com/2023/04/11/ex-biden-stenographer-says-fbi-ignored-prezs-role-in-hunters-business-dealings/. Accessed in September 2025.

3.6)   Chasmar, Jessica. "National Archives says it has 5,000 emails potentially linked to alleged Biden pseudonyms: Lawsuit." Fox News. August, 29, 2023. https://www.foxnews.com/politics/national-archives-says-5000-emails-potentially-linked-alleged-biden-pseudonyms. Accessed in September 2025.

3.7)   Boswell, Josh. 2023. "EXCLUSIVE: Hunter Biden Helped Devise Plan to 'Close Down' Viktor Shokin's Investigation into Burisma, Emails Reveal." Mail Online. Daily Mail. August 29, 2023. https://www.dailymail.co.uk/news/article-12453245/Emails-Hunter-Biden-tried-help-shut-Burisma-probe.html. Accessed in September 2025.

3.8)   Devine, Miranda. 2023. "Hunter Biden's Suspicious Email on Ukraine Raises Red Flag for Classified Doc Probe." New York Post. June 12, 2023. https://nypost.com/2023/06/11/hunter-bidens-suspicious-email-on-ukraine-raises-red-flag-for-probe/. Accessed in September 2025.

3.9)   Devine, Miranda (@mirandadevine). "Column's up: Joe has always said
          Hunter is the "smartest guy I know." But did he get so smart with the
          assistance of Dad's files?" X (formerly known as Twitter). June 12, 2023.
          https://x.com/mirandadevine/status/1668335716471042049. Accessed in
          September 2025.

3.10)   Harsanyi, David. 2019. "Wherever Joe Biden Went, Son Hunter Cashed In."
          New York Post. September 27, 2019.
          https://nypost.com/2019/09/26/wherever-joe-biden-went-son-hunter-cashed-
          in/. Accessed in September 2025.

3.11)   United States Committee on Oversight and Accountability. August 9, 2023.
          "Third Bank Records Memorandum from the Oversight Committee's
          Investigation into the Biden Family's Influence Peddling and Business
          Schemes." https://oversight.house.gov/wp-content/uploads/2023/08/Third-
          Bank-Records-Memorandum_Redacted.pdf. Accessed in September 2025.

3.12)   United States Committee on Oversight and Accountability. July 19, 2023.
          "Hearing with IRS Whistleblowers About the Bident Criminal Investigation."
          https://www.congress.gov/118/meeting/house/116254/documents/HHRG-
          118-GO00-Transcript-20230719.pdf. Accessed in September 2025.

3.13)   "About." 2019. The Oversight Project. July 3, 2019.
          https://oversightproject.org/about-us/. Accessed in September 2025.

3.14)   Balet, Nathaniel. 2025. "Double Standard for Bidens: Prominent Law Firm
          Tied to Bursima Finally Forced to Register under FARA - Oversight
          Project." Oversight Project. June 30, 2025. https://itsyourgov.org/8-years-in-
          the-making-prominent-law-firm-tied-to-bursima-finally-forced-to-register-
          under-fara/. Accessed in September 2025.

3.15)   Boswell, Josh. 2025. "DOJ Forced Top Lawyer to Register as Foreign Agent
          for Burisma...But Not Hunter Biden, Bombshell Files Reveal." Mail Online.
          Daily Mail. June 27, 2025. https://www.dailymail.co.uk/news/article-
          14851247/doj-lawyer-forced-register-foreign-agent-burisma-hunter-
          biden.html. Accessed in September 2025.

CHAPTER 4 NOTES

4.1)   "Fugitive MP Onyshchenko Claims He Secretly Recorded Talks with
          Poroshenko: Administration Calls out Report as Fake." 2018. Unian.info.
          UNIAN. April 19, 2018. https://www.unian.info/politics/10087469-fugitive-
          mp-onyshchenko-claims-he-secretly-recorded-talks-with-poroshenko-
          administration-calls-out-report-as-fake.html. Accessed in September 2025.

4.2)   "UNIAN. Watch news online." 2018. 1+1 Video. 2018.
          https://1plus1.video/unian-novosti/2018-god/aprel-opublikovani-novi-plivki-
          onishtenko. Accessed in September 2025.

4.3)   Wikipedia Contributors. 2025. "Burisma." Wikipedia. Wikimedia Foundation.
        May 25, 2025. https://en.wikipedia.org/wiki/Burisma. Accessed in September
        2025.

4.4)   Fawthrop, Andrew. 2020. "What Is Burisma? The Ukrainian Energy Firm
        Caught between US Presidential Rivals." NS Energy. October 14, 2020.
        https://www.nsenergybusiness.com/analysis/burisma-impeachment-trump/.
        Accessed in September 2025.

4.5)   PBS News Hour. "WATCH: Rep. Schiff responds to Dershowitz' argument
        that a quid pro quo would not be impeachable." January 30, 2020. YouTube
        video, 02:33. https://youtu.be/GkV9ZZqiycE?si=-3I6QgtDpxI56Xvs.
        Accessed in September 2025.

4.6)   Wikipedia Contributors. 2025. "Ministry of Environmental Protection and
        Natural Resources (Ukraine)." Wikipedia. Wikimedia Foundation. August
        13, 2025.
        https://en.wikipedia.org/wiki/Ministry_of_Environmental_Protection_and_N
        atural_Resources_(Ukraine). Accessed in September 2025.

4.7)   The Biden Ukraine Bribe Tapes. (2020, November 28). Swiss Policy Research.
        https://swprs.org/the-biden-ukraine-bribe-tapes/. Accessed in September
        2025.

4.8)   Harasymiw, Bohdan. 2023. "Party of Regions." Encyclopediaofukraine.com.
        2023.
        https://www.encyclopediaofukraine.com/display.asp?linkpath=pages%5CP%
        5CA%5CPartyofRegions.htm. Accessed in September 2025.

4.9)   Reuters Staff. 2019. "Factbox: Burisma, the Obscure Ukrainian Gas Company
        at the Heart of U.S. Political Row." Reuters, September 24, 2019.
        https://www.reuters.com/article/world/factbox-burisma-the-obscure-
        ukrainian-gas-company-at-the-heart-of-us-politic-idUSKBN1W91UG/.
        Accessed in September 2025.

4.10)   Dengi.ua. 2024. "The rating of the TOP 25 richest Ukrainians has been
        published." Dengi.ua. September 17, 2024. https://dengi.ua/finance/9749654-
        opublikovan-rejting-top-25-samykh-bogatykh-ukraintsev. Accessed in
        September 2025.

4.11)   Levine, Jon. 2023. "Hunter Biden's Daughter Naomi Repped Peru, Lived in
        White House: Public Records." New York Post. September 30, 2023.
        https://nypost.com/2023/09/30/hunter-bidens-daughter-represented-peru-
        while-living-in-the-white-house/. Accessed in September 2025.

4.12)   Bullough, Oliver. "The Money Machine: How a High-Profile Corruption
        Investigation Fell Apart." 2017. The Guardian. April 12, 2017.
        https://www.theguardian.com/world/2017/apr/12/the-money-machine-how-a-
        high-profile-corruption-investigation-fell-apart. Accessed in September 2025.

4.13)   Serious Fraud Office v. Mykola Zlochevsky. Case No. RSTO/7/2014.
         Honorable Justice Blake. (Central Criminal Court of London (Old Bailey))
         January 20, 2015. https://archive.org/details/5926342-The-Central-Criminal-
         Court-of-London-Rules-in/mode/2up. Accessed in September 2025.

4.14)   "Zlochevsky's criminal cases: out of 6 proceedings, 4 have been closed, 2 are
         'smoldering.'" 2018. Capital. March 15, 2018.
         https://www.capital.ua/ru/publication/109957-ugolovnye-dela-zlochevskogo-
         iz-6-proizvodstv-4-zakryty-2-tleyut. Accessed in September 2025.

4.15)   Interfax-Ukraine. 2013. "Tymoshenko Accepts Cox-Kwasniewski Mission's
         Proposal on Treatment in Germany, Says Vlasenko." Interfax-Ukraine.
         October 4, 2013. https://en.interfax.com.ua/news/general/169452.html.
         Accessed in September 2025.

4.16)   Wikipedia Contributors. 2025. "Aleksander Kwaśniewski." Wikipedia.
         Wikimedia Foundation. September 5, 2025.
         https://en.wikipedia.org/wiki/Aleksander_Kwa%C5%9Bniewski. Accessed in
         September 2025.

4.17)   Wikipedia Contributors. 2025. "Social Democracy of the Republic of Poland."
         Wikipedia. Wikimedia Foundation. July 5, 2025.
         https://en.wikipedia.org/wiki/Social_Democracy_of_the_Republic_of_Polan
         d. Accessed in September 2025.

4.18)   Office of Aleksander Kwasniewski. 2020."Www.kwasniewskialeksander.pl -
         Biography." Kwasniewskialeksander.pl. 2020.
         https://kwasniewskialeksander.pl/english/biography. Accessed in September
         2025.

4.19)   Wikipedia Contributors. 2019. "Yulia Tymoshenko." Wikipedia. Wikimedia
         Foundation. April 1, 2019. https://en.wikipedia.org/wiki/Yulia_Tymoshenko.
         Accessed in September 2025.

4.20)   Central European University. 2014. "Soros Explains Why He is Exerting His
         'Utmost Efforts' to Support Ukraine." December 3, 2014. Ceu.edu.
         https://www.ceu.edu/article/2014-12-03/soros-explains-why-he-exerting-his-
         utmost-efforts-support-ukraine-during. Accessed in September 2025.

4.21)   Jacobs, Sam. 2025. "Godfather of Color Revolutions: Is George Soros the Most
         Dangerous Man Alive?" n.d. Ammo.com. https://ammo.com/articles/george-
         soros. Accessed in September 2025.

4.22)   Archer, Devon. 2023. Review of "Interview of: Devon Archer." Interview by
         U.S. Committee on Oversite and Accountability. GO212551.
         https://oversight.house.gov/wp-content/uploads/2023/08/Devon-Archer-
         Transcript.pdf. Accessed in September 2025.

4.23)   "Email View | BidenLaptopEmails Terminal." 2016. Bidenlaptopemails.com.
         2016. https://bidenlaptopemails.com/biden-emails/email.php?id=20160413-
         190117_57558. Accessed in September 2025.

4.24)   Sonne, Paul, Michael Kranish, and Matt Viser. 2019. "The Gas Tycoon and the
         Vice President's Son. The Story of Hunter Biden's Foray into Ukraine." The
         Washington Post. September 29, 2019.
         https://www.washingtonpost.com/world/national-security/the-gas-tycoon-
         and-the-vice-presidents-son-the-story-of-hunter-bidens-foray-in-
         ukraine/2019/09/28/1aadff70-dfd9-11e9-8fd3-d943b4ed57e0_story.html.
         Accessed in September 2025.

Chapter 5 Notes

5.1)   "Former Georgia president now a governor of Ukraine region." 2015. Gulf
         Times. May 30, 2015. https://www.gulf-times.com/story/441293/former-
         georgia-president-now-a-governor-of-ukraine-region. Accessed in September
         2025.

5.2)   Censor.NET. 2015. "Sakvarelidze Will Head Prosecutor's Office Anti-
         Corruption Department, - Poroshenko." Censor.net. Censor.NET. December
         2015.
         https://censor.net/en/news/363194/sakvarelidze_will_head_prosecutors_offic
         e_anticorruption_department_poroshenko. Accessed in September 2025.

5.3)   Bullough, Oliver. "The Money Machine: How a High-Profile Corruption
         Investigation in Ukraine Fell Apart." 2017. Pulitzer Center. 2017.
         https://pulitzercenter.org/stories/money-machine-how-high-profile-
         corruption-investigation-ukraine-fell-apart. Accessed in September 2025.

5.4)   Wikipedia Contributors. 2025. "Marie Yovanovitch." Wikipedia. Wikimedia
         Foundation. July 10, 2025. https://en.wikipedia.org/wiki/Marie_Yovanovitch.
         Accessed in September 2025.

5.5)   Kim, Caaitlyn. 2022. "Marie Yovanovitch reflects on disinformation and her
         removal as ambassador to Ukraine." NPR Book Reviews.
         https://www.npr.org/2022/03/12/1086270962/marie-yovanovitch-reflects-on-
         disinformation-and-her-removal-as-ambassador-to-uk. Accessed in 2025.

5.6)   Axelrod, Tal. 2019. "Giuliani Asked State Dept. To Grant Visa for Ex-Ukraine
         Official at Center of Biden Allegations: Report." The Hill. October 18, 2019.
         https://thehill.com/homenews/administration/466549-giuliani-asked-state-
         dept-to-grant-visa-for-ex-ukraine-official-at/. Accessed in September 2025.

5.7)   Solomon, John. 2019. "Top Ukrainian Justice Official Says US Ambassador
         Gave Him a Do Not Prosecute List." The Hill. March 20, 2019.
         https://thehill.com/hilltv/rising/434875-top-ukrainian-justice-official-says-us-
         ambassador-gave-him-a-do-not-prosecute. Accessed in September 2025.

5.8) "Ukrainian Prosecutor General admits that US ambassador did not give him 'do not prosecute'list." 2019. Uawire.org. April 18, 2019. https://uawire.org/lutsenko-admits-that-us-ambassador-did-not-give-him-do-not-prosecute-list. Accessed in September 2025.

5.9) Zelenskyy, Vlodymyr (President of Ukraine) "telephone conversation with" Trump, Donald J. (President of the United States). July 25, 2019. https://www.documentcloud.org/documents/6429020-Ukraine-Transcript/?mode=document#document/p2/a526697. Accessed in September 2025.

5.10) Wikipedia Contributors. 2025. "George P. Kent." Wikipedia. Wikimedia Foundation. July 18, 2025. https://en.wikipedia.org/wiki/George_P._Kent. Accessed in September 2025.

5.11) United State Department of State. 2023. "George P. Kent - United States Department of State." United States Department of State. October 2, 2023. https://2021-2025.state.gov/people/george-p-kent/. Accessed in September 2025.

5.12) Golding, Bruce. 2022. "Classified 2016 Email Shows US Diplomat Warning of Hunter Biden Deals in Ukraine." New York Post. February 2, 2022. https://nypost.com/2022/02/02/us-diplomat-warned-about-hunter-biden-ukraine-deals-in-2016/. Accessed in September 2025.

5.13) Kent, George (U.S. Deputy Assistant Secretary of State) "interview with" Permanent Select Committee on Intelligence, Committee on Oversight and Reform, and Committee on Foreign Affairs (U.S. House of Representatives). October 15, 2019. https://d3i6fh83elv35t.cloudfront.net/static/2019/11/Kenttranscript.pdf. Accessed in September 2025.

5.14) Kent, George (U.S. Deputy Assistant Secretary of State) "interview with" Committee on Homeland Security and Governmental Affairs, and Committee on Finance (U.S. Senate). July 24, 2020. https://www.hsgac.senate.gov/wp-content/uploads/imo/media/doc/HSGAC_Finance_Report_FINAL.pdf. Accessed in September 2025.

5.15) Kent, George (U.S. Deputy Assistant Secretary of State) "email chain with" Herbst, John and Taylor, William (U.S. State Department). August 29, 2016. https://justthenews.com/sites/default/files/2020-09/KentYaremaAug292016.pdf. Accessed in September 2025.

5.16) Dickinson, Peter. 2020. "Ukraine's Powerful Interior Minister Avakov under Fire over Police Reform Failures." Atlantic Council. June 30, 2020. https://www.atlanticcouncil.org/blogs/ukrainealert/ukraines-powerful-interior-minister-avakov-under-fire-over-police-reform-failures/. Accessed in September 2025.

5.17)   Pyatt, Geoffrey. "U.S. Embassy Kyiv Ukraine." 2022. Facebook.com. 2022.
        https://www.facebook.com/usdos.ukraine/posts/10153248488506936?paipv=
        0&eav=AfYSlmcnKZxNQNqBMpWqyaYBnDJ7C_ByEsTsm4bWUajo-
        FWfymfxHqEkWCtLC4fnPkY&_rdr. Accessed in September 2025.

5.18)   Boswell, Josh. 2023. "EXCLUSIVE: Hunter Biden Helped Devise Plan to
        'Close Down' Viktor Shokin's Investigation into Burisma, Emails Reveal."
        Mail Online. Daily Mail. August 29, 2023.
        https://www.dailymail.co.uk/news/article-12453245/Emails-Hunter-Biden-
        tried-help-shut-Burisma-probe.html. Accessed in September 2025.

5.19)   Levine, Jon. 2022. "Exclusive | Hunter Biden Met with Dad Immediately after
        Romanian Business Meetings." New York Post. August 13, 2022.
        https://nypost.com/2022/08/13/hunter-biden-met-with-dad-immediately-after-
        romanian-business-meetings/. Accessed in September 2025.

CHAPTER 6 NOTES

6.1)   Savitsky, Alexander. "Biden urged Kiev to end its dependence on Russia."
        DW.COM. January 16, 2017. https://www.dw.com/ru/прощальный-визит-
        байден-призвал-киев-покончить-с-зависимостью-от-россии/a-37147959.
        Accessed in September 2025.

6.2)   Biden, Joseph "Remarks by Vice President Joe Biden with Ukrainian President
        Petro Poroshenko." 2017. Whitehouse.gov. Whitehouse. January 17, 2017.
        https://obamawhitehouse.archives.gov/the-press-office/2017/01/17/remarks-
        vice-president-joe-biden-ukrainian-president-petro-poroshenko. Accessed in
        September 2025.

6.3)   Biden, Joseph R., Jr, and Michael Carpenter. 2020. "How to Stand up to the
        Kremlin." foreignaffairs.com. April 16, 2020.
        https://www.foreignaffairs.com/articles/russia-fsu/2017-12-05/how-stand-
        kremlin. Accessed in September 2025.

6.4)   Crilly, Rob. 2019. "Joe Biden Visited Ukraine Six Times in Eight Years While
        Vice President." Washington Examiner. October 10, 2019.
        https://www.washingtonexaminer.com/news/joe-biden-visited-ukraine-six-
        times-in-eight-years-while-vice-president. Accessed in September 2025.

6.5)   Cheney, Dick. "Remarks by Vice President Cheney and President Yushchenko
        of Ukraine after Meeting." Transcript of speech given at Kiev, Ukraine
        September 5, 2008. https://georgewbush-
        whitehouse.archives.gov/news/releases/2008/09/20080905-3.html. Accessed
        in September 2025.

6.6)   Reuters Screen Ocean. "Ukraine: United States Vice President Al Gore Visits
        Kiev and Meets Newly Elected Ukrainian President Leonid Kuchma."
        August 2, 1994. Reuters video, 1:36,
        https://reuters.screenocean.com/record/337976. Accessed in September 2025.

6.7)   Gore, Al "Remarks at Chornobyl National Museum." Transcript of speech
        given at Chornobyl National Museum – Kiev, Ukraine on July 23, 1998.
        https://clintonwhitehouse3.archives.gov/WH/EOP/OVP/speeches/chornobyl.
        html. Accessed in September 2025.

6.8)   Biden, Joseph and Poroshenko, Petro. November 14, 2014. Review of
        "Statements to the Press by Vice President Biden and Ukrainian President
        Petro Poroshenko." Press conference at Kiev, Ukraine.
        https://obamawhitehouse.archives.gov/the-press-
        office/2014/11/21/statements-press-vice-president-biden-and-ukrainian-
        president-petro-poro. Accessed in September 2025.

6.9)   Gehrke, Laurenz. 2022. "Former German Chancellor Schröder Nominated for
        Gazprom Board." Politico. February 4, 2022.
        https://www.politico.eu/article/outrage-germany-ex-chancellor-schroder-
        gazprom-board-nomination/. Accessed in September 2025.

6.10)   United States Committee on Oversight and Government Reform. December 4,
        2020. "The Bidens' Influence Peddling Timeline."
        https://oversight.house.gov/the-bidens-influence-peddling-timeline/.
        Accessed in September 2025.

6.11)   United States Senate Committee on Homeland Security and Governmental
        Affairs and United States Senate Committee on Finance. October 2015.
        "Hunter Biden, Burisma, and Corruption: The Impact on U.S. Government
        Policy and Related Concerns."
        https://www.hsgac.senate.gov/imo/media/doc/HSGAC_Finance_Report_FIN
        AL.pdf. Accessed in September 2025.

6.12)   Vogel, Kenneth. December 16, 2020 (last updated). "Rosemont Seneca Bohai
        Bank Records Listing Payments From Burisma & To Hunter Biden (2014-
        2016)." The New York Times. Compiled report created on May 14, 2019.
        https://www.documentcloud.org/documents/6003585-Rosemont-Seneca-
        Bohai-Bank-Records-Listing/. Accessed in September 2025.

6.13)   Miller, Joshua Rhett. 2020. "Court Reinstates Fraud, Conspiracy Convictions
        of Ex-Hunter Biden Associate." New York Post. October 9, 2020.
        https://nypost.com/2020/10/09/federal-appeals-court-reinstates-convictions-
        for-hunter-bidens-ex-business-partner/. Accessed in September 2025.

6.14)   "Biography." n.d. Ron Johnson Senator from Wisconsin.
        https://www.ronjohnson.senate.gov/biography.

6.15)   "Biography." 2014. Www.grassley.senate.gov. Dece Accessed in September
        2025.mber 5, 2014. https://www.grassley.senate.gov/about/biography.

6.16) KCRG. 2020. "Senate Committees Release Report on Hunter Biden Conflicts of Interest Investigation." Https://Www.kcrg.com. KCRG. September 23, 2020. https://www.kcrg.com/2020/09/23/senate-committees-release-report-on-hunter-biden-conflicts-of-interest-investigation/. Accessed in September 2025.

6.17) Carney, Jordain. 2020. "Ron Johnson Vows to Force Burisma-Related Subpoena Vote amid Dem Opposition." The Hill. March 9, 2020. https://thehill.com/policy/national-security/486616-ron-johnson-vows-to-force-burisma-related-subpoena-vote-amid-dem/. Accessed in September 2025.

6.18) Schulz, Jacob, and Margaret Taylor. 2020. "What to Make of the Johnson-Grassley Report on Biden and Burisma." Lawfare. 2020. https://www.lawfaremedia.org/article/what-make-johnson-grassley-report-biden-and-burisma. Accessed in September 2025.

6.19) Jacobs, Emily, and Bruce Golding. 2020. "Senate Republicans Release Explosive Report on Hunter Biden, Burisma." New York Post. September 23, 2020. https://nypost.com/2020/09/23/gop-senators-release-explosive-report-on-hunter-biden-burisma/. Accessed in September 2025.

6.20) Mascaro, Lisa. 2024. "Hunter Biden's Years of Personal Grief and Public Missteps Are Focus of House Impeachment Probe." AP News. February 27, 2024. https://apnews.com/article/hunter-biden-impeachment-investigation-congress-testimony-republicans-3b5573341b260713c2a637df24edf5fc. Accessed in September 2025.

6.21) Levine, Jon. 2022. "Exclusive | Who Is Eric Schwerin? What to Know about Hunter Biden's Business Partner." New York Post. April 30, 2022. https://nypost.com/2022/04/30/who-is-eric-schwerin-what-to-know-about-hunter-bidens-business-partner/. Accessed in September 2025.

6.22) Winter, Tom. 2020. "Email to Hunter Biden Raises Fresh Questions about His Tax Dealings." NBC News. December 11, 2020. https://www.nbcnews.com/politics/politics-news/email-hunter-biden-raises-fresh-questions-about-his-tax-dealings-n1250973. Accessed in September 2025.

6.23) Jansen, Bart. 2020. "Hunter Biden's Taxes under Investigation by US Attorney's Office in Delaware." USA TODAY. December 9, 2020. https://www.usatoday.com/story/news/politics/2020/12/09/hunter-bidens-taxes-under-investigation-u-s-attorneys-office/3869793001/. Accessed in September 2025.

6.24) Kerr, Andrew. 2019. "Investigation: Hunter Biden Had IRS Lien for $113k in Unpaid Taxes during Time on Burisma Board." The National Interest. December 30, 2019. https://nationalinterest.org/blog/buzz/investigation-hunter-biden-had-irs-lien-113k-unpaid-taxes-during-time-burisma-board-109481. Accessed in September 2025.

6.25)   Linton, Caroline. 2024. "Read Hunter Biden's Pardon and President Biden's Full Statement." Cbsnews.com. CBS News. December 2, 2024. https://www.cbsnews.com/news/hunter-biden-pardon-joe-biden-statement/. Accessed in September 2025.

6.26)   CBC News. "The real impact of Joe Biden's pardon of his son Hunter | About That." December 2, 2024. YouTube video, 08:39. https://youtu.be/vva46CoTkpQ?si=9xB8YsuGJtN7iaHz/. Accessed in September 2025.

6.27)   Fox News. "'LEGAL JEOPARDY': 'Unprecedented' details surrounding Biden autopen investigation." September 6, 2025. YouTube video, 04:09. https://youtu.be/iY2QaaYEfCM?si=fmWaeMLtP7_IP_n8. Accessed in September 2025.

6.28)   Real America's Voice. "EXPLOSIVE NEW DOCUMENTS THAT EXPOSE BIDEN'S AUTOPEN USE." September 5, 2025. YouTube video. 00:56. https://youtu.be/s4E-vMTjosc?si=mHhkReBP_o44Bof1. Accessed in September 2025.

6.29)   "Email View | BidenLaptopEmails Terminal." 2016. Bidenlaptopemails.com. 2016. https://bidenlaptopemails.com/biden-emails/email.php?id=20160413-190117_57558. Accessed in September 2025.

6.30)   Christenson, Josh. 2025. "Hunter Biden Begged DNC to Pay His Legal Fees for Tax, Gun Cases: New Book." New York Post. July 4, 2025. https://nypost.com/2025/07/04/us-news/hunter-biden-begged-dnc-to-pay-his-legal-fees-for-tax-gun-cases-new-tome/. Accessed in September 2025.

Chapter 7 Notes

7.1)   Wolfe, Robert L. , ed. 1976. "All the President's Men." Film. Directed by Alan J. Pakula. United States: Warner Bros.

7.2)   Solomon, John. "Latvia Flagged 'Suspicious' Hunter Biden Payments in 2016." 2016. Just the News. 2016. https://justthenews.com/accountability/political-ethics/latvia-flagged-suspicious-hunter-biden-payments-2016. Accessed in September 2025.

7.3)   Colen, Aaron. 2019. "Latvia Was Investigating 'Suspicious' Payments to Hunter Biden, Burisma in Potential Laundering Scheme: Report." Blaze Media. December 17, 2019. https://www.theblaze.com/news/latvia-was-investigating-suspicious-payments-to-hunter-biden-burisma-in-potential-laundering-scheme-report. Accessed in September 2025.

7.4)   Committee on Oversight and Government Control. May 25, 2022. "Comer Probes Hunter Biden's Suspicious Foreign Business Transactions Flagged by U.S. Banks." https://oversight.house.gov/release/comer-probes-hunter-bidens-suspicious-foreign-business-transactions-flagged-by-u-s-banks/. Accessed in September 2025.

7.5)   Vogel, Kenneth. December 16, 2020 (last updated). "Rosemont Seneca Bohai
        Bank Records Listing Payments From Burisma & To Hunter Biden (2014-
        2016)." The New York Times. Compiled report created on May 14, 2019.
        https://www.documentcloud.org/documents/6003585-Rosemont-Seneca-
        Bohai-Bank-Records-Listing/. Accessed in September 2025

7.6)   "Unnamed Witness Testimony." Unpublished. Prosecutor General's Office of
        Ukraine. (Testimony of Anonymous testimony of a person who provided
        Zlochevsky with services for legalizing money through Latvian banks and
        companies).

7.7)   State Financial Monitoring Service of Ukraine. "Summary material No.
        0145/2016/DSK of the State Financial Monitoring Service of Ukraine."
        Publication date Unknown. (Evidence to criminal case No.
        4201400000000159)

CHAPTER 8 NOTES

8.1)   "Russia's Actions 'a Land Grab.'" March 18, 2014. Dw.com. Deutsche 2025.
        Welle. https://www.dw.com/en/biden-russias-actions-in-crimea-nothing-
        more-than-a-land-grab/a-17503768. Accessed in September 2025.

8.2)   Whalen, Jessica. 2014. "Rookie CEO Takes Over Ukraine Gas Monopoly."
        March 28, 2014. The Wall Street Journal. 2014.
        https://www.wsj.com/articles/SB10001424052702304688104579467610934
        906866?msockid=1ea70dc7d9d56bd918071874d83b6a30. Accessed in
        September 2025.

8.3)   Naftogaz. 2014. "Naftogaz Urges Expansion of Slovakia-Ukraine Gas
        Transmission Interconnector Capacity." October 22, 2014. Euro-Petrole.com.
        2025. https://www.euro-petrole.com/naftogaz-urges-expansion-of-slovakia-
        ukraine-gas-transmission-interconnector-capacity-n-i-10375. Accessed in
        September 2025.

8.4)   Ukraine. Verkhovna Rada. Law of Ukraine About the Natural Gas Market.
        April 9, 2015 adopted. No. 329-VIII.
        https://cis-legislation.com/document.fwx?rgn=75452. Accessed in September
        2025.

8.5)   Belyakova, Olega. 2016. "Ukraine: Establishment of Independent Supervisory
        Boards in State-Owned Companies." November 18, 2016. Cms-
        Lawnow.com. CMS Law-Now. 2016. https://cms-
        lawnow.com/en/ealerts/2016/11/ukraine-establishment-of-independent-
        supervisory-boards-in-state-owned-companies. Accessed in September 2025.

8.6)   Venk. Victoria. 2020. "How Biden ruled Ukraine. Full text of Poroshenko's
        scandalous tapes." Archive.org. Strana.ua. May 19, 2020.
        https://strana.news/news/268104-bajden-i-poroshenko-stenohramma-vsekh-
        zapisej-video-i-tekst.html#google_vignette. Accessed in September 2025.

8.7)   Ukraine. Verkhovna Rada. On Amendments to Certain Legislative Acts of Ukraine Regarding the Management of State-Owned Property. Commercial Code. September 9, 2015 draft. No. 3062. https://rpr.org.ua/en/draft-laws/3062-en/. Accessed in September 2025.

8.8)   Naftogaz Group. 2021. "About Naftogaz Group." 2021. Naftogaz.com. https://www.naftogaz.com/en/about-naftogaz. Accessed in September 2025.

8.9)   Wikipedia Contributors. "Overview | Naftogaz Ukraine." n.d. wikiwandland.com. https://www.wikiwand.com/en/articles/Naftogaz. Accessed in September 2025.

8.10)   Kitsoft. 2016. "Cabinet of Ministers of Ukraine - Supervisory Boards to Supervise Activity of State-Owned Enterprises instead of Ministries." Kmu.gov.ua. February 19, 2016. https://www.kmu.gov.ua/en/news/248843712. Accessed in September 2025.

8.11)   Ukrinform. 2019. "Sevki Acuner, Chairman of Supervisory Board of JSC 'Ukrainian Railways.'" Ukrinform.net. Укрінформ. February 15, 2019. https://www.ukrinform.net/rubric-economy/2641162-sevki-acuner-chairman-of-supervisory-board-of-jsc-ukrainian-railways.html. Accessed in September 2025.

8.12)   Interfax-Ukraine. 2016. "Ex-Head of IMF Strauss-Kahn, Economists Aslund, Saltiel Become Members of Supervisory Board of Pinchuk's Bank Credit-Dnepr." Interfax-Ukraine. February 3, 2016. https://en.interfax.com.ua/news/economic/322067.html. Accessed in September 2025.

8.13)   Naftogaz. "Amos Hochstein Leaves Naftogaz Supervisory Board | Naftogaz Ukraine." 2020. Naftogaz.com. October 12, 2020. https://www.naftogaz.com/en/news/amos-hohshtayn-zalyshae-naglyadovu-radu-nak-naftogaz-ukrainy. Accessed in September 2025.

8.14)   Wikipedia Contributors. 2025. "Amos Hochstein." Wikipedia. Wikimedia Foundation. August 25, 2025. https://en.wikipedia.org/wiki/Amos_Hochstein. Accessed in September 2025

8.15)   Sun, Lena H. 2006. "A CONVERSATION with AMOS HOCHSTEIN Interview by Michael Grunwald." The Washington Post. April 23, 2006. https://www.washingtonpost.com/archive/opinions/2006/04/23/a-conversation-with-amos-hochstein-interview-by-michael-grunwald/eaef2aa4-909d-4407-9fc6-d92a2b39c8a3/. Accessed in September 2025.

8.16)   Raymond, Adam K. 2019. "Everything We Know about the Joe Biden–Ukraine Controversy." Intelligencer. May 7, 2019. https://nymag.com/intelligencer/2019/05/joe-biden-ukraine-controversy.html. Accessed in September 2025.

8.17) Naftogaz. "Andrew Favorov Resigns as Head of Naftogaz Integrated Gas Business Unit | Naftogaz Ukraine." 2020. Naftogaz.com. April 2020. https://www.naftogaz.com/en/news/andriy-favorov-zalyshae-post-dyrektora-z-integrovanogo-gazovogo-biznesu-naftogazu. Accessed in September 2025.

8.18) Сташинський Яків. 2020. "Poroshenko Boasted to Biden That He Had Raised Tariffs by 100% instead of the Required 75%, – a Record of Conversation Was Made Public." Ukrainian News. May 19, 2020. https://ukranews.com/en/news/703227-poroshenko-boasted-to-biden-that-he-had-raised-tariffs-by-100-instead-of-the-required-75-a-record. Accessed in September 2025.

8.19) Energy Resources of Ukraine. "ERU Trading." 2016. Eru.com.ua. 2016. https://eru.com.ua/en/press_centr/news/eru_trading_s_first_billion/. Accessed in September 2025.

8.20) Interfax-Ukraine. 2017. "US Company Is Sole Private Supplier to Ukrainian State-Owned Ukratransgaz." Interfax-Ukraine. December 13, 2017. https://en.interfax.com.ua/news/press-release/469598.html. Accessed in September 2025.

8.21) bne IntelliNews. 2025. "Interview: Ukraine's Gas Traders Open Taps on a Brighter Future." Intellinews.com. 2025. https://www.intellinews.com/interview-ukraine-s-gas-traders-open-taps-on-a-brighter-future-107703/. Accessed in September 2025.

8.22) The White House Office of the Vice President. 2016. "Readout of Vice President Biden's Call with President Petro Poroshenko of Ukraine." December 19, 2016. https://obamawhitehouse.archives.gov/the-press-office/2016/12/19/readout-vice-president-bidens-call-president-petro-poroshenko-ukraine. Accessed in September 2025.

8.23) "'Save our asses.' Full transcript of the new Biden-Poroshenko tapes." 2020. Sumy.ua. 2020. https://debaty.sumy.ua/ukraine-and-world-news/spasti-nashi-zadnitsy-polnaya-rasshifrovka-novyh-plenok-bajdena-poroshenko. Accessed in September 2025.

8.24) "ERU Trading Dropped Twofold in Power Exports in 1H of 2018 - to 27.3 Mil KWh — EXPRO Consulting." 2018. Expro.com.ua. 2018. https://expro.com.ua/en/tidings/eru-trading-dropped-twofold-in-power-exports-in-1h-of-2018-to-273-mil-kwh. Accessed in September 2025.

CHAPTER 9 NOTES

9.1) U.S. Agency for International Development (USAID). "ABOUT USAID PROJECT - Municipal Energy Reform Project in Ukraine (MERP)." 2018. Merp.org.ua. 2018. https://merp.org.ua/us/layout-2.html. Accessed in September 2025.

9.2) Markey, E., Wayden, R., Shaheen, J. & Murphy, C. Letter to Obama, Barack. June 27, 2014. Washington, D.C. U.S.A. Media Collection of Senator Markey. United States Senate. https://www.markey.senate.gov/imo/media/doc/2014-06-27_PresidentObama_Ukraine_energy.pdf . Accessed in September 2025.

9.3) Payne, Daniel & Solomon, John. "Hunter Biden's Ukraine Firm Landed Deal with USAID Program While under Corruption Investigation." 2020. Just the News. 2020. https://justthenews.com/accountability/russia-and-ukraine-scandals/ukraine-official-implicated-6-million-burisma-bribe. Accessed in September 2025.

9.4) "Memorandum of Understanding," signed 13 October 2014, between The Municipal Energy Reform Project of Ukraine (MERP) and Burisma Holdings Limited, located in the U.S. Agency for International Development (USAID) internal records. https://justthenews.com/sites/default/files/2020-06/DoSMERPBurismaMOU.pdf. Accessed in September 2025.

9.5) Schwartz, Eric P. (U.S. Assistant Secretary, Bureau of Population, Refugees, and Migration) teleconference with Frist, Bill (U.S. Senator) and Smith, Gayle (Special Assistant to the President Gayle). 2011. "Briefing on Dr. Jill Biden's Recent Visit to Kenya." August 11, 2011. Washington D.C. https://2009-2017.state.gov/j/prm/releases/remarks/2011/181085.htm. Accessed in September 2025.

9.6) U.S. Agency for International Development (USAID). "Winners of Journalist Contest Rewarded in Kyiv - Municipal Energy Reform Project in Ukraine (MERP)." 2015. Merp.org.ua. 2015. https://merp.org.ua/us/for-media/80-articles-eng/194-winners-of-journalist-contest-rewarded-in-kyiv.html. Accessed in September 2025.

9.7) "About Ed." n.d. Senator Ed Markey. https://www.markey.senate.gov/about.3. Accessed in September 2025.

9.8) Reuters Staff. 2014. "Bill Would Boost Ukraine's Energy Efficiency, Drilling." Reuters, June 5, 2014. https://www.reuters.com/article/world/us-politics/bill-would-boost-ukraines-energy-efficiency-drilling-idUSKBN0EG2KY/. Accessed in September 2025.

9.9) Ron Wyden. 2014. "Wyden on Ukraine in Senate Energy Hearing." March 25, 2014. YouTube video, 06:02. https://youtu.be/7ByvJlepT5g?si=U34kWDjj3-qoIy3Y. Accessed in September 2025.

9.10) "Senate Passes Markey Bill to Help Ukraine Withstand Energy Crunch, Become More Energy Efficient | U.S. Senator Ed Markey of Massachusetts." 2014. Senate.gov. Edward Markey. December 11, 2014. https://www.markey.senate.gov/news/press-releases/senate-passes-markey-bill-to-help-ukraine-withstand-energy-crunch-become-more-energy-efficient. Accessed in September 2025.

9.11)   United States Senate (113TH Congress 2D Session). 2014 "Ukrainian
        Independence from Russian Energy Act" (MRW14373 SLC). December 11m
        2014. https://www.markey.senate.gov//imo/media/doc/2014-06-
        05_UkraineBill_Energy_Markey.pdf. Accessed in September 2025. Accessed
        in September 2025.

9.12)   RTI International. 2025. "Paul Weisenfeld." Rti.org. January 9, 2025.
        https://www.rti.org/expert/paul-weisenfeld. https://www.rti.org/expert/paul-
        weisenfeld. Accessed in September 2025.

9.13)   Weisenfeld, P. (2011). Successes and challenges of the Haiti earthquake
        response: The experience of USAID. Emory International Law Review,
        25(3), 1097-1120. http://law.emory.edu/eilr/content/volume-25/issue-
        3/symposium/index.html. Accessed in September 2025.

9.14)   Beeton, Dan. 2022. "Press Release: Twelve Years After Haiti's Devastating
        Earthquake, New Report Recommends Key USAID Reforms." January 12,
        2022. Center for Economic and Policy Research.
        https://cepr.net/newsroom/twelve-years-after-haitis-devastating-earthquake-
        new-report-recommends-key-usaid-reforms/. Accessed in September 2025.

9.15)   U.S. International Development Finance Corporation. "Paul Weisenfeld |
        DFC." 2025. Dfc.gov. 2025. https://www.dfc.gov/who-we-are/development-
        accountability-council-dac/paul-weisenfeld. Accessed in September 2025.

9.16)   Devine, Miranda. 2021. "Exclusive | Hunter Biden Brought vp Joe to Dinner
        with Shady Business Partners." New York Post. May 26, 2021.
        https://nypost.com/2021/05/26/hunter-biden-arranged-secret-dinner-with-
        business-partners-and-vp-joe/. Accessed in September 2025.

9.17)   The Eisenhower School. "People." 2025. Ndu.edu. 2025.
        https://es.ndu.edu/People/Academic-Faculty/FacBio/Article/3246524/mr-
        stephen-gonyea. Accessed in September 2025.

9.18)   Kent, George (U.S. Deputy Assistant Secretary of State) "interview with"
        Committee on Homeland Security and Governmental Affairs, and
        Committee on Finance (U.S. Senate). July 24, 2020.
        https://www.hsgac.senate.gov/wp-
        content/uploads/imo/media/doc/HSGAC_Finance_Report_FINAL.pdf.
        Accessed in September 2025.

9.19)   Brown, Nick. "Foreign Assistance: Where Does the Money Go?" 2025.
        Congress.gov. 2025. https://www.congress.gov/crs-product/R48150.
        Accessed in September 2025.

9.20)   FD-1023. 2020. "First Meeting with Burisma Executives in Kyiv, Ukraine
        201S/2016." (Unclassified by Senator Chuck Grassley). June 30, 2020.
        https://www.grassley.senate.gov/imo/media/doc/fd_1023_obtained_by_senat
        or_grassley_-_biden.pdf. Accessed in September 2025.

9.21) "Grassley Obtains & Releases FBI Record Alleging vp Biden Foreign Bribery Scheme | U.S. Senator Chuck Grassley of Iowa." 2023. Senate.gov. Chuck Grassley. July 20, 2023. https://www.grassley.senate.gov/news/news-releases/grassley-obtains-and-releases-fbi-record-alleging-vp-biden-foreign-bribery-scheme. Accessed in September 2025.

9.22) United States House Committee on Oversight and Government Reform. 2023. "Comer Demands Suspicious Activity Reports Related to Burisma and Alleged Biden Bribery Scheme." United States House Committee on Oversight and Government Reform. October 2, 2023. https://oversight.house.gov/release/comer-demands-suspicious-activity-reports-related-to-burisma-and-alleged-biden-bribery-scheme%ef%bf%bc/.. Accessed in September 2025.

9.23) Raskin, Jamie. 2023. "Fact v. Fiction: FBI FORM FD-1023." United States House Committee on Oversight and Accountability Democrats Ranking Member. n.d. https://oversightdemocrats.house.gov/sites/evo-subsites/democrats-oversight.house.gov/files/FD-1023%20Fact%20Sheet%20FINAL%20PDF.pdf. Accessed in September 2025.

9.24) Research Triangle Institute. Enhancing Ukraine's Energy Security through Municipal Energy Efficiency. (2019, March 5). Rti.org. https://www.rti.org/impact/enhancing-ukraine-energy-security-municipal-efficiency. Accessed in September 2025.

9.25) Grayer, Annie, Marshall Cohen, and Jeremy Herb. 2023. "Grassley Releases Internal FBI Document about Unverified Biden Bribery Allegations." CNN. July 20, 2023. https://edition.cnn.com/2023/07/20/politics/chuck-grassley-fbi-document. Accessed in September 2025.

9.26) Cabinet of Ministers of Ukraine. August 5, 2015. "Resolution No. 553: On Amendments to the Procedure for Attracting, Using and Monitoring International Technical Assistance." https://zakon.rada.gov.ua/laws/show/553-2015-%D0%BF#n2. Accessed in September 2025.

9.27) 15 min. 2015. "Former Head of Price Commission Diana Korskayte: There are Those Who Think I Should Not Work in Lithuania." January 21, 2015. 15.min.it. https://www.15min.lt/verslas/naujiena/bendroves/diana-korsakaite-yra-mananciu-kad-netureciau-dirbti-lietuvoje-663-480036. Accessed in September 2025.

9.28) Kent, George (U.S. Deputy Assistant Secretary of State) "interview with" Permanent Select Committee on Intelligence, Committee on Oversight and Reform, and Committee on Foreign Affairs (U.S. House of Representatives). October 15, 2019. https://d3i6fh83elv35t.cloudfront.net/static/2019/11/Kenttranscript.pdf. Accessed in September 2025.

9.29)   Levine, Jon. 2021. "Exclusive | Biden Hired Rosemont Seneca Employee to
         His Private vp Office Staff." New York Post. May 29, 2021.
         https://nypost.com/2021/05/29/biden-hired-rosemont-seneca-employee-to-
         private-vp-office/. Accessed in September 2025.

9.30)   Solomon, John. 2019. "Solomon: These Once-Secret Memos Cast Doubt on
         Joe Biden's Ukraine Story." The Hill. September 26, 2019.
         https://thehill.com/opinion/campaign/463307-solomon-these-once-secret-
         memos-cast-doubt-on-joe-bidens-ukraine-story/. Accessed in September
         2025.

9.31)   Kent, George (U.S. Deputy Assistant Secretary of State) "interview with"
         Permanent Select Committee on Intelligence, Committee on Oversight and
         Reform, and Committee on Foreign Affairs (U.S. House of Representatives).
         October 15, 2019.
         https://d3i6fh83elv35t.cloudfront.net/static/2019/11/Kenttranscript.pdf.
         Accessed in September 2025.

CHAPTER 10 NOTES

10.1)   Oprysko, Caitlin & Lippman, Daniel. 2022. "Blue Star Registers Retroactively
         for Burisma Work." POLITICO. May 17, 2022.
         https://www.politico.com/newsletters/politico-influence/2022/05/17/blue-
         star-registers-retroactively-for-burisma-work-00033202. Accessed in
         September 2025.

10.2)   Grassley, Chuck. "Grassley, Johnson to DOJ: Did Burisma's U.S. Lobbying
         Firm File Misleading Information on Foreign Agent Form? | U.S. Senator
         Chuck Grassley of Iowa." 2022. Senate.gov. Chuck Grassley. May 24, 2022.
         https://www.grassley.senate.gov/news/news-releases/grassley-johnson-to-
         doj-did-burismas-us-lobbying-firm-file-misleading-information-on-foreign-
         agent-form. Accessed in September 2025.

10.3)   Quinn, Ben. 2019. "Tim Bell, Margaret Thatcher's Spin Doctor, Dies at 77."
         The Guardian. The Guardian. August 26, 2019.
         https://www.theguardian.com/media/2019/aug/26/tim-bell-margaret-
         thatchers-spin-doctor-dies-at-77. Accessed in September 2025.

10.4)   Gaffey, Conor. 2017. "The Pentagon, Pinochet, and Assad: Bell Pottinger's
         Most Controversial Clients." Newsweek. September 13, 2017.
         https://www.newsweek.com/bell-pottinger-pentagon-al-qaeda-south-africa-
         assad-664180. Accessed in September 2025.

10.5)   Erielle Azerrad. 2019. "Top Romney Adviser Worked with Hunter Biden on Board of Ukrainian Energy Company." The Federalist. September 26, 2019. https://thefederalist.com/2019/09/26/top-romney-adviser-worked-with-hunter-biden-on-board-of-ukrainian-energy-company/. Accessed in September 2025.

10.6)   "Blue Star Strategies | the Firm." 2018. Bluestarstrategies.com. 2018. https://bluestarstrategies.com/the-firm/#thefirm-about. Accessed in September 2025.

10.7)   Jordon, Jim (U.S. House of Representatives Chairman Committee on the Judiciary) and Comer, James (U.S. House of Representatives Chairman Committee on Oversight and Accountability) Letter to Tramontano, Karen A. (C hief Executive Officer Blue Star Strategies, LLC). November 29, 2023. Congress of the United States. Washington D.C. https://judiciary.house.gov/sites/evo-subsites/republicans-judiciary.house.gov/files/evo-media-document/2023-11-29-jdj-jc-to-tramontano-blue-star-strategies-re-ti-request.pdf. Accessed in September 2025.

10.8)   Otten, T., Otten, T., Houghtaling, E. Q., Otten, T., Otten, T., Houghtaling, E. Q., Houghtaling, E. Q., Houghtaling, E. Q., Otten, T., & Otten, T. (2024, March 26). James Comer Finally Admits Defeat in His Biden Impeachment Crusade. The New Republic. https://newrepublic.com/post/180126/james-comer-admits-defeat-biden-impeachment. Accessed in September 2025.

10.9)   "Burisma закрыла сделку о покупке сервисной компании 'Геоюнит.'" 2020. Enkorr.ua. 2020. https://enkorr.ua/ru/news/burisma_zakryla_sdelku_o_pokupke_servisnoy_ko mpanii_geoyunit/241536. Accessed in September 2025.

10.10)   Boswell, Josh. 2025. "DOJ Forced Top Lawyer to Register as Foreign Agent for Burisma...But Not Hunter Biden, Bombshell Files Reveal." Mail Online. Daily Mail. June 27, 2025. https://www.dailymail.co.uk/news/article-14851247/doj-lawyer-forced-register-foreign-agent-burisma-hunter-biden.html. Accessed in September 2025.

10.11)   Ackley, Kate, and Justin Wise. 2024. "Cravath Reveals Work for Ukraine Entities Tied to Hunter Biden." @BLaw. January 5, 2024. https://news.bloomberglaw.com/business-and-practice/cravath-reveals-work-for-ukraine-entities-tied-to-hunter-biden. Accessed in September 2025.

10.12)   United States Department of Justice, Form NSD-1 Revised 10/23: Registration Statement Pursuant to the Foreign Agents Registration Act of 1938, as amended (filing for John Buretta on Behalf Craveth, Swaine & Moore on January 4, 2024) LLP https://efile.fara.gov/docs/7358-Registration-Statement-20240104-1.pdf. Accessed in September 2025.

10.13) Buretta, John (Craveth,Swain and Moore LLP) Letter to Yovanovitch, Marie.
        September 15, 2016. Document Cloud Legacy.
        https://www.documentcloud.org/documents/6937275-In-a-Letter-to-
        Ambassador-Yovanovitch-Burisma-s/. Accessed in September 2025.

10.14) Rojas, Francisco. 2016. "Burisma Group & Prince Albert II of Monaco
        Foundation Announce Event: 'Energy Security for the Future.'" Think
        GeoEnergy - Geothermal Energy News. ThinkGeoEnergy. April 21, 2016.
        https://www.thinkgeoenergy.com/burisma-group-prince-albert-ii-of-monaco-
        foundation-announce-event-energy-security-for-the-future/. Accessed in
        September 2025.

10.15) "Electric Marathon 2015 | Kiev - Monte-Carlo | 03.06-10.06.2015 | Route
        Map." 2015. Ukraine-Kiev-Tour.com. 2015. https://ukraine-kiev-
        tour.com/electric-marathon-2015-kiev-monte-carlo.html. Accessed in
        September 2025.

CHAPTER 11 NOTES

11.1)   Olivier, Berruyer. Dir. 2020. UkraineGate – Inconvenient Facts, Documentary
        Video Series. Released January 13, 2020-February 17, 2020 on   Les-Cres.Fr
        & Consortium News. https://consortiumnews.com/2020/02/17/part-four-of-
        ukrainegate-inconvenient-facts/. Accessed in September 2025.

11.2)   Carroll, Oliver. 2019. "Viktor Shokin: The inside Story on Ukraine's 'Very
        Good' Prosecutor at Centre of Trump Scandal | the Independent." The
        Independent. October 9, 2019.
        https://www.independent.co.uk/news/world/europe/viktor-shokin-ukraine-
        prosecutor-trump-biden-hunter-joe-investigation-impeachment-
        a9147001.html. Accessed in September 2025.

11.3)   Pyatt, Geoffrey. "U.S. Embassy Kyiv Ukraine." 2022. Facebook.com. 2022.
        https://www.facebook.com/usdos.ukraine/posts/10153248488506936?paipv=
        0&eav=AfYSlmcnKZxNQNqBMpWqyaYBnDJ7C_ByEsTsm4bWUajo-
        FWfymfxHqEkWCtLC4fnPkY&_rdr. Accessed in September 2025.

11.4)   Torkington, Patrick (International Affairs at the National Crime Agency British
        Embassy in Ukraine) "correspondence to" Main Investigation Department of
        the Prosecutor General's Office. September 23, 2015. Accessed in September
        2025.

11.5)   "Bulletproof Glass Saves Ukraine's Top Prosecutor." 2015. Sky News. Sky.
        November 3, 2015. https://news.sky.com/story/bulletproof-glass-saves-
        ukraines-top-prosecutor-10340887. Accessed in September 2025.

11.6)   Poroshenko, Petro (President of Ukraine) "telephone conversation with" Kerry,
        John (United Sates Secretary of State). December 2015.[phone records].

11.7)   Cawthorne, Jessica and Cameron Chasmar. 2023. "Burisma's Devon Archer
          Met with Then-Secretary of State Kerry Just Weeks before Shokin Was
          Fired." Fox News. August 27, 2023.
          https://www.foxnews.com/politics/burismas-devon-archer-met-secretary-
          state-kerry-weeks-before-shokin-fired. Accessed in September 2025.

11.8)   Clemons, Steve. 2016. "The Biden Doctrine." The Atlantic. August 22, 2016.
          https://www.theatlantic.com/international/archive/2016/08/biden-
          doctrine/496841/. Accessed in September 2025.

11.9)   Council on Foreign Relations. "Joe Biden on Defending Democracy." Council
          of Foreign Relations Conference Washington D.C., streamed live on January
          23, 2018. YouTube video. 59:49.
          https://www.youtube.com/live/Q0_AqpdwqK4?si=TMDe4tLTR4HNgIvE.
          Accessed in September 2025.

11.10)   Hudson, John, Rachael Bade, and Matt Viser. 2019. "Diplomat Tells
          Investigators He Raised Alarms in 2015 about Hunter Biden's Ukraine Work
          but Was Rebuffed." The Washington Post. October 18, 2019.
          https://www.washingtonpost.com/politics/diplomat-tells-investigators-he-
          raised-alarms-in-2015-about-hunter-bidens-ukraine-work-but-was-
          rebuffed/2019/10/18/81e35be9-4f5a-4048-8520-0baabb18ab63_story.html.
          Accessed in September 2025.

11.11)   International Monetary Fund. "IMF Annual Report 2015." n.d. Www.imf.org.
          https://www.imf.org/external/pubs/ft/ar/2015/eng/spotlight-ukraine.htm.
          Accessed in September 2025.

11.12)   Ukraine Today. "Calling for Resignations: Ukrainian President asks Prime
          Minister & General Prosecutor to resign." http://uatoday.tv., Febuary 16,
          2016. YouTube video. 0:26. https://youtu.be/tFFxxw-
          tQk0?si=EZ6eWxgETK3nFpCB. Accessed in September 2025.

11.13)   Biden, Joe (United States Vice President) "telephone conversation with"
          Poroshenko, Petro (President of Ukraine). February 18, 2016.
          https://www.rev.com/blog/transcripts/joe-biden-leaked-call-transcript-with-
          petro-poroshenko. Accessed in September 2025.

11.14)   Volker, Kurt (U.S. Special Representative for Ukraine Negotiations) "interview
          with" Permanent Select Committee on Intelligence, Committee on Oversight
          and Committee on Foreign Affairs (U.S. House of Representatives). October
          3, 2019. https://apps.npr.org/documents/document.html?id=6540391-Kurt-
          Volker-Testimony. Accessed in September 2025.

11.15)   Sukhov, Oleg. 2016. "Onyshchenko Makes Sweeping Claims about
          Poroshenko Graft." Kyiv Post. December 9, 2016.
          https://www.kyivpost.com/post/9333. Accessed in September 2025.

11.16)   Kaleniuk, Daryna. 2018. "Zlochevsky paid to have his cases closed, says director of the Anti-Corruption Center." Channel24. February 8, 2018. https://24tv.ua/zlochekvskiy_zaplativ_shhob_yogo_spravi_buli__direktor_tsentru_protidiyi_koruptsiyi_n924178. Accessed in September 2025.

11.17)   RFE/RL. 2016. "Ukrainian President's Ally Approved for Top Prosecutor's Post." RadioFreeEurope/RadioLiberty. RFE/RL. May 12, 2016. https://www.rferl.org/a/ukraine-prosecutor-general-lutsenko-no-legal-background/27731069.html. Accessed in September 2025.

11.18)   Daria, Zubkova. 2020. "Shokin Hopes for His Reinstatement by Court as Prosecutor General." Ukrainian News. February 7, 2020. https://ukranews.com/en/news/682636-shokin-hopes-for-his-reinstatement-by-court-as-prosecutor-general. Accessed in September 2025.

11.19)   Ukrinform. 2019. "Supreme Court Rejects Shokin's Reinstatement as Prosecutor General." Ukrinform.net. Укрінформ. October 24, 2019. https://www.ukrinform.net/rubric-polytics/2805169-supreme-court-rejects-shokins-reinstatement-as-prosecutor-general.html. Accessed in September 2025.

11.20)   Viktor Mikalovych Shokin v Ukraine. 2022. Application no 77117/17, European Court of Human Rights. September 8, 2022. https://www.stradalex.eu/en/se_src_publ_jur_eur_cedh/document/echr_77114-17. Accessed in September 2025.

11.21)   Devine, Miranda. 2023. "Despite Biden's Claim, Europeans WEREN'T Trying to Oust Ukraine Prosecutor Targeting Hunter's Firm." New York Post. September 8, 2023. https://nypost.com/2023/09/08/despite-bidens-claim-europeans-werent-trying-to-oust-ukraine-prosecutor-targeting-hunters-firm/. Accessed in September 2025.

11.22)   Ilya Timtchenko. 2015. "British Court Unfreezes Accounts of Yanukovych-Era Ecology Minister Zlochevsky." Kyiv Post. January 23, 2015. https://www.kyivpost.com/post/10119. Accessed in September 2025.

11.23)   Oleg Sukhov. 2015. "Release of 'Diamond Prosecutor' Shows Fatal Flaws of Law Enforcement - Jul. 31, 2015." Kyiv Post. July 31, 2015. https://archive.kyivpost.com/kyiv-post-plus/release-of-diamond-prosecutor-shows-fatal-flaws-of-law-enforcement-394791.html. Accessed in September 2025.

11.24)   Ukraine Media Center. 2016. "Investigators on 'diamond prosecutors' case face a threat of dismissal. UCMC-24-03-16." YouTube video, 22:41. March 24, 2016. https://youtu.be/i3UhejOi6Bk?si=WGC90IvcAAPLDBi0. Accessed in September 2025.

12.1)   Kramer, Andrew. 2016. "Ukraine Ousts Viktor Shokin, Top Prosecutor, and Political Stability Hangs in the Balance," The New York Times. March 29, 2016. https://www.nytimes.com/2016/03/30/world/europe/political-stability-in-the-balance-as-ukraine-ousts-top-prosecutor.html. Accessed in September 2025.

12.2)   Guiliani, Rudy (@RudyGiuliani). "I can't believe how blind our media has become.They are blindly using the prosecutor who corruptly dismissed the cases against Biden's son and his corrupt company. There was no investigation. Where's the report? Use your common sense for those who haven't lost it. Analyze it...." September 30, 2019. https://x.com/RudyGiuliani/status/1178600915043008512. Accessed in September 2025.

12.3)   National Museum of Organized Crime and Law Enforcement. "Rudolph Giuliani." n.d. The Mob Museum. https://themobmuseum.org/notable_names/rudolph-giuliani/. Accessed in September 2025.

12.4)   Sager, Monica. 2024. "Rudy Giuliani's Relationship with Trump Officially Costs Him His Legal Career." Newsweek. September 26, 2024. https://www.newsweek.com/rudy-giuliani-disbarred-lawyer-donald-trump-relationship-1959903. Accessed in September 2025.

12.5)   Edwards, Sophie. 2017. "Trump's 'America First' Budget Slashes Foreign Aid, Multilateral Funding." Devex. March 16, 2017. https://www.devex.com/news/trump-s-america-first-budget-slashes-foreign-aid-multilateral-funding-89850. Accessed in September 2025.

12.6)   Zelenskyy, Vlodymyr (President of Ukraine) "telephone conversation with" Trump, Donald J. (President of the United States). July 25, 2019. https://www.documentcloud.org/documents/6429020-Ukraine-Transcript/?mode=document#document/p2/a526697. Accessed in September 2025.

12.7)   Face the Nation. 2021. "Rudy Giuliani on Ukraine dealings." Facebook (now Meta) video, 01:35. April 28, 2021. https://www.facebook.com/FaceTheNation/videos/rudy-giuliani-on-ukraine-dealings/1317559815297604/. Accessed in September 2025.

12.8)   Asawin Suebsaeng, and Erin Banco. 2020. "Rudy: Only '50/50' Chance I Worked with a 'Russian Spy' to Dig Dirt on Bidens and Ukraine." The Daily Beast. October 17, 2020. https://www.thedailybeast.com/rudy-giuliani-says-theres-only-5050-chance-i-worked-with-a-russian-spy-to-dig-dirt-on-bidens/. Accessed in September 2025.

12.9)   CSPAN. 2019. "Marie Yovanovitch Complete Opening Statement." YouTube video, 21:21. November 15, 2019. https://youtu.be/UK5yRVzKWXw?si=scrGGva8xayB7CCT. Accessed in September 2025.

12.10)   Reuters Staff. 2019. "Factbox: Burisma, the Obscure Ukrainian Gas Company at the Heart of U.S. Political Row." Reuters, September 24, 2019. https://www.reuters.com/article/world/factbox-burisma-the-obscure-ukrainian-gas-company-at-the-heart-of-us-politic-idUSKBN1W91UG/. Accessed in September 2025.

12.11)   Donald J. Turmp (@realDonalTrump), "Where are all of the arrests? Can you imagine if the roles were reversed? Long term sentences would have started two years ago. Shameful!" Twitter (now X), October 6, 2020. https://x.com/realDonaldTrump/status/1313842083606802435. Accessed in September 2025.

12.12)   MSNBC. 2023 "Rudy Giuliani's bad week continues as he files for Chapter 11 bankruptcy in New York." YouTube video, 06:52. December 21, 2023. https://youtu.be/cTGsXhU-VNk?si=mshoFgOxX93jEFpt. Accessed in September 2025.

12.13)   Pavel Polityuk, and Matthias Williams. 2016. "Ukrainian Chief Prosecutor Back at Work despite Resignation." Reuters, March 16, 2016. https://www.reuters.com/article/world/ukrainian-chief-prosecutor-back-at-work-despite-resignation-idUSKCN0WI1UA/. Accessed in September 2025.

12.14)   RFE/RL. 2016. "Ukrainian President's Ally Approved for Top Prosecutor's Post." RadioFreeEurope/RadioLiberty. RFE/RL. May 12, 2016. https://www.rferl.org/a/ukraine-prosecutor-general-lutsenko-no-legal-background/27731069.html. Accessed in September 2025.

12.15)   lawForUkraineIsMoreImportantThenBread. 2018. "4 Years of Changes in the Prosecutor's Office of Ukraine: Two Steps Forward, One Back." Центр політико правових реформ. October 23, 2018. https://pravo.org.ua/en/4-years-of-changes-in-the-prosecutors-office-of-ukraine-two-steps-forward-one-back/. Accessed in September 2025.

12.16)   Oleg Sukhov. 2016. "UPDATES: Poroshenko Appoints Lutsenko as Prosecutor General - May. 12, 2016." Kyiv Post. May 12, 2016. https://archive.kyivpost.com/article/content/ukraine-politics/parliament-approves-appointing-lutsenko-as-prosecutor-general-413590.html. Accessed in September 2025.

12.17)   RFE/RL. 2012. "Ukraine's Lutsenko Gets Two Years." RadioFreeEurope/RadioLiberty. RFE/RL. August 17, 2012. https://www.rferl.org/a/ukraine-lutsenko/24679808.html. Accessed in September 2025.

12.18)   Counsel of Europe. Democratic Society - Consultative Council of European
         Judges - Www.coe.int." 2021. Consultative Council of European Judges.
         2021. https://www.coe.int/en/web/ccje/opinion-no.-12-on-the-relations-
         between-judges-and-prosecutors-in-a-democratic-society. Accessed in
         September 2025.

12.19)   Counsel of Europe. 2009. Opinion No.12 (2009) of the Consultative Council of
         European Judges (CCJE) AND Opinion No.4 (2009) of the Consultative
         Council of European Prosecutors (CCPE). Strasbourg. December 8, 2009.
         https://rm.coe.int/1680747391. Accessed in September 2025.

12.20)   Censor.NET. 2016. "Hundreds of Employees of Prosecutor's Office to Be Laid
         Off, - Deputy Prosecutor General Telychenko." Censor.net. Censor.NET.
         June 4, 2016.
         https://censor.net/en/news/391757/hundreds_of_employees_of_prosecutors_o
         ffice_to_be_laid_off_deputy_prosecutor_general_telychenko. Accessed in
         September 2025.

12.21)   Lutsenko v. Ukraine. Application no. 6492/11, European Court of Human
         Rights, FINAL, Strausburg. November 19, 2012.
         https://hudoc.echr.coe.int/eng#{%22itemid%22:[%22001-112013%22]}.
         Accessed in September 2025.

12.22)   Raczkiewycz, Mark. 2011. "Yurii Lutsenko is indicted." The Ukrainian
         Weekly. July 31, 2011. https://archive.ukrweekly.com/wp-
         content/uploads/The_Ukrainian_Weekly_2011-31.pdf. Accessed in
         September 2025.

12.23)   RFE/RL. 2012. "Ukraine's Lutsenko Gets Two Years."
         RadioFreeEurope/RadioLiberty. RFE/RL. August 17, 2012.
         https://www.rferl.org/a/ukraine-lutsenko/24679808.html. Accessed in
         September 2025.

12.24)   Coynash, Halya. 2016. "Selective prosecutions as weapons in Prosecutor's war
         against reform?" Human Rights in Ukraine. April 15, 2016.
         https://khpg.org/en/1460641177. Accessed in September 2025.

12.25)   Russian Crimes Daily News. 2012. "Vitaly Kasko – a swindler, a corrupt
         official, a "shot down pilot." September 9, 2016. Russian Crimes Daily
         News. https://ruscrime.com/vitaly-kasko-a-swindler-a-corrupt-official-a-shot-
         down-pilot.html. Accessed in September 2025.

12.26)   Daryna Krasnolutska, Kateryna Chursina, and Stephanie Baker. 2019. "Ukraine
         Prosecutor Says No Evidence of Wrongdoing by Bidens." Bloomberg.com.
         Bloomberg. May 16, 2019. https://www.bloomberg.com/news/articles/2019-
         05-16/ukraine-prosecutor-says-no-evidence-of-wrongdoing-by-bidens.
         Accessed in September 2025.

CHAPTER 13 NOTES

13.1)   "The Detective Story of Mr. Zlochevsky." 2022. Newsessentials Blog. March
        29, 2022. https://newsessentials.wordpress.com/2022/03/29/the-detective-
        story-of-mr-zlochevsky. Accessed in September 2025.

13.2)   Leshchenko, Sergii. "Ukraine's Corrupt Counter-Revolution." 2016.
        OpenDemocracy. 2016. https://www.opendemocracy.net/en/odr/ukraine-s-
        corrupt-counter-revolution/. Accessed in September 2025.

13.3)   Oleg Sukhov. 2018. "Onyshchenko Releases Alleged Recording Implicating
        Poroshenko, Zlochevsky in Graft." Kyiv Post. April 20, 2018.
        https://www.kyivpost.com/post/10319. Accessed in September 2025.

13.4)   Vimont, Pierre. "Ukraine's Indispensable Economic Reforms." 2016. Carnegie
        Endowment for International Peace. 2016.
        https://carnegieendowment.org/research/2016/04/ukraines-indispensable-
        economic-reforms?lang=en. Accessed in September 2025.

13.5)   "Flourishing Businesses of Mykola Zlochevskyi - Investigation -
        Anticorruption Action Centre." 2020. Anticorruption Action Centre. March
        5, 2020. https://antac.org.ua/en/news/flourishing-businesses-of-mykola-
        zlochevskyi/. Accessed in September 2025.

13.6)   Яків Сташинський. 2020. "Yuriy Lutsenko: NABU Closes Case of
        Zlochevsky and Biden without Any Investigative Actions." Ukrainian News.
        February 11, 2020. https://ukranews.com/en/news/683404-yuriy-lutsenko-
        nabu-closes-case-of-zlochevsky-and-biden-without-any-investigative-actions.
        Accessed in September 2025.

13.7)   Wikipedia Contributors. 2024. "Igor Kononenko." Wikipedia. Wikimedia
        Foundation. October 30, 2024.
        https://en.wikipedia.org/wiki/Igor_Kononenko. Accessed in September 2025.

13.8)   Leshchenko, Sergii. 2016. "Sergii Leshchenko: Poroshenko creates his own
        'family' clan." Kiyv Post. October 25, 2016.
        https://www.kyivpost.com/article/opinion/op-ed/sergii-leshchenko-weve-
        returned-to-the-family-poroshenko-creates-his-clan-419429.html. Accessed
        in September 2025.

13.9)   Antac.org.ua. 2017. "Repeated failures by Ukraine General Prosecutor's Office
        show politics at work, serious reform needed." Antac.org.ua. January 18,
        2017. https://antac.org.ua/en/news/burisma-group-of-companies-are-still-
        under-criminal-investigation-in-ukraine-despite-case-against-mykola-
        zlochevskyi-was-dumped-by-the-general-prosecutor-s-office/. Accessed in
        September 2025.

13.10) United States Congress. 2019. "Repeated failures by Ukraine General Prosecutor's Office show politics at work, serious reform needed." Meeting. December 11, 2019. https://www.congress.gov/116/meeting/house/110331/documents/HMKP-116-JU00-20191211-SD1032-U1.pdf. Accessed in September 2025.

13.11) Onyshchenko, . Oleksandr January Peter the Fifth: The True Story of the Ukrainian Dictator. Germany: Verlag am Park, 2018. Accessed in September 2025.

13.12) Selivanova, Ekaterina. "Бывший украинский прокурор, который вел дело Burisma, сообщил о первоначальном предложении взятки в 50 миллионов долларов за закрытие дела." 2025. OCCRP. 2025. https://www.occrp.org/ru/novosti/byvsii-ukrainskii-prokuror-kotoryi-vel-delo-burisma-soobshhil-o-pervonacalnom-predlozenii-vziatki-v-50-millionov-dollarov-za-zakrytie-dela. Accessed in September 2025.

13.13) Vogel, Kenneth P., and Iuliia Mendel. 2019. "Biden Faces Conflict of Interest Questions That Are Being Promoted by Trump and Allies (Published 2019)." The New York Times, May 2, 2019, sec. U.S. https://www.nytimes.com/2019/05/01/us/politics/biden-son-ukraine.html. Accessed in September 2025.

13.14) Wikipedia Contributors. 2025. "Kostiantyn Kulyk." Wikipedia. Wikimedia Foundation. July 5, 2025. https://en.wikipedia.org/wiki/Kostiantyn_Kulyk. Accessed in September 2025.

13.15) Karamanau, Yuras. 2020. "Ukraine to Investigate Leaked Tapes with Ex-President, Biden." AP News. May 20, 2020. https://apnews.com/article/02895b0ffce2b6c6f11c20333fe7ba3d. Accessed in September 2025.

13.16) Bullough, Oliver. 2017. "The Money Machine: How a High-Profile Corruption Investigation Fell Apart." The Guardian. April 12, 2017. https://www.theguardian.com/world/2017/apr/12/the-money-machine-how-a-high-profile-corruption-investigation-fell-apart. Accessed in September 2025.

13.17) Serious Fraud Office v. Mykola Zlochevsky. Case No. RSTO/7/2014. Honorable Justice Blake. (Central Criminal Court of London (Old Bailey)) January 20, 2015. https://archive.org/details/5926342-The-Central-Criminal-Court-of-London-Rules-in/mode/2up. Accessed in September 2025.

13.18) Цензор.НЕТ. 2020. "50 млн долларов, - Кулик назвал изначальную сумму взятки за закрытие дела против 'Burisma' и семьи Байденов." Censor.net. Цензор.НЕТ. June 22, 2020. https://censor.net/ru/news/3203528/50_mln_dollarov_kulik_nazval_iznachalnuyu_summu_vzyatki_za_zakrytie_dela_protiv_burisma_i_semi_bayidenov. Accessed in September 2025.

13.19) "MP behind 'Poroshenko Tapes' Addresses Sytnik on Burisma Group Case."
        2020. Unian.info. UNIAN. June 23, 2020.
        https://www.unian.info/politics/mp-behind-poroshenko-leak-addresses-
        sytnik-on-burisma-group-case-11046845.html. Accessed in September 2025.

13.20) Kateryna Chursina, and Daryna Krasnolutska. 2020. "Ukraine Official Says
        Bribe Was Offered to Close Zlochevsky Case." Bloomberg.com. Bloomberg.
        June 13, 2020. https://www.bloomberg.com/news/articles/2020-06-
        13/ukraine-official-says-bribe-was-offered-to-close-zlochevsky-case-
        kbdqr8f3. Accessed in September 2025.

13.21) Ilya Zhegulev. 2020. "Ukraine Alleges $5 Million Bribe over Burisma, No
        Biden Link." Reuters, June 13, 2020.
        https://www.reuters.com/article/world/ukraine-alleges-5-million-bribe-over-
        burisma-no-biden-link-idUSKBN23K0KH/. Accessed in September 2025.

13.22) "The largest bribe in the history of Ukraine. The VAKS approved the
        agreement between ex-Minister of Ecology Zlochevsky and the
        investigation." 2023. New Voice Ukraine. August 1, 2023.
        https://nv.ua/ukraine/events/delo-zlochevskogo-vaks-utverdil-soglashenie-so-
        sledstviem-o-priznanii-vinovnosti-50343196.html. Accessed in September
        2025.

13.23) Wikipedia Contributors. 2024. "Artem Sytnyk." Wikipedia. Wikimedia
        Foundation. December 17, 2024.
        https://en.wikipedia.org/wiki/Artem_Sytnyk. Accessed in September 2025.

13.24) Olha Bereziuk. 2024. "Artem Sytnyk Became the Deputy Head of the Defense
        Procurement Agency." Babel.ua. Babel. June 21, 2024.
        https://babel.ua/en/news/108323-artem-sytnyk-became-the-deputy-head-of-
        the-defense-procurement-agency. Accessed in September 2025.

13.29) Weiss, Debra Cassens. 2021. "Afternoon Briefs: Search of Giuliani's Home Is
        'Legal Thuggery,' Says His Lawyer; Top Legal Officer Earns $50.9M." ABA
        Journal. April 28, 2021. https://www.abajournal.com/news/article/afternoon-
        briefs-search-of-giulianis-home-deemed-legal-thuggery-top-legal-officer-
        gets-50.9m. Accessed in September 2025.

13.25) "LDaily." 2020. LDaily. April 9, 2020. https://ldaily.ua/en/interviews/vadym-
        pozharsky-the-macro-goal-of-all-players-in-the-gas-production-market/.
        Accessed in September 2025.

13.26) Contributors. 2024. "Vadym Pozharskyi." Historica Wiki. Fandom, Inc. 2024.
        https://historica.fandom.com/wiki/Vadym_Pozharsky. Accessed in
        September 2025.

13.27)   Richards,Steven and John Solomon. 2020. "Impeachment Evidence Counters Biden's Claims, Shows He Met with Many of Son's Major Foreign Clients." Just the News. 2020. https://justthenews.com/accountability/political-ethics/joe-biden-met-nearly-all-his-sons-foreign-business-associates. Accessed in September 2025.

13.28)   Today. "FBI Raids Rudy Giuliani's Home and Office | TODAY." NBC Today streamed April 29, 2021. YouTube video 2:43, https://youtu.be/rLLOiJVp-Fw?si=3XL5Vct4GWPvE2wn. Accessed in September 2025.

13.29)   Weiss, Debra Cassens. 2021. "Afternoon Briefs: Search of Giuliani's Home Is 'Legal Thuggery,' Says His Lawyer; Top Legal Officer Earns $50.9M." ABA Journal. April 28, 2021. https://www.abajournal.com/news/article/afternoon-briefs-search-of-giulianis-home-deemed-legal-thuggery-top-legal-officer-gets-50.9m. Accessed in September 2025.

13.30)   Baker, Stephanie, and Greg Farrell. 2020. "FBI Raids US Company with Ties to Ukrainian Oligarch Igor Kolomoisky." Bloomberg.com. Bloomberg. August 4, 2020. https://www.bloomberg.com/news/articles/2020-08-04/fbi-raids-u-s-company-with-ties-to-ukrainian-oligarch. Accessed in September 2025.

13.31)   Beck, Glenn. 2019. "UKRAINE OFFICIALS CAN'T GET VISAS: Ambassador Yovanovitch Blocks Entry for Trump Investigation." Glenn Beck. October 11, 2019. https://www.glennbeck.com/radio/ukraine-officials-cant-get-visas-ambassador-yovanovitch-blocks-entry-for-trump-investigation. Accessed in September 2025.

13.32)   CNN Newsource. 2019. "Marie Yovanovitch Testifies She Was 'Shocked and Devastated' after Being Removed from Her Post." WCPO 9 Cincinnati. November 15, 2019. https://www.wcpo.com/news/national/marie-yovanovitch-testifies-she-was-shocked-and-devastated-after-being-removed-from-her-post. Accessed in September 2025.

13.33)   United States Department of Justice. "Frequently Asked Questions." 2017. Www.justice.gov. August 21, 2017. https://www.justice.gov/nsd-fara/frequently-asked-questions. Accessed in September 2025.

13.34)   Morris, Emma-Jo, and Gabrielle Fonrouge. 2020. "Smoking-Gun Email Reveals How Hunter Biden Introduced Ukrainian Businessman to vp Dad." New York Post. October 14, 2020. https://nypost.com/2020/10/14/email-reveals-how-hunter-biden-introduced-ukrainian-biz-man-to-dad/. Accessed in September 2025.

CHAPTER 14 NOTES

14.1)   "Natalie A. Jaresko." 2023. World Bank Live. 2023. https://live.worldbank.org/en/experts/4/48001. Accessed in September 2025.

14.2)   Wikipedia Contributors. 2025. "Natalie Jaresko." Wikipedia. Wikimedia
         Foundation. August 23, 2025. https://en.wikipedia.org/wiki/Natalie_Jaresko.
         Accessed in September 2025.

14.3)   Emerging Europe Staff. 2019. "Horizon Capital Closes Third Ukraine Fund at
         200 Million-US Dollar Hard Cap - Emerging Europe." Emerging Europe.
         January 25, 2019. https://emerging-europe.com/business/horizon-capital-
         closes-third-ukraine-fund-at-200-million-us-dollar-hard-cap/. Accessed in
         September 2025.

14.4)   Western NIS Enterprise Fund. Annual Report 2017: ADVANCING CHANGE
         THAT LASTS. 2017. www.USAID.gov/Ukraine. https://wnisef.org/wp-
         content/uploads/2018/09/2017-WNISEF-AR_ENG_FINAL.pdf. Accessed in
         September 2025.

14.5)   Адміністратор. 2015. "Новый министр финансов Наталья Яресько.
         Информация к размышлению." Вишгород Газета ONLINE. January 14,
         2015. https://vyshgorod.in.ua/novini/1607-novyj-ministr-finansov-natalya-
         yaresko-informatsiya-k-razmyshleniyu. Accessed in September 2025.

14.6)   "The head of the Ministry of Finance of Ukraine, Yaresko, earned more than $2
         million in 2014." 2015. INTERFAX.RU. April 9, 2015.
         https://www.interfax.ru/world/435316. Accessed in September 2025.

14.7)   Natalya Yaresko's v Igor Figlus. Case № 2-9816/11. Proceedings
         №2/761/864/2013. Shevchenkiv District Court of. Kyiv (2013).
         http://reyestr.court.gov.ua/Review/29731301. Accessed in September 2025.

14.8)   EMERGING EUROPE GROWTH FUND, L.P., and HORIZON CAPITAL GP
         LLC, a Delaware limited liability company v Igor Figlus. C.A. No. 7936-
         VCMR. COURT OF CHANCERY OF THE STATE OF DELAWARE
         (2018). https://courts.delaware.gov/Opinions/Download.aspx?id=282190.
         Accessed in September 2025.

14.9)   Igor Figlus v NATALIE A. JARESKO, and HORIZON CAPITAL GP LLC, a
         Delaware limited liability company, and EMERGING EUROPE GROWTH
         FUND, L.P., Nominal Defendant C.A. No. 2017-0373-TMR. COURT OF
         CHANCERY OF THE STATE OF DELAWARE (2018).
         https://courts.delaware.gov/Opinions/Download.aspx?id=282190. Accessed
         in September 2025.

14.10)   Parry, Robert. 2015. "How Ukraine's Finance Chief Got Rich." Truthout.
         November 13, 2015. https://truthout.org/articles/how-ukraine-s-finance-chief-
         got-rich/. Accessed in September 2025.

14.11)   "TREATIES AND OTHER INTERNATIONAL ACTS SERIES 15-526
         Loan Guarrantee," Agreement Between the UNITED STATES OF
         AMERICA and UKRAINE with Annexes, signed May 18, 2015.
         https://www.state.gov/wp-content/uploads/2019/02/15-526-Ukraine-Loan-
         Guarantee.pdf. Accessed in September 2025.

14.12) Сташинський Яків. 2020. "Poroshenko Boasted to Biden That He Had Raised Tariffs by 100% instead of the Required 75%, – a Record of Conversation Was Made Public." Ukrainian News. May 19, 2020. https://ukranews.com/en/news/703227-poroshenko-boasted-to-biden-that-he-had-raised-tariffs-by-100-instead-of-the-required-75-a-record. Accessed in September 2025.

14.13) Reuters Staff. 2015. "Ukraine Completes Debt Restructuring of around $15 Billion." Reuters, November 12, 2015. https://www.reuters.com/article/business/ukraine-completes-debt-restructuring-of-around-15-billion-idUSKCN0T12FS/. Accessed in September 2025.

14.14) АТН. 2013. "Арбузов и Колобов улетели в США искать средства." АТН. January 16, 2013. https://atn.ua/business/arbuzov-i-kolobov-uleteli-v-ssha-iskat-sredstva-90866/. Accessed in September 2025.

14.15) "Арбузов и Колобов отправились в США с целью поиска альтернативных источников инвестиций." 2019. РБК-Украина. 2019. https://www.rbc.ua/rus/news/arbuzov-i-kolobov-otpravilis-v-ssha-s-tselyu-poiska-alternativnyh-16012013151200. Accessed in September 2025.

14.16) Kulikov, Anton. 2013. "Americans Buy 20 Percent of Ukraine's Public Debt." PravdaReport. November 11, 2013. https://english.pravda.ru/news/business/126110-ukraine_public_debt/. Accessed in September 2025.

14.17) Emmanuel. 2015. "Ukraine vs. Franklin Templeton Investments, Round 77." Data:blog.title. 2015. https://ipezone.blogspot.com/2015/06/ukraine-vs-franklin-templeton.html. Accessed in September 2025.

14.18) Rao, Sujata. 2017. "Ukraine's Growth-Linked Bonds - When Recovery Becomes Painful." Reuters, September 15, 2017. https://www.reuters.com/article/world/uk/ukraines-growth-linked-bonds-when-recovery-becomes-painful-idUSKCN1BQ1UW/. Accessed in September 2025.

14.18) Interfax-Ukraine. 2020. "Payments on GDP Warrants of $40 Mln in 2021 with Moderate GDP Growth Potentially Could Reach $22 Bln by 2040 – Finance Minister." Interfax-Ukraine. September 9, 2020. https://en.interfax.com.ua/news/economic/686624.html. Accessed in September 2025.

14.19) Financial Oversight and Management Board for Puerto Rico. Fiscal Year 2022 Report. 2022. San Juan, PR: July 31, 2022. https://drive.google.com/file/d/1e7TdoBoBI5rnHk8BGlWDGCVqNMPhn_5X/view. Accessed in September 2025.

14.20) Rivera, Maria Mercedes Rodriguez. 2019. "The Board: More Transparency and Less Conflict of Interest." Espaciosabiertos.org. 2019. https://espaciosabiertos.org/en/la-junta-mas-transparencia-y-menos-conflicto-de-interes/. Accessed in September 2025.

14.21) "Despite Harm to Ratepayers, Puerto Rico Oversight Board Opens Door to Increases." 2025. Ieefa.org. 2025. https://ieefa.org/resources/despite-harm-ratepayers-puerto-rico-oversight-board-opens-door-increases. Accessed in September 2025.

CHAPTER 15 NOTES

15.1) Венк, Виктория. 2020. "Как Байден Украиной управлял. Полный текст скандальных пленок Порошенко." Archive.org. Strana.ua. May 19, 2020. https://web.archive.org/web/20200601111256/https://strana.ua/news/268104-bajden-i-poroshenko-stenohramma-vsekh-zapisej-video-i-tekst.html. Accessed in September 2025.

CHAPTER 16 NOTES

16.1) Cabinet of Ministers of Ukraine. August 5, 2015. "Resolution No. 553: On Amendments to the Procedure for Attracting, Using and Monitoring International Technical Assistance." https://zakon.rada.gov.ua/laws/show/553-2015-%D0%BF#n2. Accessed in September 2025.

16.2) Irene. 2020. "U.S., Soros-Funded Ukrainian HIV Charity under Criminal Probe for Embezzlement - Judicial Watch." Judicial Watch. February 26, 2020. https://www.judicialwatch.org/u-s-soros-funded-ukrainian-hiv-charity-under-criminal-probe-for-embezzlement/. Accessed in September 2025.

16.3) AnTAC. 2025. "About Center." 2025/ Anticorruption Action Centre. https://antac.org.ua/en/about-us/. Accessed in September 2025.

16.4) EN, Pravda. 2025. "Cars for the Army and Combat Allowances – for Yourself, Cover – from NABU: The Media Showed Shabunin's 'Anti-Corruption' Scheme." Pravda EN. July 19, 2025. https://news-pravda.com/world/2025/07/19/1529081.html. Accessed in September 2025.

16.5) "100% Life: 20 Years of Fighting | UNAIDS." 2021. Unaids.org. 2021. https://www.unaids.org/en/resources/presscentre/featurestories/2021/may/20-years-of-fighting. Accessed in September 2025.

16.6) Kateryna Chursina. 2025. "Ukraine Anti-Graft Activist Vitaliy Shabunin Accused of Dodging Army Service." Bloomberg.com. Bloomberg. July 11, 2025. https://www.bloomberg.com/news/articles/2025-07-11/ukraine-anti-graft-activist-accused-of-dodging-army-service. Accessed in September 2025.

16.7)   "The companies "BaDM" and "Optima-Pharm" earned billions on inflated prices during the war." 2025. Nenka.info. August 9, 2025. https://nenka.info/en/badm-and-optima-farm-companies-earned-billions-on-high-prices-during-the-war/. Accessed in September 2025.

16.8)   "Ukraine: Light of Hope's Work Improving Social Services for Marginalized Groups." 2016. International Budget Partnership. October 31, 2016. https://internationalbudget.org/publications/case-study-improving-social-services-ukraine/. Accessed in September 2025.

16.9)   Postolovska, Iryna. 2016 Ukraine: Combating Corruption Disguised as Charity. (Harvard School of Public Health: International Budget Partnership, October 2016.) https://internationalbudget.org/wp-content/uploads/ibp-case-study-combating-corruption-ukraine-2016.pdf. Accessed in September 2025.

16.10)   Розенфельдт София. 2021. "Опецькуватий и марудний зульдер: прокуроры возмутились процедурой переаттестации." Наблюдатель. October 7, 2021. https://nabludatel.od.ua/vlada/opeckyvatii-i-marydnii-zylder-prokyrory-vozmytilis-procedyroi-pereattestacii/. Accessed in September 2025.

16.11)   Government Executive. 2021. State Department Faulted for Lax Oversight of Afghanistan Justice Contract - Government Executive." Govexec.com. 2021. https://www.govexec.com/oversight/2014/01/state-department-faulted-lax-oversight-afghanistan-justice-contract/77510/. Accessed in September 2025.

16.12)   Войко, Дмитрий. 2020. "Команда Рябошапки официально уничтожила документы по переаттестации прокуроров." Archive.org. Strana.ua. April 4, 2020. https://web.archive.org/web/20200413142217/https://strana.ua/news/259354-komanda-eks-henprokurora-rjaboshapki-unichtozhila-dokumenty-pereattestatsii-prokurorov.html. Accessed in September 2025.

16.13)   The Accounting Chamber. Annual Report 2017. (Kyiv: Supreme Audit Institution of Ukraine, 2018). https://rp.gov.ua/Activity/Reports/?lang=eng. Accessed in September 2025.

16.14)   U.S. Embassy Kyiv. 2021. "Remarks by Chargé d'Affaires, A.i. Kristina A. Kvien at the Kyiv Security Forum." U.S. Embassy in Ukraine. March 12, 2021. https://ua.usembassy.gov/remarks-by-charge-daffaires-a-i-kristina-a-kvien-at-the-kyiv-security-forum/. Accessed in September 2025.

CHAPTER 17 NOTES

17.1)   Verkhovna Rada of Ukraine. 2015. "The Criminal Procedural Code of Ukraine." 2015. Official Website of the Parliament of Ukraine. https://zakon.rada.gov.ua/laws/anot/en/4651-17. Accessed in September 2025.

17.2)   "The Prosecutor's Office Has Lost Powers of Pre-Trial Investigation of Crimes Prosecuted by the State Bureau of Investigations." 2016. Kmp.ua. 2016. https://kmp.ua/en/analytics/infoletters/the-prosecutor-s-office-has-lost-powers-of-pre-trial-investigation/. Accessed in September 2025.

17.3)   National Anti-Corruption Bureau of Ukraine (NABU). "History of NABU | NABU Official Website." 2014. Nabu.gov.ua. 2014. https://nabu.gov.ua/en/about-the-bureau/struktura-ta-kerivnitctvo/istoriya-stanovlennya/. Accessed in September 2025.

17.4)   Ekodia. 2019. "The Land Question: land concentration and the agricultural land moratorium in Ukraine." ecoaction.org.ua. Feburary 22, 2019. https://en.ecoaction.org.ua/the-land-question.html. Accessed in September 2025.

17.5)   "Elite Leisure in Rivne Region: Court Finds NABU Head Sytnyk Guilty of Corruption." 2019. Unian.info. UNIAN. December 13, 2019. https://www.unian.info/politics/10794095-elite-leisure-in-rivne-region-court-finds-nabu-head-sytnyk-guilty-of-corruption.html. Accessed in September 2025.

17.6)   Wikipedia Contributors. 2025. "National Anti-Corruption Bureau of Ukraine." Wikipedia. Wikimedia Foundation. August 19, 2025. https://en.wikipedia.org/wiki/National_Anti-Corruption_Bureau_of_Ukraine. Accessed in September 2025.

17.7)   "Cabinet Endorses Bill Set to Sack NABU Chief Sytnyk." 2021. Unian.info. UNIAN. February 15, 2021. https://www.unian.info/politics/nabu-cabinet-endorses-bill-set-to-sack-director-sytnyk-11322158.html. Accessed in September 2025.

17.8)   Ukrainska Pravda. 2022. "Sytnyk Completes His Work at NABU. What Were the 7 Years and What to Expect Next?" Ukrainska Pravda. April 16, 2022. https://www.pravda.com.ua/eng/columns/2022/04/16/7340018. Accessed in September 2025./.

17.9)   Ukrinform. 2020. "Constitutional Court Declares Unconstitutional Certain Provisions of Law on NABU." Ukrinform.net. Укрінформ. September 17, 2020. https://www.ukrinform.net/rubric-polytics/3101188-constitutional-court-declares-unconstitutional-certain-provisions-of-law-on-nabu.html. Accessed in September 2025.

17.10) Fornusek, Martin. 2024. "NABU First Deputy Director Suspended amid Leak Investigation." The Kyiv Independent. May 24, 2024. https://kyivindependent.com/nabu-first-deputy-director-suspended-amid-leak-investigation/. Accessed in September 2025.

17.11) "Говда Роман." 2025. LIGA.net. 2025. https://file.liga.net/ua/public/index.php/ua/persons/govda-roman. Accessed in September 2025.

17.12)   Віка Карпінська. 2020. "Head of SAPO Nazar Kholodnytskyi Resigned -
           Transparency International Ukraine." Transparency International Ukraine -
           Світ без корупції. August 21, 2020. https://ti-ukraine.org/en/news/head-of-
           sapo-nazar-kholodnytskyi-resigned/. Accessed in September 2025.

CHAPTER 18 NOTES

18.1)   Zimmermann, David. 2025. "CIA Finds 'Anomalies' in 2016 Report on
           Russian Election Interference." Washington Examiner. July 2, 2025.
           https://www.washingtonexaminer.com/news/3460833/cia-2016-election-
           report-russian-interference-anomalies/. Accessed in September 2025.

18.2)   Madhani, Aamer and Colleen Long. 2020. "Trump Ups Pressure on Barr to
           Probe Bidens as Election Nears." AP News. October 21, 2020.
           https://apnews.com/article/election-2020-joe-biden-donald-trump-william-
           barr-elections-20fd56b64801dd83b1657c630a1ebdfa. Accessed in September
           2025.

18.3)   Donald J. Turmp (@realDonalTrump), "Where are all of the arrests? Can you
           imagine if the roles were reversed? Long term sentences would have started
           two years ago. Shameful!" Twitter (now X), October 6, 2020.
           https://x.com/realDonaldTrump/status/1313842083606802435. Accessed in
           September 2025.

18.4)   Patel, Kash "Government Gangsters: The Deep State, the Truth, and the Battle
           for Our Democracy," (Post Hill Press: Tennessee, 2023). pg, 56.

18.5)   Horwitz, Jeff, and Chad Day. 2016. "Trump Campaign Chairman Paul
           Manafort Resigns." AP News. August 19, 2016. https://apnews.com/united-
           states-presidential-election-events-ec32c7bae99246c195bef49fee920c7d.
           Accessed in September 2025.

18.6)   CBC. 2017. "Why Washington Post's Anne Applebaum Warned of the
           'Ukrainization of American Politics.'" CBC. October 31, 2017.
           https://www.cbc.ca/radio/thecurrent/the-current-for-october-31-2017-
           1.4378789/why-washington-post-s-anne-applebaum-warned-of-the-
           ukrainization-of-american-politics-1.4378812. Accessed in September 2025.

18.7)   Єрмоленко, Володимир, and Наталя Гуменюк. 2016. "'Трампа та його
           оточення чомусь дуже цікавить питання України' — пулітцерівська
           лауреатка." Hromadske. August 2, 2016. https://hromadske.ua/posts/trampa-
           ta-ioho-otochennia-chomus-duzhe-tsikavyt-pytannia-ukrainy-pulittserivska-
           laureatka. Accessed in September 2025.

18.8)   Kramer, Andrew E, Mike McIntire, and Barry Meier. 2016. "The Black Ledger
           in Ukraine Lists Cash for Trump's Campaign Chief." The New York Times,
           August 15, 2016. https://www.nytimes.com/2016/08/15/us/politics/paul-
           manafort-ukraine-donald-trump.html?ref=world&amp. Accessed in
           September 2025.

18.9)   Hohmann, James. 2020. "The Daily 202: Can Trump Chairman Paul Manafort Survive New Ukraine Revelations?" The Washington Post. July 17, 2020. https://www.washingtonpost.com/news/powerpost/paloma/daily-202/2016/08/15/daily-202-can-trump-chairman-paul-manafort-survive-new-ukraine-revelations/57b0ec7ccd249a2fe363ba20/?utm_term=.a1c8614ed0ce. Accessed in September 2025.

18.10)   Interfax-Ukraine. 2016. "NABU Says Trump's Campaign Chief Could Get $12.7 Million from Regions Party's 'Black Ledger.'" Kyiv Post. August 15, 2016. https://www.kyivpost.com/article/content/ukraine-politics/nabu-says-trumps-campaign-chief-could-get-127-million-from-regions-partys-black-ledger-421095.html. Accessed in September 2025.

18.11)   Vogel, Kenneth P. 2016. "Manafort's Man in Kiev." POLITICO. Politico. August 19, 2016. http://www.politico.com/story/2016/08/paul-manafort-ukraine-kiev-russia-konstantin-kilimnik-227181. Accessed in September 2025.

18.12)   NABU. 2016. "Роз'яснення щодо згадування ім'я Пола Манафорта у 'чорній бухгалтерії' ПР | НАБУ офіційний вебсайт." Nabu.gov.ua. August 18, 2016. https://nabu.gov.ua/novyny/rozyasnennya-shchodo-zgaduvannya-imya-pola-manaforta-u-chorniy-buhgalteriyi-pr. Accessed in September 2025.

18.13)   Melkozerova, Veronika. 2017. "Black Ledger' Investigation Appears to Come to a Halt." Kyiv Post. June 15, 2017. https://www.kyivpost.com/post/10731. Accessed in September 2025.

18.14)   NABU. Criminal Case No. 52016000000000166 [Pre-Trial Investigations of Black Ledger], May 30, 2016. Accessed in September 2025.

18.15)   BBC News. 2014. "Ukraine: Pro-Russians Storm Offices in Donetsk, Luhansk, Kharkiv," April 6, 2014, sec. Europe. https://www.bbc.com/news/world-europe-26910210. Accessed in September 2025.

18.16)   DENISOVA, Oksana. 2016. "VIKTOR TREPAK: "I HANDED OVER TO NABU EVIDENCE OF TOTAL CORRUPTION OF THE AUTHORITIES." Zerkalo nedeli (Eastview on Demand). May 20, 2016: No. 19. https://on-demand.eastview.com/browse/issue/2732274/udb/3. Accessed in September 2025.

18.17)   Ukrainska Pravda. 2016. "Manafort 'Received Cash Payments through Party of Regions MPs.'" Ukrainska Pravda. August 19, 2016. https://www.pravda.com.ua/eng/news/2016/08/19/7118143/. Accessed in September 2025.

18.18)   Ukrayinska Pravda. 2016. "NABU Publishes Party of Regions 'Black Cash' Ledger Entries for Manafort." Ukrayinska Pravda. August 18, 2016. https://www.pravda.com.ua/eng/news/2016/08/18/7118109/. Accessed in September 2025.

18.19)   NABU. "Clarification regarding the mention of Paul Manafort's name in the Party of Regions' 'black ledger' | NABU official website." 2016. Nabu.gov.ua. August 18, 2016. https://nabu.gov.ua/novyny/rozyasnennya-shchodo-zgaduvannya-imya-pola-manaforta-u-chorniy-buhgalteriyi-pr. Accessed in September 2025.

18.20)   Wikipedia Contributors. 2025. "Serhiy Leshchenko." Wikipedia. Wikimedia Foundation. June 24, 2025. https://en.wikipedia.org/wiki/Serhiy_Leshchenko. Accessed in September 2025.

18.21)   Leshchenko, Sergii. 2021. "Sergii Leshchenko: Yulia Tymoshenko's Swan Song Is Fitting – a Corruption Scandal - Aug. 27, 2021." Kyiv Post. August 27, 2021. https://archive.kyivpost.com/article/opinion/op-ed/sergii-leshchenko-yulia-tymoshenkos-swan-song-is-fitting-a-corruption-scandal.html. Accessed in September 2025.

18.22)   Donald J. Turmp (@realDonalTrump), "Ukrainian efforts to sabotage Trump campaign – 'queitly working to boost Clinton.' So where is the investigation A.G. " Twitter (now X), July 25, 2017. https://x.com/realDonaldTrump/status/889788202172780544. Accessed in September 2025.

18.23)   Vogel, Kenneth P, and David Stern. 2017. "Ukrainian Efforts to Sabotage Trump Backfire." POLITICO. Politico. January 11, 2017. https://www.politico.com/story/2017/01/ukraine-sabotage-trump-backfire-233446. Accessed in September 2025.

18.24)   Panetta, Grace. 2019. "Mike Pompeo: US Should Investigate Ukraine, 2016 Election Conspiracy." Business Insider. November 26, 2019. https://www.businessinsider.com/mike-pompeo-us-should-investigate-ukraine-2016-election-conspiracy-2019-11. Accessed in September 2025.

18.25)   Interfax-Ukraine. 2017. "Kyiv Court Opens Case against NABU Chief, MP Leschenko on Manafort Leaks." Interfax-Ukraine. October 24, 2017. https://en.interfax.com.ua/news/general/456824.html. Accessed in September 2025.

18.26)   Ukrainska Pravda. 2018. "Court rules that NABU illegally wiretapped Rosenblatt." Ukrainska Pravda. September 20, 2018. https://www.pravda.com.ua/rus/news/2018/09/20/7192684/. Accessed in September 2025.

18.27)   "UPDATE: Publication of Manafort payments violated law, interfered in US election, Kyiv court rules." 2018. Kyiv Post. December 12, 2018. https://docs.house.gov/meetings/JU/JU00/20191022/110106/HHRG-116-JU00-20191022-SD002.pdf. Accessed in September 2025.

18.28)   Borislav Rosenblatt. "Yesterday, at an extraordinary meeting of the Temporary Investigative Commission, I made an official statement about the commission of evil..., Facebook (now Meta) [includes video], March 13, 2019. https://www.facebook.com/boryslav.rozenblat/videos/2301343333249593/. Accessed in September 2025.

18.29)   NABU. "NABU and SAP are not authorized to investigate Paul Manafort's activities as a political consultant for the Party of Regions (joint statement) | NABU official website." 2017. Nabu.gov.ua. June 29, 2017. https://nabu.gov.ua/news/novyny-nabu-i-sap-ne-upovnovazheni-rozsliduvaty-diyalnist-pola-manaforta-yak-politychnogo/. Accessed in September 2025.

18.30)   "Head of Ukraine's CEC Faces Corruption Charges in Case of Party of Regions' 'Black Accounts.'" 2016. Unian.info. UNIAN. December 13, 2016. https://www.unian.info/politics/1677382-head-of-ukraines-cec-faces-corruption-charges-in-case-of-party-of-regions-black-accounts.html. Accessed in September 2025.

18.31)   Sukhov, Oleg. 2018. "Kholodnytsky has dismal record as anti-corruption prosecutor since 2015." 2018. Kyiv Post. April 13, 2018. https://archive.kyivpost.com/ukraine-politics/kholodnytsky-dismal-record-anti-corruption-prosecutor-since-2015.html#:~:text=Andriy%20Pasishnik%2C%20a%20deputy%20CEO,owned%20by%20Poroshenko%20and%20Kononenko. Accessed in September 2025.

18.32)   Wikipedia Contributors. 2024. "Mykhaylo Okhendovsky." Wikipedia. Wikimedia Foundation. October 21, 2024. https://en.wikipedia.org/wiki/Mykhaylo_Okhendovsky. Accessed in September 2025.

18.33)   Interfax-Ukraine. 2016. "Kyiv Appeals Court Nixes SAPO Pretrial Confinement Request for Okhendovsky." Interfax-Ukraine. December 28, 2016. https://en.interfax.com.ua/news/general/393673.html. Accessed in September 2025.

18.34)   Interfax-Ukraine. 2017. "SAPO Continues Okhendovsky Investigation." Interfax-Ukraine. February 15, 2017. https://en.interfax.com.ua/news/general/403320.html. Accessed in September 2025.

18.35)   Kryukova, Svetlana. 2018. "'They're just adding a one to the protocols.' Former Central Election Commission head Mikhail Okhendovsky spoke to Stana about election fraud schemes and foreign influence." Strana.ua. December 4, 2018. https://strana.news/articles/interview/174706-eks-hlava-tsik-ukrainy-mikhail-ohkendovskij-rasskazal-o-delakh-protiv-neho-i-o-vyborakh-prezidenta-2019.html. Accessed in September 2025.

18.36)   Strana.ua. 2020. "Poroshenko told Biden about Trump's 'bad idea' to bring Manafort onto his team." Strana.today. Strana.ua. July 9, 2020. https://strana.today/news/277678-plenki-derkacha-poroshenko-nazval-plokhoj-ideej-vzjat-manforta-v-komandu-trampa.html#google_vignette. Accessed in September 2025.

CHAPTER 19 NOTES

19.1)   Wikipedia Contributors. 2025. "David Sakvarelidze." Wikipedia. Wikimedia Foundation. July 29, 2025. https://en.wikipedia.org/wiki/David_Sakvarelidze. Accessed in September 2025.

19.2)   Monroe, Derek. 2016. "The U.S. Is 'Missing' Millions in Ukraine." Observer. May 17, 2016. https://observer.com/2016/05/the-u-s-is-missing-millions-in-ukraine/. Accessed in September 2025.

19.3)   "Problems with Chronology: Lutsenko Told the Lie Accusing U.S. Ambassador - Anticorruption Action Centre." 2020. Anticorruption Action Centre. March 5, 2020. https://antac.org.ua/en/news/problems-with-chronology-lutsenko-told-the-lie-accusing-u-s-ambassador/. Accessed in September 2025.

CHAPTER 20 NOTES

20.1)   Lisova, Justyna. 2024. "NABU dismisses deputy director Uglava, who was involved in the 'leaks' case." Hromadske. September 3, 2024. https://hromadske.ua/ru/politika/230597-v-nabu-uvolili-zamestitelya-direktora-uglavu-kotoryy-figuriroval-v-dele-slivov/. Accessed in September 2025.

CHAPTER 21 NOTES

21.1)   Komendantova, Nadiya. 2020. "Viktor Shokin on his poisoning: I have no obvious enemies except Joe Biden." Ukrainian News. February 7, 2020. https://ukranews.com/interview/2315-viktor-shokin-o-svoem-otravlenii-u-menya-net-yavnyh-vragov-krome-dzho-bajdena. Accessed in September 2025.

www.ingramcontent.com/pod-product-compliance
Lightning Source LLC
Chambersburg PA
CBHW070906130626
46555CB00001B/26